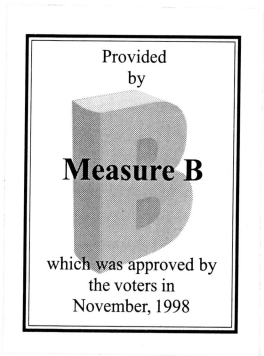

Provided
by

Measure B

which was approved by
the voters in
November, 1998

BEHIND Bars

BEHIND Bars

THE STRAIGHT-UP TALES OF A BIG-CITY BARTENDER

Ty Wenzel

THOMAS DUNNE BOOKS   ST. MARTIN'S PRESS   🅜   NEW YORK

The names and identifying characteristics of some individuals depicted in this book have been changed.

THOMAS DUNNE BOOKS.
An imprint of St. Martin's Press.

www.stmartins.com

Library of Congress Cataloging-in-Publication Data

Wenzel, Ty.
    Behind bars : the straight-up tales of a big-city bartender / by Ty Wenzel.—1st ed.
        p.   cm.
    ISBN 0-312-31102-8
    1. Wenzel, Ty.   2. Bartending.   I. Title.
TX950.5.W45 A3   2003
641.8'74—dc21

                                                            2002156181

First Edition: August 2003

10   9   8   7   6   5   4   3   2   1

For my boys,
Kyle and Kurt

INGREDIENTS

Give strong drink unto him that is ready to perish, and wine unto those that be of heavy hearts. Let him drink, and forget his poverty, and remember his misery no more.

—PROVERBS 31:6–7

Shaken but Not Stirred

Work is the curse of the drinking class.

OSCAR WILDE

MANHATTAN

(Marion's style)
Down South Bourbon Manhattans are the choice.

2 oz. blended whiskey
1 oz. Italian sweet Vermouth
2 dashes Angostura bitters

Pour all ingredients over ice in a mixing glass and stir
as you would a martini. Strain into a chilled
cocktail glass. Garnish with a cherry. Note: If you
prefer a dry Manhattan, use dry vermouth and garnish
with a lemon peel.

My last day on the job, a chilly December night in 2001, didn't turn out the way I had long pictured it in my mind. It had been ten years, two months, and six days since I had started my illustrious career as an award-winning bartender at the kitschy fifties-knockoff Marion's Continental Restaurant and Lounge in New York City. I had pictured my final night to be like the ones I'd grown fond of there: surly gum-snapping waitresses doing shots with me, cigarette smoke wafting between glances like in a Goddard film, and the vibe of a packed speakeasy from the days of Prohibition. Instead the waiters folded napkins and piled into booth number thirty-five, the staff retreat, smoking and sipping their last cocktails of the night, hoping I'd hurry up and close already.

I was about to call final call for the last time. For me this was momentous; fuck the waiters. At a quarter past 2 A.M. I wiped off the sticky bar and, like an aged sales manager retiring after thirty-five years, I collected remnants of my decade-plus in this godforsaken fantasy of a place: pictures I'd taped to the wall behind the shiny retro register, the first tip I ever made (on which someone had written in black marker "DIRTY MONEY" and given George Washington a Salvador Dali mustache and beard), glitter makeup I kept in the drawer for Swing Tuesdays, bits and pieces of costumes I was made to wear on other special theme nights (a coconut bra, a bunny tail, a Farrah Fawcett wig and other hairpieces, blue glitter nail polish, a lei and grass skirt, ripped-up fishnets, two Wonderbras, a garter, a tutu, and a large stash of MAC lipsticks); when I couldn't fit any more of my past into the small box, I ditched the rest.

There would be no gold watch for this retiree. I had made a big stink about not standing for any celebration or salute of service, no teary-eyed good-byes or meaningful hugs. It wasn't really good-bye, after all; I wasn't moving to Siberia. But in all honesty, I had no plans ever to come back, even for a drink or the proverbial free dinner. When you really got down to it, I was sick of this place, these people—despite our familial love—and, like even the best of burnt-out love affairs, we needed to break up. The bar craved fresh talent, and, God knows, I was becoming as jaded as the bouffant-coiffed waitresses at the fifties restaurant Marion's pretended to be.

Still, I was hurt. None of the owners or managers came to bid me good luck and farewell. One waitress and her friend, a dining regular, came by and I really appreciated that. But I still felt cheated. I wondered if I'd ever meant anything to the people here, to the colleagues and patrons whom I considered my chosen family.

I had secretly imagined a multitude of lonely souls, walk-ins, bridge-and-tunnel types, and the usual suspects, six deep, each on their third drinks, professing their sadness at seeing me go: the boys who told me they had been in love with me all these years, the girls who said I'd been the big sister they never had. Looking around on that crisp night, I decided that it was particularly slow for a Friday. Perhaps people had left for their Christmas jaunts already. There was not a regular to be found nursing a usual—and at Marion's that was downright eerie.

Usually, on any given night I expected the crowd to be one of two things. On weekends, the music was upbeat with the croonings of Sinatra, Ella, or Nancy Wilson; the energy was frenetic and often chaotic, with strangers intermingling with regulars, celebrities peppering the dining room, drag queens making a Cosmo pit-stop, and, on the rare occasion, customers dancing on tables. Not a lot of my advice-giving on those nights; there just wasn't any time. I was mostly shaking cocktails, flirting like a whore, and making more money than I ever had in the real world.

On weekdays it was much more mellow, often resembling a scene from a Tom Waits video: heartbreaking drinking music resounding in the air; martinis and scotch shots lining the bar; customers piling in, looking as if they'd found salvation from the aloof New York undercurrent outside; connections being made; and me giving advice to anyone who needed a cheap shrink. After ten years of sob stories, pickup lines, and personal revelations, I'd learned to judge people instantly from where I stood. It was beginning to get to me.

Much to my husband's distress, I no longer enjoyed going out on my nights off. After all, I was *out* every time I went to work and often felt hypersocialized. My drinking ebbed, as I saw the effect it had on people. The countless evenings of projectile vomiting turned me off for good. Thankfully I was married, since I didn't trust men anymore, watching many of them come in and predatorily con women into their lairs with games and lines they'd use on every Marion's excursion. Being a bartender was making a recluse out of this one-time party girl. It was time to leave.

When I finally did last call there were six people left at the bar and a deuce sitting at a table. Although I'd always imagined this moment in a mythological way, in reality I found myself left with drunk NYU types glaring at their watches with the universal collective comment, "What time is it?"

"Time to go," I replied as I always did. They ordered last-call cocktails—a couple of whiskey sours, one Suburban, two Cosmos, and a Brassy Blonde—as they always did. I made their drinks knowing they'd be the last, kicked everyone out, and hailed a cab.

The cord was cut, and it took everything I had not to break down in that taxi.

pet peeve no. 1 ....➤

> If I've done last call, that's it. Don't beg. I'm not about to take the gear back out and start mixing for you. I've been working up to ten hours so give me a fucking break. Plus, it makes you look like an alcoholic.

◄---

Being Muslim only complicated matters. I was born in a mud-packed house in a tiny village outside Konya, Turkey, the same place where the whirling dervishes are from. I'm no slick New York bartender, despite what people think they're seeing as I place that drink in front of them. I am, in fact, a first-generation immigrant from a village that isn't even acknowledged in most world atlases. I was sent to a type of Sunday school to learn to read the Koran, kneel and pray in Arabic, and understand my place as a worshipping second-class human being. To this day I still say my prayers at night, finding solace in my own version of Islam, and I give alms when they are called for during certain holidays. I don't eat pig meat in any form and, yes, I *still* believe in God. So you say, *Alcohol is a sin according to Islam?* No shit, Sherlock. There's the rub.

In the mid-eighties it was a minor scandal that a young Muslim girl would live in the big, bad city. After a couple of years I wore down my family in Jersey and they—mostly my mother—found a kind of frustrated acceptance. She started to boast to her friends about her highly talented daughter in the Big Apple. It was nice to see her carrying around a picture of me from the cover of *The New York Times* Arts and Leisure section when I was a student at the Fashion Institute of Technology, which I will refer to as F.I.T. from this point forth (or Fags-in-Training, which will give you an inkling of what life was like for a straight girl in this particular school and profession). She showed anyone who would bother to look: cashiers, the mailman, coworkers, relatives, the bank teller; not even the newspaper boy was spared.

But I dropped out after three semesters, figuring I'd learned all I needed to know. I was quickly launched into the dazzling environs of über-models, photographers, and stylists—a young girl's wet dream. Being the receptionist at a notoriously chic public-relations firm wasn't exactly an exalted title, but I got to circulate with the likes of Yohji Yamamoto, Katherine Hamnett, Jean-Paul Gaultier, Marc Jacobs, and Stephen Sprouse all day long, by phone and in the office. Then there were the full-blown fashion shows that I got to help with. At twenty years of age there wasn't anything more captivating than the buzz of frenzied divas, reporters, and celebrities running about, as well as the feuding fashion editors, raving stylists, half-naked models throwing fits, and designers on the verge of a nervous breakdown.

The dream job lost its reverent status with me when I realized that I couldn't make it in New York on seventeen thousand dollars a year. And after being refused a raise I started asking the callers of the office if they knew of anyone looking for the hippest up-and-comer around. A stylist indulged a lead and said that a certain bigwig fashion director at Bloomies was looking for an assistant. Off I went and got the job! On my last day at the publicity firm, one of the owners invited me into his office for a chat. He told me straight, "The fashion world is shallow and harsh. Don't ever lose your sweetness. Don't ever change."

Bloomies was pretty much the same deal, only I got paid agreeably and could exist in Manhattan tolerably. My diva boss was a holy trip to work for. Imagine Diana Vreeland meets Emma Peele and you've got her down. She let me smoke in the office and treated me with an abundance of respect, alluding to me as her assistant only when she wanted to impress someone.

Still, it was a thorny experience, spiraling in and out of this vacuous abyss. Despite all my efforts to fit in, I couldn't relate to the insipid lifestyle that was expected of me: ass-kissing sessions at showroom parties, designer events, and restaurant and club openings; mingling with Condé Nasty assistants who thought it was great to work for minimum wage as long as they were given free clothes and beauty products. I was barely able to stay awake at the desk, let alone act the part of the fashion princess. Everyone I knew told me how lucky I was, how people would kill for my job, but *really*, what were we talking about here? Clothing. The hype that accompanied the genre was boring: colleagues cherishing their Gaultier sample sale finds, salivating over Manolo shoes, and killing each other to sit in the front rows at fashion shows. Models were taking on a celebrity of rock-star proportions, and designers were throwing hissy fits, much to everyone's delight. Were shoulder pads really that important or was I just crazy? A voice kept telling me there was more to life than this goddamn department store.

I was being courted by *Cosmopolitan* magazine to take over the fashion editor post. After five months of interviews I left Bloomies for what was to be the straw that broke the camel's back. I was to help give *Cosmo* a hip, young look. I called on hot designers who ordinary wouldn't loan clothes to the cheap-end, low-brow *Cosmo* of those days and got them involved.

Even with my new post, I was increasingly crestfallen about the fashion trade. How many times could one clash about the length of a skirt? Was it seventeen inches or twenty-one this season? What's the new black, for chrissakes? And how long did I have to watch my back?

I'd never met so many scheming people in my life. I even found a note on a coworker's desk detailing my activities to the office head—the bitch was spying on me! When the woman who hired me abandoned me for another magazine with no intention of bringing me along, I had had enough. The antics of this office were a microcosm of what the trade was about—it was de rigueur not to trust anyone. It was a shallow and harsh world indeed, and it wasn't for me.

After a stint at two less glamorous companies and freelancing, I got myself on unemployment and did a lot of clubbing, drugging, smoking, and daydreaming of what to do next.

My boyfriend at the time owned a nightclub on Sixth Avenue that primarily catered to the hip-hop and house scene. He'd been beaten up by a group of young thugs (they alleged he was a homosexual cruising them) and dodged many a bullet at that club. Put young macho Latinos and African Americans into a blustering, dark club—bass pounding, drugs and alcohol everywhere—then someone looks at someone else's girl, the next thing you know, we're all ducking for cover and running for our lives. The fire marshall was an ambitious intruder, always trying to seal the doors permanently shut. The infamous Michael Alig—the clubkid who dismembered his drug-dealer sidekick during an opiate binge—was a constant friend and promoter. There was Ecstasy in the punch, and everywhere the drop-dead-gorgeous drag queens that I loved so dearly. In hindsight, it was both a fun *and* self-indulgently depraved environment.

My unemployment was running out after three extensions, and like a lot of people who are in transition, I thought bartending would be the perfect short-term job for me. Hell, I was in New York, where there seemed to be a bar on every block. My boyfriend told me that I could make a great deal of money. Plus, I needed to recover from fashion burnout. God knows I had frequented enough bars and clubs in my life to make a go of it, and remembering how much fun I'd had made the idea even more appealing. I asked one of the bartenders at the club to teach me a thing or two. John generously let me come in early one night for a quick lesson. I was worried when all he taught me was the margarita, martini, and Manhattan, assuring me they were all I needed to commit to memory.

I had a huge bartender fetish, thanks to the divine mixers at Lucky Strike, a regular destination for my friends and me, given the view! I wanted to be the rock stars they became when they were serving up their gorgeous drinks and making me weak at the knees. Digesting their flawless cocktails and signature winks, I knew I could pull it off. They were my first inspiration.

When it became time to find a job, I went to a dubious (Mafia?) nightclub in Tribeca. George, the manager, was a weasel. (His hand was always in the bartender's till, an ethical no-no for any supervisor even if he's desperate for singles to put in his register. I recall slapping his hand quite a few times, to no avail.) But he bought the deception that I was an experienced bartender and gave me the job.

pet peeve no. 2 --➤

> Never, ever touch bartenders to get their attention. I'd rather you
> snapped your fingers like a French tourist than touch me. We deal with
> hundreds of people a week—sometimes in a day—and get pawed at
> endlessly, leaving us feeling violated and defensive. It will also
> guarantee you the slowest service you've ever had.

◄--

The world of mixing was completely different from the cold and bulimic fashion life, which I was still recuperating from. I was having more fun than I'd had in years. I hadn't danced so much since my club days, and I sampled as many drinks as I could, even daring to invent a few. With my new friends I attended parties that didn't involve me kissing up to vapid models and garish designers, and we even began promoting our own parties, which netted me even more income. We threw events at the Palladium and various downtown restaurants and invited the most marvelous people that Manhattan could offer.

And best of all, for the first time, *I* was the one people clamored to, not the fools of fashion. People came to me for their evening's entertainment and I doled it out. I had forgotten that I had a pretty good sense of humor, not having used it in eons. This newfound sense of adoration may have been an illusion, but it felt great.

I'm not saying that the bar scene can't be harsh, but at least people can let it all hang out. Most of us were laid-back, happy, and creative individuals. And unlike my experience in fashion, I didn't catch bartenders trying to stab me in the back—in fact, we had the utmost respect for one another. And we received that admiration twofold from the majority of our customers. The stress of deadlines, business meetings, and performance evaluations didn't exist in the world of mixology.

For someone whose only experience with liquor was many nights of clubbing saturated by Absolut and cranberry juice, I was in for a shock. Bartending at the nightclub in Tribeca was one of the most frightening and exhilarating experiences of my life. It was a boundless divergence from the potentially civilized restaurant-bar gig. I was, along with everyone else, in the weeds from the moment they opened the doors until the lights were turned on, blinding everyone at four in the morning.

I had purchased *The Bartending Bible*, which had every conceivable drink recipe laid out in alphabetical order. Since all I knew how to make were the martini, Manhattan, and margarita, I compiled Cliff notes on a tiny piece of paper for twenty well-known drinks I had heard of, along with their garnishes. I kept it at my register, and when someone ordered a Long Island Iced Tea I just pretended to do something at the till and checked the recipe. Because it was a nightclub, I didn't need to know which glass a drink had to be served in, since everything went into a tacky plastic cup.

Reality check, people. That's how bartenders learn how to make drinks. One by one. And over and over, until people stop complaining and we seem to have gotten the proportions down. There's no magic, Harry Potter–esque school (well, unless you're dense enough to pay for one) and no elderly wizard doling out wisdom, so be patient when we're new, okay? You didn't learn how to drink overnight either.

The most difficult duty at first was to learn bar slang or aliases for certain liquors. The first time someone ordered a Seven and Seven, I had to scratch my head. The jig was up—he knew I was a complete novice. I asked him what it was and, while shaking his head, he told me he wanted a *Seagram's* Seven and 7-Up. Who knew that "White Label" meant Dewars, or "Black Label" meant Johnnie Walker Black? Why the hell weren't they just ordering Dewars or Johnnie Walker Black? People would get upset if they got two olives in their martini instead of one or three—two were bad luck, they'd heard. Same response if they didn't get coffee beans in their Sambuca. The little rituals around the act of libation seemed to mean a lot to the people ordering, and I realized I had more to learn than a few drink recipes.

Every night at the club was a raucous adventure. People clawing the bartenders for attention was not unusual, and I was forced to throw a drink into the face of one dolt after he nabbed me hard twice. If I couldn't get to a drinker in faster-than-light time, he'd sometimes jump the bar to make his own cocktails, and would then get ejected unceremoniously by the mighty black bouncers who peppered the joint.

Phone numbers, from celebrities to faceless men, were scribbled for me drunkenly on napkins. One man who claimed to be the manager for an internationally famous rock band known for tearing hotel rooms apart tried seducing me while sporting a shiny wedding band.

"Won't the wife mind?" I asked.

"Not particularly" was his response.

pet peeve no. 3

> If you're going to have dinner or a snack at the bar, don't expect service of the kind you'd get from a waiter. If we wanted to be waiters, we wouldn't be bartending. It's not that we don't want to serve you, but have patience, as we have a lot of drinkers to deal with—our first priority. Don't send us back to the kitchen for every little thing. P.S. Most bartenders are not up to date on the menu since we deal primarily with alcohol, so don't ask me silly questions about sauces, vegetarian concerns, and sides. I know bartenders who just tell you what they think you want to hear.

Despite the chaos, I managed to learn a few tricks of the trade early on at this club. Nightclub drink prices are astronomical, so there were always the scoundrels trying to get away with smuggling in their own booze. When a club bartender would hear, "Can I have a glass of ice?" she'd pull out a plastic cup with holes pierced into the bottom, prepared just for this occasion. The clubber would then pour the liquor he'd sneaked in under his clothes into the cup—only to find his hooch draining out onto his clothes.

But if we really loathed someone, we would turn to the bottle of Visine we kept handy. A tiny squirt into a cocktail would send a lush bolting to the john with the most violent diarrhea he'd ever experienced.

Here's my Visine story. One busy night, an exceptionally annoying lush was downing Absolut tonics as if they were shots. I could barely keep up with him and the throng of clubbers who were piled on top of each other. But he didn't care. His way of getting my attention was to wave a dollar bill in the air and scream "Bartender!" at the top of his lungs. Just to shut him up, I'd get his drinks as fast as I could and move on.

In between cocktails he hit on every unaccompanied woman at the bar. The poor things were looking to me for help but I could offer none. I was just too slammed to intervene. By drink number five he was snapping his fingers to get my attention and his tips were getting smaller and smaller. He was becoming my worst enemy and he could sense it. My usual practice of acknowledgment, a good-natured wink, had turned into a glare of hatred. By drink number seven I shoved my hand to his face and said, "You'll have to wait!" as I got to other clubbers who were drinking at a normal rate and had been waiting patiently as he continued to aggravate me. I was hoping he'd fall over in a pool of his own vomit at that point, but no such luck.

After approximately eight or nine cocktails, I had had enough. He was drunk enough to screw around with, and the only way I thought I could lose him was to get him sick—pronto. The alcohol obviously wasn't enough to do it. Hoping he'd go home to his bed, I pulled out the Visine and squeezed out a few drops into his next drink. Handing it to him I said, "This one's on me. Enjoy!"

He grabbed it like a bloodthirsty hyena, stiffed me, and downed it like the others—in three giant swigs. (I have never understood why some people don't tip on the comp drink. It's not as if the drink appears out of thin air—a service grat is expected by all mixers, and a good one at that, considering the drink is free. Needless to say, it made it a helluva lot easier on my conscience that I had pulled the Visine trick on him.)

Within minutes he began wobbling and turning green. I said, "Hey, you don't look so good. Maybe you've had enough, no?"

"Nah! I just need a minute."

Within thirty seconds he bolted to the bathroom, weaving through the throng of oblivious bacchants. He pushed a few people in line for the toilets out of the way and pounded on one of the doors. A girl emerged, and he threw her aside and jumped in. I watched as a man and two women angrily banged on the door—but he was in there but good. Ten minutes later he came out. He was white as a ghost, weak, and barely able to make it to the door. I yelled out for Cedric, the bouncer, who hustled over. "Make sure he gets into a cab."

Mr. Finger Snapper/Dollar Waver/Cheapskate finally went home. Never challenge a bartender to a duel—we always play dirty.

Everyone hears how some bartenders make truckloads of money. Well, it's true. At least where nightclubs are concerned. After putting in over forty hours a week in the fashion biz bringing home about four hundred dollars (after taxes), I was now carting home between five and seven hundred dollars *a night* and only working two days a week! I had freedom like I'd never known and more money than I knew what to do with—plus I was having fun! True, there was no security in it, let alone health insurance or a 401K, but hell, at twenty-four years of age, who gives a shit? It was mind-boggling.

But, like all things that seem too good to be true, my gig at this club began falling apart, slowly, at the seams. After a small mention in *New York* magazine, the place became wildly successful, the crowd got less fabulous for it, and the fire marshall got wind of the masses. They began closing the place every other night, citing overcrowding. It didn't help that it was a rumored Mafia-backed establishment.

As the climate got more fragile, the bartenders began experiencing a silent hostility toward the manager, George. We were told to watch our tip jars by Annie, the bar manager. I began counting my tips hourly—not an easy feat when you're still running to your recipe cheat sheet all night, beating off horny customers, and feeling so busy you can't breathe. George would appear at the most engrossing moments and say he was out of singles and would help himself to my tip jar, leaving me with twenties and removing the dollar bills. I realized that I was missing between one and two hundred dollars a night from my jar after he had made "change." If he was helping himself to all the bar tip jars, he was pocketing about a thousand dollars a night—in cash! That was one of the first trade lessons I learned. The manager stealing from his own bartenders, besides qualifying him as pure scum, was another clue that the place would be closed down sooner than we thought.

It was a great start anyway. Nightclubs in particular taught me about the requisite importance of speed and the bare basics of the craft. How to make a drink in general and, most important, how to get addicted to the money. Bartending is a love-hate thing, and don't make believe the love is much more than the wad of cash you're going to take home. Usually it's not. But there are nights when there's a certain magic in the air, you're giddy about life, you love *all* of your regulars, you dance with your coworkers because of a favorite song on the stereo, you fall in love with a stranger. Just for one night.

I got busy looking for another bar gig and landed one at a celebrated eatery on the Upper West Side. I never made as much cash as I did at the nightclub, but I also vowed never to work in such an insane environment ever again. Within two weeks of starting at my new job, the nightclub closed for various violations cited by the fire marshall.

But hell, as a bartender I was in!

People thought I was crazy for becoming a bartender. Some even looked down on me for it (what could prompt a successful woman to stoop so low?). I could see the condescension in their eyes, the disappointment in my mother's brow. According to her, Muslim girls were supposed to get married and push out three kids by the age of twenty-two. I took it all in stride, never explaining it to people of the yuppie mind-set or to my family. They wouldn't have understood. Couldn't a girl try something new without everyone coming down on her?

True, the new job wasn't without its pitfalls. My friends and I started drifting apart. My new hours didn't allow me to mix with nine-to-fivers. There were the embarrassing nights when I served my old contemporaries their cocktails, sensing the pity in their corporate gazes *(she was so promising)*. They couldn't see how satisfied I was. Or they wouldn't. I was different—I had changed. Like leaving a husband who wouldn't grow with me, I left my desk and took up the bottle.

Time is incredibly underrated in a world of IPOs and Roth IRAs. I could finally take a stab at writing the great American novel, become an actress, try painting—all things I'd dreamed about doing one day. For a long time I'd cursed my Seventh Avenue existence for crowding my creative yearnings. It hadn't given me enough time to sleep six hours a night, let alone pursue an artful life.

No more cubicle, no more sunshine wasted on business lunches. Yeah, the bar scene can be harsh, but I finally got to be me.

I was free.

Sex with a Twist

I drink to make other people interesting.

GEORGE JEAN NATHAN

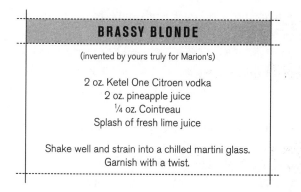

BRASSY BLONDE

(invented by yours truly for Marion's)

2 oz. Ketel One Citroen vodka
2 oz. pineapple juice
¼ oz. Cointreau
Splash of fresh lime juice

Shake well and strain into a chilled martini glass.
Garnish with a twist.

Throughout most of the twentieth century the Bowery, located on Manhattan's Lower East Side, was known as the last port for drunks. Flophouses and seedy bars, liquor stores and the Salvation Army, all vied for the tobacco-stained men and women who had nowhere else to go. Since the mid-1990s, interest in the Bowery has taken on epic proportions, mainly because it has endured a massive amount of gentrification. Now we have à la mode restaurants taking on the look of L.A., with palm trees, bouncers, and velvet ropes, and trendy handbag shops squeezed in between restaurant supply chains. Skid Row has cashed in beyond recognition. Nowadays, the Salvation Army looks curious, out of place. The last liquor store on the Bowery was bulldozed in the spring of 2001. Something is wrong with the world when a liquor store doesn't exist on the Bowery.

I hadn't been on the Bowery since my clubkid days. Area, the Pyramid, the World, and the Michael Todd room at the Palladium were places to be seen, after which we'd eat brownie ice-cream sundaes with alluring drag queens at Jerry's 103 on Second Avenue at 6 A.M. *every morning.* We climbed over bums to get to our sundaes, and I could have never imagined their extinction back then. However annoying, dusty, and rude, they were Bowery fixtures.

From 1984 until 1990 my friends and I lived the New York fantasy. When walking into a club, I'd be handed a bunch of drink tickets—I didn't even pay for booze!—and would be given free drugs, fall in love every night, and dance for hours. There was a debauched and venomous excitement that permeated the air as we experimented with life. During our adventures, we put on trial our sexuality, played with illicit opiates, and coexisted with art; and though many of us didn't survive, the memories remain golden. I don't think anyone would regret a single moment of those magical days, despite the consequences. We didn't need a Woodstock, and I like to think we didn't turn into stock-greedy yuppies. I think I idealize this period like some do the sixties, but the people who were there also reminisce as if the heart of New York stopped beating when Steve Rubell—the coowner of Studio 54 and the Palladium—bit the dust.

Today, sadly, I think of Manhattan as a giant Duane Reade. One big homogenized disaster. Its shimmer is more like a corporate fluorescent bulb flickering a deadened beat, and, sure, it may be safer, but the streets seem fueled by mediocrity instead of inventive juices. The innocence has faded. We worry too much to deeply enjoy Manhattan: anthrax, terrorism, and the stock market crash into our lives every other day. There's no time for art. We're too busy watching CNN.

Back in the day, chatting with Andy Warhol, Jean-Michel Basquiat, Francesco Clemente, Julian Schnabel, and Keith Haring on a single night was routine. It was like an elephantine art orgasm. Fresh bands like Rita Mitsouko from France or ABC played for you, and banal girlies like Britney couldn't get into these establishments. The drag queens did runway every evening—before Madonna heisted Vogueing—at closing time when the lights turned on. Gay, straight, white, black, purple, and green coexisted beautifully, and I had more fun than I ever had in my life or ever hope to again.

Toward the end of that lustrous era, Marion's Continental Restaurant and Lounge sprung up on the Bowery, just off East Fourth. It was July of 1990, and it took a lot of balls to open on this spot. The owners took advantage of the cheap real estate and parked themselves on what turned out to be a gold mine. They were pioneers when they debuted on this shady street—and in doing so, began a cycle that picked away at the very character of the neighborhood. Whether they knew it or not.

Other than the burgeoning club scene, not much else in the way of refined socializing was going on in the area. A semiserious restaurant on the Bowery was sure to fail. Who would brave walking over passed-out winos and drug addicts just for some grub? Grade-C prostitutes and drug dealers abounded, and the buildings had the famous gray tinge. The punk rockers and clubbers did come to get into CBGB's, but for fine dining? We're talking pre-Giuliani here.

A fifties lounge–style establishment with jazz reverberating, and waiters in red vests and crisp white shirts: attitude that redefined ornery—but with a sense of humor. Then there were the bartenders, impassioned about their soon-to-be award-winning, almighty martini, armed with a demeanor that was tough but never too cool to listen to people's problems. I'm proud to include myself among them. We created a decade-plus following that just won't quit.

It must have cost practically nothing to create Marion's. Nearly everything on the walls and anything considered decor must have been bought at flea markets and auctions. Walls were covered with cheesy paintings, collectible U.S. state plates, a mock Andy Warhol portrait of Marion, cocker spaniel figurines, knickknacks, and bric-abrac. But for some inexplicable reason, when the lights were dimmed into their carefully chosen combination of gold and red, everything looked priceless. Even the orange booths and tufted black leather banquettes, purchased at a Howard Johnson's auction, added a nostalgic touch. And when the place really got going, the disco ball would shower silvery flecks over the diners and drinkers, who were then transferred to a magical place in another time.

In the back of the room, located in front of the Sky Lounge, is a large round table (#1) that sits six to eight people. It's called the Kennedy Booth, and the walls around it are festooned with a collection of pictures and paintings of the president and his family. Often diners called to reserve it by name, embracing the dub since it created the history they yearned for: the rumor was that Marion had had a fling with the sexy president back in the day. When John John dined at Marion's, the topless painting of Jackie O was tastefully draped with a black velvet cloth, and when she died, the space was adorned with black ribbons.

Music is critical to the vibe of Marion's. What easier way to transport people to the fifties than playing the melodies that defined the era? Michael, a waiter who used to mix the tapes, was a connoisseur of the period; through him I learned to really appreciate this music, which I had never acknowledged before. His eclectic selections featured the likes of Ella, Frank, Tony, Billie, Sarah, Rosemary, and the many other vocalists who made our evenings romantic and memorable. Though the fifties were our schtick, the owners permitted all music up until 1970. With this concession, we listened to blues, sixties rock, early disco, light classical, bluegrass, Broadway musicals, and other retro-sounding tunes. I did, however, get my own music on the sound system when it was late enough and the room consisted mostly of drinkers. My tapes were of current alternative/indie music (Tom Waits, Radiohead, Elliott Smith, Guided by Voices, Ryan Adams, Nirvana, etc.) and people did appreciate the change of pace. There's just so much Sinatra we could listen to before wanting to run into oncoming Bowery traffic.

The most treasured part of the look is unequivocally the hundreds of celebrity plates that line the walls of the bar area. Instead of asking celebrities to sign head shots of themselves, we invited them to autograph dinner plates. Sometimes they would get creative. Beautiful pictures were made by Matt Dillon, Ed Harris, Patty Smith, Tim Robbins, Tabitha Soren, and Drew Barrymore, to name a few. Others enjoyed penning poetry (sometimes charming and sometimes bizarre), including Ethan Hawke, Sean Penn, Annie Liebowitz, Marisa Tomei, Billy Corgan of the Smashing Pumpkins, and Spalding Gray. The only celebrity who deigned it inappropriate to sign a plate while dining out was the brilliantly banal Keanu Reeves, who got a lot of flack from his table for acting so precious.

One afternoon Ernesto, the dishwasher, was asked to clean the plates since they had gotten ashen and brownish from all the cigarette smoke that stained the walls. He didn't speak any English at the time so he thought he was supposed to bleach off the autographs. He accidentally destroyed the plates of Chuck Close, Roy Lichtenstein, and Robert Rauschenberg. That broke my heart.

In the front of the restaurant by the bar is our lounge. It was technically considered a section of my workstation, where people could sit at the two small café tables and have appetizers with their martinis. The walls displayed photos of Marion with a variety of notable fifties stars. A framed photograph of Audrey Hepburn used to hang among them, with the scribble, "To Cary, I'll never forget our little secret." It was unceremoniously stolen the day after she passed away. So many of the celebrity photos were lifted that in my final year at Marion's, they were bolted down. In fact, I once had a customer chase down a bandit who filched a framed glossy of Doris Day for two blocks—and return it! Now *that's* a devoted regular.

I have never seen a bar look more different from day to night as Marion's. In the daytime the place was grubby and disoriented, like the many flophouses it neighbored. But in the evenings (those divine evenings!) it changed into something glorious, like a night on the town with Frank Sinatra—Peggy Lee serenading and the gold light casting martini glasses luminous.

The legend was that Marion Nagy, an ex-model, Olympic swim-mer, and mother to three eccentric children (who went on to launch other restaurants), had opened the joint in 1950. The walls were dressed up with photos of Marion and Sinatra. Marion and Clark Gable. Marion, Ava Gardner, and Judy Garland. Flanked on the wall across the bar were framed glossies of stars with scribbles, always "To Marion." Burt Reynolds's says, "You're one classy gal . . ." Her beloved drink was the Stolichnaya Gibson, so it became the house cocktail. Sometime in the late seventies, the infamous Ms. Nagy closed the joint. No one knows why. One of her sons, along with his boyfriend, reopened it on the same spot. They continue to swear by this story. We, the staff, were told to stick to it. So we did. The crowd that came in week after week reveled in the idea that they were hanging in the same digs as Tony Bennett and Nancy Wilson. I always doubted if Sinatra and Bennett, Hepburn and Davis, would actually undertake an outing to the Bowery back then. I mean, *really.* In the eighties, you could hardly get anyone but clubkids and drag queens past Lafayette.

These fantasies coupled with the space's location and retro set-ting—the history, the glamour, and the forbidden—are what give Marion's its resolve. Much like a speakeasy during prohibition, the place has an aura of the illicit. Anyone who comes has the feeling he is drinking at the best-kept secret of Manhattan. And he is.

Before getting the job at Marion's I worked on the Upper West Side serving an awful lot of bland white people killing time before the curtain went up at Lincoln Center. Watching the celebrities who frequented the place in herds provided me with some diversion from the aching boredom of that job, until I realized the $200 a week I was making just wouldn't cut it. A waiter told me there was an open bar gig at the Bowery's only restaurant and that they were looking for a female mixer. I had nothing to lose so I asked for a recommendation and called.

The reference did the trick; I was asked to come by. Jumping on my bicycle I rode to no-man's-land, my old stomping grounds. Locking the bike on a meter I noticed two shaggy men inspecting it. I responded by gaping back at them. They realized it was a crappy vehicle and strode on. They were right—I had bought it on St. Marks Place for five bucks.

It seemed an eternity when a small Mexican man reeking of tequila answered the doorbell that I'd been ringing. He didn't understand a word I said, so I enunciated the owner's name slowly and loudly. He finally got that and disappeared to the back room to get him. I waited. And waited. After a few minutes I began perusing the place.

It was dark. The only sounds were the industrial dishwasher in back and the occasional ringing of the phone—and the unmistakable scurrying sounds of mice running amok. The dull light from the cloudy sky filtered through the large window up front, the only light available in the whole place. The stools were upside down on the bar and only the bottles glistened. The place still reeked of the previous night's revelry.

An attractive man finally came to the booth I was sitting at. He was the straightest-looking gay man I'd ever met. My days at Fags-in-Training had misled me into thinking that gay men were forever sporting boas and pumps, air-snapping their fingers. This guy was J. Crew straight-looking. He didn't ask a lot about my experience, which was great since there wasn't much, but did ask when I could start. I said immediately, and the next thing I knew I was thrust upon a scene I was not prepared for—one that lasted well into the next decade.

The owner disappeared into the coat-check room that hid the stairs to the basement. I had gotten up to leave when I noticed the back of the restaurant flashed a large aquarium filled with floating plants and a sunken treasure chest that was illuminated by its waters. Two dead goldfish floated on top, their mouths gaping open and their eyes staring into space. There was a third still clinging to life.

Typical Marion's.

pet peeve no. 4

If you're a regular at my bar and you have a crush on another regular, please don't ask me to fix you up. I don't mind playing matchmaker, but if it doesn't pan out, or she ends up burning an effigy of you with your entire wardrobe, don't come to my bar and expect free drinks for the rest of your life because I fixed you up and it failed. Leave me out of it.

My new life suited me well as I made fascinating new friends and began discovering a fresh New York. As an exiled corporate lackey I was downright light-headed. I have never known a mixologist who didn't start out utterly psyched to tend bar. We're always fervent and privileged to be a part of it. There's a history and nobility attached to it. After the prostitute, it's got to be one of the oldest professions.

There's all the interesting people you're going to meet, all the free booze you're going to imbibe, your days off to walk about in the city's sunshine while people are imprisoned in their cubicles, all that time to pursue your writing/acting/painting/dancing dreams, not to mention getting laid. All that getting laid!

Here's what I now know. People are positively *not* that interesting, especially after a few drinks. Most bartenders are in AA because of the free liquor. Or else they end up loathing its effects after witnessing their customers destroy themselves. (I was once asked by a cab-driver, "Would you want to drive on your days off if you were me?") Or they become obnoxious connoisseurs about wine, single-malt scotches, or wheat beers, get obsessed about Robert Parker and get gout. You're actually too tired from your busy shift the night before to wake up before three in the afternoon, so if you get in a good three hours of daylight, consider yourself lucky. And *forget* making it to that audition. You're depleted and your eyes are too puffy. And, interestingly enough, you don't get laid that much. Never mind Tom Cruise flipping glass bottles with pecs throbbing under his guinea-T. The girls dancing on top of the bar at Hogs and Heifers for Harrison Ford are miserable (a few "heifers" had applied for jobs at Marion's and they told me so—dancing on bars is exhausting; plus the owner is a bitch, or so I hear). The closest facsimile of bar culture I've ever seen in a film was *Barfly:* miserable drunks, awkward sexual alliances made after too many cocktails, and enough small talk to choke a horse.

But here's the trick: like the lure of Frank Sinatra at Marion's, it's about the promise of something more. Despite the fact that my illusions of bartending came to a crashing pile of martini glasses, I was stuck on waiting for the prospects to come through. And while patiently waiting, Marion's allowed me the autonomy and cash to experiment with all the dreams I ever held through childhood. Corporate America never allowed me to dream of anything more than a paltry check at the end of the week. And for me, that was never enough.

And so people came in droves, day after day, to see if we were hiring for a coveted position behind the bar. At one point we hadn't booked a bartender in over ten years—*that's* how good the gig was. It is the rare bar job when the bartenders are around that long, anyone who has ever mixed knows that. I always acknowledged how damn lucky I was.

Bartenders are quick to describe the imperfections of their patrons. They like to feel untouchable and in control because most of the time, they are deluged by drunken rubes. To cope they learn to desensitize themselves against their patrons' failures and infectious melancholy. It really does get to you after a while.

Russell, an ex-bartender at my steady haunt, Lucky Strike, once told me how a regular of his had come in with a nasty cold one January afternoon. When Russell told him that he looked green at the gills, his customer said he could use a bourbon to clear his throat. He just needed to "anesthetize" the pain so he could feel "human" again. And that pretty much says it all. Numbing oneself goes a long way in neurotic New York City. What better way to get over an ex *or* a cold, for that matter? You can drown your sorrows in that drink, and there's always brandy for your coffee for that sniffle that won't go away.

I have seen a lot of good excuses for getting lit, loneliness being at the top of the list. And after a couple of cocktails everyone starts looking pretty good. A friend once told me he read somewhere that statistically the same person you found unattractive at the beginning of the night looks 60 percent better by last call. Let's face it, God invented bars so people could get laid. Psychologically it's a setup; that promise of a human connection. Of sex. Maybe even love.

Foodies like to decree that a fine meal is tantamount to sex, hence the existence of restaurant groupies, star chefs, and designer *intercourse* cookbooks. We like to feed our lovers in erotic ways. We go on dinner dates and observe the way our potential lover eats. We enjoy licking the dribble off his chin. I've dumped people for chewing with their mouths open or making strange noises when they swallow. We've given sexual meanings to hundreds of foods. There have been foodies from the beginning of time.

For better or worse, despite all the exotic, elaborate, and hard-to-get edibles we've assumed (or deluded ourselves into believing) make oneself more tempting to another, there is absolutely *nothing* that will get two people into the sack like ALCOHOL. Food may be the way to a man's heart, but it's the Sapphire Gibson that will get you into his pants. There isn't an oyster in the world that can get you laid faster than an ice-cold dry martini in a dimly lit, jazz-infused bar.

It's not all flirtations and the possibility that a stranger could jump-start one's life. There's a serious dark side. Alcohol contributes to many unwanted sexual advances as well. A lot of data illustrate that the inability to control one's drinking can lead to vast misadventures as well as the cheap passionate encounter. I know when a man is taking advantage and when a woman is headed for trouble. I've pulled as many people apart as I've played matchmaker for. Some may disagree, but I considered it part of my job.

One of our hostesses at Marion's, Pam, had a drinking problem, and that's a colossal understatement. Despite the fact that she was living with her boyfriend, I found her drunk and brazenly hitting on men nearly every night. I put my foot down during one particular episode when she was practically sitting on a stranger's lap. That evening, as usual, she was a helpless lush not in control of her faculties. He, also really drunk, was elbowing his buddies and they were cheering him on. Everything about him spelled "date-rape."

I tried to pull her aside several times, and in the end I pleaded with her to stop egging him on. She waved her hand, saying she was just having some fun, not to worry. Eventually they were making out, Pam barely standing at this point. Finally she wobbled to the bathroom for a touch-up. I went to Mr. Date Rape and told him straight, "You're cut off. Take your friends and get out."

Bartenders are required by law and moral code to stop serving people they deem inebriated enough to harm themselves or someone else. It's usually met with a lot of outrage. In this case, Mr. Date Rape said he wasn't drunk and that I had no right to cut him off. Besides, he said, he was hanging out with the manager.

"She's the hostess, not the manager," I said. "You know she's loaded and you're an asshole for using her. If you so much as say one more word to her I am going to have you thrown out."

Luckily, several regulars backed me up and the guys begrudgingly walked out before Pam returned. I took her aside and told her she was an alcoholic and that if she pulled that crap again I would have to go above her. She soon stopped hostessing and assumed an office position.

Liquor can lead you to a seemingly lustful evening with someone you later wish you had seen in daylight at least once. It seems odd that so many people continue to depend on bars for sex—especially when the stats show that after a few shots your performance lacks the athletic stamina required to dazzle a total stranger. How hot can sex get when a guy can't maintain an erection—referred to as "whiskey dick"? One fallacy is that it's a stimulant and can increase one's performance. Wrong. Alcohol is a depressant and will, instead, put you to sleep—not so fun when trying to bag a lover. For the gals, alcohol often leads to painful sex because they can't stay lubricated, and in addition to slowing arousal time it cuts any chance in hell for orgasm. It can also kill sperm count should anyone like to procreate. That third Cosmo can also make you stupid enough to believe that ex-lovers are really dying for you to telephone them at four in the morning.

In the end, what alcohol is really good for, sexually speaking, is lowering inhibitions, which is obviously why so many people go to bars to get laid in the first place. Liquor makes us vulnerable. It makes us initially feel lucid and approachable. Most people just aren't capable of boldly walking up to someone they find attractive and striking up a conversation—especially in the United States, where sex is a confusing mix of puritanical repression and a Madison Avenue, in-your-face T-and-A fest. Maybe bad sex is better than no sex at all.

Another side effect of booze: it causes you to tell the same boring story over and over again until your date wants to *smash your head in*. I should know.

It all started with the singles bar, and Maxwell's Plum is still considered the pioneer of this setup. Pickup lines like "What's your sign?" came out of this burger-beer-and-babe haunt on Sixty-Fourth Street and First Avenue, in the spring of 1966. We're talking fake ferns, mirrored walls, and brass detailing; Don Juans sporting thick, gold chains over their fashionably hairy chests with Harvey Wallbangers or Screwdrivers lined up in front of them. It was a Mecca for all of New York City's horny social classes: stewardesses, dancers, actors, millionaires, and wanna-be urchins that had nowhere to congregate. Donald met Ivana there. Owner LeRoy (who went on to open Tavern on the Green) had wanted to design a communal meeting spot on the grand scale of a Roman arena—and it worked. It took six policemen to control the masses on opening night.

Maxwell's Plum was also where bartenders broke out with pseudo-celeb distinction. They were all attractive and were as much in demand for dates as the patrons were—they poured glamour.

If there's anything they taught us it's that the three things that make a bartender successful are sex, sex, and, lest I forget, *sex*. What it boils down to is, how much money do you want to make? There is a plenitude of notable barkeeps who do just fine churning out the cocktails, attending to everyone's worries, and generally keeping the good vibes rolling. There isn't a whole lot of flirting going on, but their professionalism keeps their business steady. They're probably making the standard dollar per drink and it affords them a decent lifestyle.

Then there are the bartenders who rake it in. You know, the ones you hear about who walk home with twelve hundred dollars working two or three nights a week, who can afford that share in the Hamptons, and who go on vacation every six months. They work hard, can't feel their feet ("waiter's foot"), are in a sort of fog from exhaustion, hungover, and spent, but, hey, they made twelve hundred dollars in less than thirty hours and you're in a cubicle, paying taxes up the arse, hoping for that one week of paid vacation with no hopes of affording a share at Jones Beach, let alone the Hamptons.

What are these bartenders doing that the other, less financially successful ones aren't? They're selling their sex appeal, at least as much as their establishment's trendy cocktails, and the promise that you will feel like the most adored person in the world. It sounds trite, but sex sells, especially when there's alcohol involved.

In my single days I frequented Lucky Strike two or three times a week in the late eighties and early nineties. They had a marvelous selection of male bartenders, Rob and Brendan, whom I had befriended on my regular jaunts there. A girlfriend and I would drop in and would be entertained merely by watching them work their magic. It wasn't that they were model handsome or even extreme bartenders, but they radiated a flirty charm and sultriness that had all the stools holding up a bevy of beautiful women, head in hands, literally wiping the drool off their faces. The competition for Rob and Brendan's attention was ruthless. I'd seen many digits left on their bar, and I imagined the two had a sort of contest going every night. In the beginning, I was one of those girls: early twenties, frustrated by the lack of straight men in my circle, and pretty damn desperate. In my feeble attempts at trying to get to know these two, we all just ended up becoming pals, which wasn't exactly my first choice; but Rob in particular became a bar ally in the ensuing years of my new career. I had even gotten him his next job at B Bar after he left Lucky Strike.

It was my days as a patron at Lucky Strike, watching the hottie pros in action, knowing they were getting laid left and right, knowing they were making a fortune, knowing they were getting a kind of attention that only rock stars get, that ignited my fascination with mixology, and I was hooked.

Appraise Manet's *A Bar at the Folies-Bergeres* and his interpretation of the barmaid. Reverence from a great painter. She looks detached, motherly, and like a whore all at once. It's still what managers look for when hiring women to tend bar, one of the few fields where women make more money than men.

There are a few things that every female bartender knows. The less she wears the more money she makes. It's just common insider knowledge—I'm not trying to tick NOW off by saying this. I had a vast collection of indispensable Wonderbras, tube tops, and tight dresses. When I heard that drag queens wore MAC Lipglass (the shiniest known to man) I knew it would round out the look. When drag queens swear by a lip gloss, you listen!

The "less is more" concept was especially difficult during the winter months. Our heaters would collapse from overwork by Thanksgiving and couldn't keep me warm, let alone the customers. Casey was bartending with a sweater on and Ida, one of the ex-fill-ins, once wore a down coat and scarf during her shift. I was a trooper. There I was, tube top and microscopic skirt, mixing as my breath evaporated into thick chunks mingling with cigarette smoke. The goose bumps were impossible to conceal and my erect nipples brought in more than a few lowered glances—and large tips. "Aren't you freezing?" I'd be asked every night.

"No. Are you?" would be my immediate response, through chattering teeth. My shivering told another story. I would count out my tips for the night, quickly don a Gap sweater to layer me toasty, and call last call before hurling the last of the frozen nightcappers out into the snow.

It worked, all right. The men got something to dream about that night. I didn't mind the rubbernecking leers at first—fielding men was a fun way to pass the time. I got paid very well for it and it made me feel attractive, even if all the adoration was directed toward my chest. Perhaps I had a touch of latent exhibitionism to express.

As you now know, it's about the promise. It's the rare man who comes to a bar by himself looking to go home alone. Newcomers would cast their desperate eyes on me as I plodded through my shift. When I would look over, they wouldn't turn away like the lovesick regulars do. As things quieted down, they would ask for my name and another drink. When the next drink was put down, they would incorporate the overplayed conversation. Batting eyelashes, confident that the Lipglass was working overtime, I would try to humor them. When it was time to leave there was always the huge tip on the bar with a phone number scrawled drunkenly on a napkin. It was sad that their techniques never varied ... just the number on the crumpled napkin, never to be dialed.

Regulars were customized. They were classic Bowery—downtrodden at times, shabby-chic at others, East Village glamorous with tattered edges all the way. They lived in frayed loft or studio apartments, had great taste in music, and were lonely beyond belief. Most were artists—painters, actors, and the usual gamut of strugglers—though there was a smidgen of frustrated cubicle worker bees who needed a regular hit of fantasy. Marion's was where they could pretend something legendary was going on in New York besides being parked on a couch watching reruns with a pint of Ben & Jerry's Chunky Monkey.

Needing their steady business, making customers feel privileged became one of the unavoidable tasks I had to attend to. After asking "The usual?" I readied their cocktail and placed it before them. This was always the first attack: *She knows my drink! Cool!* Other customers would notice I was playing favorites. Some would get a kiss on the cheek. When the bar was slow and there was breathing room, these regulars got most—if not all—of my attention. The compliments they showered on me were unending, seemingly sincere. If I truly liked the person, I gave it right back. These lonesome souls usually stayed until last call and then there it was: a twenty, fifty, or hundred dollar bill on the bar. I can't deny that many times there was a twinge of guilt as I put the cash into the tip jar as they walked out the door, rejected, into the night.

Anyone reading this is probably going to think my behavior is callous, even malicious. But consider this. Corporate suits regularly rent hookers and lap dancers to impress their clients and automobile manufacturers still use bikini-clad women to sell cars. The most popular magazine covers feature half-naked models and celebrities (at *Cosmopolitan* magazine we even airbrushed more cleavage onto the already ample forms). Porn stars are becoming mainstream and soap operas are out of control. Madison Avenue sells sex by the boatload, and movies celebrate exploited actresses who peel off their clothes as part of the show. Get real—*sex sells*.

At the very least, I cared about my customers. But in the end it's a business just like anything else

----

There are tricks we use to make more money at the bar and, hopefully, a regular out of you—of course, the easiest tactic is the ability to flirt. You should know we usually aren't the least bit attracted to you, but we want to spark your interest. I made a lot of regulars this way, and it's a great way to get to know people. I've been duped by many a male bartender myself and I didn't mind that they were playing me. Maybe it was about rebelling against my Islamic background or a feigned attempt at boosting my ego, but hell, it was a great distraction. I hear time flies when you're having fun—and boy, was it fun.

Some mixers use tactics that are downright cold. A bartendress I met at a local hangout once let me in on a trick that always worked for her. I thought it was overly manipulative, not to mention extremely high-maintenance, but she swore by it.

Whenever a newcomer came to her bar, she would flirt until the drinker was frequenting the bar regularly. She said the tips were great but the jackpot was in pushing it further. On the fourth or fifth visit, she would set things up to the point where he would ask her out on a date. She would accept and they would exchange phone numbers. Now the lush was hooked. He would depart that night leaving a gigantic tip and dreams of a rendezvous, one which she never intended to keep. He would call her and they would arrange the date. Her ruse was to cancel it at the last minute with some "urgent problem" she had to attend to. He would "understand" and come to the bar again to chat—and leave another large tip. She would set up more dates, only to cancel them until he would decide that she was too flakey to date but fun enough to be his favorite bartender. She ends up with a loyal drinker and he ends up with a fun way to spend his evening—and his cash.

My poker face isn't good enough to pull that off, nor would I want to. For me, the most profitable strategy was to get to know as many restaurant and bar workers as I could. Nobody tips like other service professionals. After spending time hashing out the business, gossiping, and sharing work anecdotes, they will always leave the best tip of the night—which I reciprocate in a courtesy call within a few weeks. It's common service-industry etiquette. And we *always* come back.

If I listen to your saga about how you had to put your mother into a nursing home last week, then you will probably leave me a stellar grat. It's really important for bartenders to find time to listen to a customer's rant. I even had a drinker once tell me, after I told him I didn't have time to chat, that it was my *job* to listen to his story. I told him to get a life, but actually, he was right to an extent. They don't call us the poor man's psychiatrist for nothing. And much like soap opera story lines, these narratives almost always continue on the next visit.

I liked to use the phrase "I'm on it" all the time. It gave patrons the idea that I was going to take care of them before anyone else and give them special treatment. Even if I didn't. The term could mean a variety of things, but the connotation was what was important. I even took their order before someone who was at the bar first, but I didn't always *make* their drink first. It's the illusion that they're first, even if they're not.

If I really despised a customer—a serial cheapskate, for example— and he was intent on getting my phone number and exasperating me to the point where I began fantasizing tearing his eyes out of their sockets with my paring knife, I had a simple trick that usually worked. I would appear to *lightheartedly* give in and scribble my phone number on a napkin. Tightwad would triumphantly stuff the digits into his wallet and walk out the door feeling like a champ. When he finally got around to calling me, he'd be greeted with a machine that said, "You must be eighteen years or older to use this service. Please have your credit card ready. . . ." Basically my tactic for these tenacious morons was to give them an escort rental's number. Hey, at least I gave them the chance to finally score!

Another technique that frequently worked was to convert a Cosmopolitan drinker to a similar cocktail that only Marion's specialized in. This trick worked especially well with women. For example, I had a local woman who came in for Cosmos every month, so I suggested the Suburban. It was very similar in that it was fruity and came in a martini glass, but it also employed blood-orange juice. She loved them so much that she began coming every week. I mean, who else is going to have blood-orange juice at their bar?

pet peeve no. 5 ···➤

> Take a look around you. Don't tell me your life story when I'm in the weeds. Yeah, I'm nodding my head, evidently riveted by whatever it is you're saying, but if you really must know, I didn't hear a single word you said. I was too busy trying to remember the drinks that the last eight people asked for and in which order to serve them. Your sob story really isn't that important to me at the moment.

◄···

But back to sex. The "Platform" theory is the main reason why a bartender is both revered and capable of making large amounts of cash. When she is standing back behind the bar, she generally acts as the entertainment for the place. There I'd be, mixing drinks with as much knack as I could muster, regaling the throngs of patrons with my (hopefully not too boring) stories and jokes, decked out in full gear (with sparkly makeup and coiffed hair), performing like a trollop and, most of all, listening to everyone' gripes. People loved to comment on the way I made a martini. One woman even came to me once, handing me a twenty dollar bill and saying, "You bartend like a ballerina. I love watching you!"

Watching me work meant watching an actress in a role that didn't draw upon aspects of her real life. I've never been into the Method technique—my performance every night was improvisational with an underlying continuity. Especially the flirting.

When a newcomer sat himself down and it was rather busy, the most important first step was eye contact. There's that certain way to look (or wink) at a man you're interested in—I would transfer that to the patron. It put the *Hey, sailor!* on the *I'll be right over!* That little glance in acting is called a "button." Ever see a commercial that ends with the actress turning to the camera and giving a little wink? That's a button. Or in a soap opera when the scene ends with a close-up of the actor's face and all you see is a drawn-out shot of a glare? The button, or tag, is a strong emphasis on a brief gaze or expression. It's meant to make a point. At the bar, the point being made was always "Hey, handsome, want a blow job?"

All the dependable trappings came into play: batting eyelashes, demure smirk, twisting of hair, wetting of lips, and the like. If I really wanted to make some money I would engage in a conversation that included topics of interest to men: sports, architecture, music (the Bob Dylan type), and male lit. Mentioning books by Henry Miller was always a crowd pleaser, as most men couldn't believe a woman would appreciate his work—after all, he frequently referred to women as "cunts" and I reckon I'm supposed to be insulted by this. For some odd reason, this turned some men on.

I did everything I wasn't supposed to do as a Muslim woman; I was aware while sending out those vibes and inflections that hell was definitely in my distant future. It wasn't rocket science—all the weapons a woman has stored up came in handy when going the extra mile for the tip jar (despite it condemning me as Satan's martini-master for eternity). Hey, I had to eat and it gave the customer something to dream about. Plus, it was a fun role to play.

The lady who compared me with a ballerina was a perfect example of how closely a bartender is watched sometimes. I often enjoyed observing a customer oversee my technique. In a common scene, she would sit very still as I pulled out her martini glass and piled it high with ice cubes. Then I'd fill it with water. If she was a novice she'd shriek, "I said I wanted it straight up!" To which I'd quietly reply, "I know. I'm chilling your glass."

Her look of relief would suddenly turn to awe. The clear mixing glass would appear and I'd fill that up with ice cubes and pull the bottle of liquor without even looking behind me. Filling it a perfect four-count, I'd twirl the glass with my left hand to let it settle. In tandem, my right hand would be reaching for the dry vermouth, which was kept on the speed rack below. With my right pointer finger I would cover the spout and let exactly one bead of Vermouth plunge into the liquor. To this, she would smile. The large metal mixing glass would be put over the glass and the shaking would commence. I would shake the concoction for about fifteen seconds over my shoulder until the metal mixing glass was freezing to the touch. It would sweat when it was ready; with my hand numbed I would remove it. With my left hand the strainer would be placed on the top of the glass and I would twirl it around some more. During that time, my right hand would be reaching for a napkin to be placed in front of the customer. I would then pour out the ice that had been chilling the martini glass and put the cold glass on the napkin. Now with that free hand I would pull out an olive that had been prespeared while my left hand began pouring the chilled cocktail into the frosty glass. Presto!

She would look privileged to be drinking such a lovingly made cocktail and I would flicker with pride as I put the fiver into the tip jar. The trick was to keep both hands engaged on a different job the whole time. I became ambidextrous not by choice, but necessity. I also employed stylistic affectations: shaking over my shoulder, letting the vermouth drop from very high above the mixing glass, pulling out multiple bottles without having to look. It has to look seamless— as if I could do it in my sleep. Which I can.

That's the "Platform" theory—if you want to impress someone, get them to see you on some kind of pedestal. Even if it's just hosting a fabulous party or making a speech of some kind. Get yourself on television or a stage—they'll never see you the same way again.

Mind you, this was work, but there was a payoff. The regulars were my bread and butter, and the men who developed crushes on me showered me with praise and cold, hard cash. I wasn't necessarily exploiting them, because to be a good bartender you really must enjoy flirting, but there are nights when it's just not in you. If you're good, they'll never know you're premenstrual and ready to stab them in the heart with a broken bottle of Heineken. A professional bartender will smile, however difficult, and give them what they came for—after all, the show must go on!

Watching Rob and Brendan at Lucky Strike also taught me how to sell sexuality but still have the all-important protective wall. Those boys could and would lower that wall when they wanted to, but it was always there. A good bartender, especially women bartenders, know to keep that wall up at *all* times.

I have had my share of customers who have gotten hold of my unlisted phone number and called my home to ask me out on dates. There are those who hung up on me every two or three hours, and the ones who left bizarre messages on my machine without leaving their names or digits—leaving me guessing in fear. Those who left sordid poems at the bar letting me know what they'd like to do to me. Those who have waited for me outside the bar so that I had to beg a waiter to take me home. While we played Liar's Poker on a slow night I once had a regular tell me flat out he enjoyed masturbating to me. One elderly gentleman from a halfway house down the street from Marion's told me no one had ever fucked me like he could and began to tell me in minuscule detail what he'd do to me. *Trust me*, female bartenders need to make the wall their friend.

Working at Bloomingdale's I never had to worry about stalkers or creepy phone calls in the middle of the night. At one point, literally every man I worked with was gay. After a decade of bartending, turning down crusty men nearly every night left me depleted and disillusioned. Perhaps it would have been a different story had they been interesting or even mildly attractive. Those men almost never approached me (I approached *them*). It was always the drunk foreigners, cheapskates, vagrants, drug addicts, and general East Village oddballs who dared to hit on me.

It boils down to defending oneself, which is why dating patrons isn't a wise way to go. All too often when it doesn't work out the bartender will be at work and the dumped boyfriend will pop in at the bar for "a drink." She is relatively ambushed behind that invisible wall, obliged to look at and, worst of all, *serve* some guy she's discarded. He will inevitably sit there for hours ogling her, brooding, and in some cases showing signs of a potential stalker.

If you work in an office, imagine some guy you just unloaded last night showing up at your job, sitting by your desk, and staring at you for hours. There's nothing you can do about it. You're trapped. That's what it's like, sometimes, when bartenders date customers. I made it a policy never to put myself in that position after countless creepy interludes.

At my first restaurant job on the Upper West Side, I was forced to bartend the dreaded brunch shift. I had to start at the bottom and that meant serving geriatrics, families with kids, and hungover sots that came for my famous Bloody Bulls and mimosas at what seemed like the break of dawn. It was no small feat to make it to the job by nine-thirty in the morning since I had to work the Saturday-night shift there as well.

One of my brunch regulars was a rather creepy-looking heroin addict who lived in the neighborhood. He would never engage in small talk and always came in solo. The only time he would speak was to order a vodka on the rocks (hair of the dog?) and the bagel-with-lox entrée. I could never shake the ominous feeling that I was being examined. Every time I glanced over to see if he required anything, his shaggy blond hair would be covering his face but not his bloodshot eyes—which were glued to me in a permanent stare.

I tried to be rude, annoying, and even grotesque by picking my nose in front of him in hopes of turning him off. I would talk to other transient customers about "my husband" and began wearing a borrowed wedding band to work, the oldest trick in the book to discourage a customer's infatuation. None of it worked. Ignoring him became the only thing I could do, so when he demanded service I made him wait a long time for everything, took other drinkers' orders instead, or just plain "forgot" what he needed. Somehow I got the feeling that he sensed my agitation and got off on it.

After four months of this—on the sixteenth brunch!—he took it to another level. With a grimace I dropped his check and went back to the espresso machine to churn out what seemed like a hundred cappuccinos. When I returned to collect the cash he had already disappeared, much to my great relief. Under the twenty-dollar bill was a note folded into a neat little square. It read:

> I want to be your boy toy
> I want you to play with me
> Wind me up and watch me go
> Sick of being coy
> (212) ***-8732
>   —Elliott

Was that supposed to be him asking me out on a date? I presented it to the waiters, who were mostly gay (except for the one I had just begun dating). They thought it harmless even though we all agreed he was creepy. I threw it out and began dreading the following Sunday.

I all but begged every bartender to trade me for the shift, but the looming brunch finally arrived. When all else failed, I offered to pay one of the girls fifty dollars to take the shift off my hands. No luck.

Deciding to pretend I never saw the note, I served Elliott like I always did. He was filthy and sunglasses-clad, with his hair in matted clumps and his patchy beard unshaven. He smacked of a bike messenger on a busy, hot August day—that's how bad he stank. The stench was so bad that I began calling him Smelliott.

Never mentioning the note, he behaved quietly and surly as always, drinking his vodka on the rocks and eating his bagel. When he left, once again there was another note under the twenty-dollar bill. Mind you, his bill always came to around eighteen dollars, so we're not talking about a big tipper here. Had he looked like Harrison Ford I still wouldn't have considered him, with a showing like that. The gall in trying to court me while stiffing me was beyond reproach.

The "poem" was far more bizarre the second time around:

I'd like to make you brunch
I smash eggs on your body
Smear them while you grunt
I laugh and shut the door
And eat them off your cunt
    —Elliott
P.S. I know you're not married

Haiku it was not. I was officially freaked out and showed the note to the manager. He seemed hardly concerned and gave it to one of the owners, who laughed it off. After all, he said, he's a regular. I screamed in disbelief, bawling that Smelliott was someone I would never serve again; I didn't care if he was the president of the free world! They begrudgingly agreed to 86 him the following Sunday.

That whole week I began getting phone calls at home in which I was met with silence on the other end. I began to panic and asked the waiter I was seeing to spend the next few nights with me so that he could answer the phone. He happily obliged, even changed my outgoing message, thinking the male voice would deter whoever was calling; I was sure it was Smelliott.

That Sunday morning I had such blinding anxiety that I could think of nothing but the confrontation that was to ensue. When Smelliott eventually dragged his dilapidated self in, he was met by the manager and my boyfriend. They took him outside the restaurant and informed him civilly that he was officially cut off. He shook his head in distress and peered through the window. The manager angrily stepped in front of him, obstructing his view of me. My waiter boyfriend was becoming furious and pointed, signaling him to leave. Smelliott finally sauntered away but not without one last glare through the large windows.

I thanked them and went back to serving what seemed like every blue-haired snob on the Upper West Side.

The following week was blissfully mundane until I began packing it in to head home. While counting out my tips I was overcome by a chilling hunch and took a look out to the street. Smelliott was outside, leaning against a parked car. I officially had my very own stalker!

My boyfriend was livid and I had to plead with him not to make a scene. The manager and every male server said they would "take care of it." As they converged to the front of the restaurant, all eight of them (including the dishwasher, bless his little heart), my disheveled stalker flashed a look of trepidation and swiftly walked away. I had never seen such a chivalrous group of queens in my life—and it was the last time I ever saw Smelliott.

pet peeve no. 6

> If a bartender is nice to you, don't take advantage. If she indulges you in a buy-back or even lets you drink for free, it doesn't mean show up *every single night* she bartends. Pace yourself. We bore easily. We don't want to see anyone that much and you will wear out your welcome (and kiss those free drinks good-bye).

In dealing with regulars, one discovers that they drink to find a brand of intoxicated redemption. An ex-Marion's bartender, Maryanne, once called bars a church for the quaffing zealots, a place where everyone is accepted. (Think of Norm from *Cheers* and you get the picture loud and clear.) My regulars, when they were drinking at

Marion's, were no longer just men or women; they *found* themselves in the crystal effects of spirits, and in turn found the courage
to *be* themselves. In this clarity, they also discovered the gumption to
love.

Marion's maintained a "sex is in the air" vibe that couldn't help
but arouse our patrons. Having gotten to know many of our drinkers
so intimately, we regularly interjected them in our shenanigans.
Sometimes we rubbed up against them, much to their erogenous
delight. *Ca-ching!* They were often included in our gossipy sex talk
and knew *almost* as much as I did about who in the bar was shagging
whom.

Getting this chummy with the staff meant some infatuations
resulted. Many of the customers made falling in lust with their waiters and bartenders a habit. For a handful it became a bonafide fetish.
One particular lush comes to mind immediately.

Remy, a film publicist, came to Marion's on such a regular basis
that I anticipated him on certain days. He was *very* mod in his black
turtlenecks and, like all publicity people, a fast talker. He had suc-
cessfully befriended everyone I worked with. He fit the new and
improved Bowery perfectly—chic tethered to a churlish, leering
quality that bums from the fifties wore with style. The kind Humbert Humbert boasted in my imagination, checking out the girlies.

If Remy didn't show up for a while I'd get worried about him, and
dispatch e-mails asking if he was ill. He was someone I had become
friends with despite his showing up nearly every night I worked.
That's rare. Usually I would need breaks from the chronic patrons,
but I never tired of Remy.

He was the master of flirtation, able to bring anyone to his or her
knees. Many times throughout a night, as I was toiling away, I would
catch him giving me *that* look. Imperceptibly his blue eyes would
narrow, lips got lightly licked. He would bring his fingers up to his
mouth in the form of a V and lick them as if he were giving head.
Then he'd mouth a kiss and lick his lips again. I always laughed,
though I can't say it didn't get me hot now and again.

He claimed he was looking for love though his behavior was more predatory than innocent, pouncing on new workers male and female, the first week they arrived. My husband secretly called him the Marquis de Sade—though there were times when I think Remy could have made the Marquis blush. We confessed to each other our sexual fantasies, along with the realities of our love lives (my husband would kill me if he knew how much Remy knew about us) and anything else that related to the delicious topic.

It wasn't unusual for him to come in with a date and return after he'd bagged him or her to relate every petty detail to my burning ears. The doors would swing open and the dauntless Remy would prance in like a proud peacock. I'd stop whatever I was doing and sprint over for the juice. There would be no "Hello" or "I'm back." I knew why he'd returned—to regale me with the details of the sexual romp he'd just finished five minutes before. The stories always launched with lines like "She doesn't swallow. Can you believe it? I'm never going to see her again!" Or "I was hoping he was the one, but he's a top too. Tsk tsk, it's definitely not going to work. Too bad, though, he's so cute!"

An explosive match for him was Michelle, a petite waitress who dripped sex appeal, leaving puddles in her wake. She was a recovering sexaholic, in a twelve-step program for alcohol, and had severe family traumas that would make great material for another book someday. Remy asked me about her. I told him she was trouble, trying to dampen the match from igniting. Needless to say, Remy cornered her by the bathrooms in the back of the restaurant and when he got back a few minutes later, he casually informed me that Michelle had just given him the blow job of his life.

I myself had my share of crushes on regulars. One such instance was the solemn Brian. More often than not, he would arrive alone and shine those wet brown lamb eyes at me—and I will admit that I melted a few times. I didn't have to fake the itch like I did so often with the others.

Things took a turn for the worse when his beloved girlfriend, the stoic Lydia, abruptly dumped him for a business partner. Brian practically moved into the bar. Other regulars spotted him in the afternoons drunk and hobbling all over city parks. I was beginning to worry, and marvel at how he was maintaining his corporate job. Whenever I voiced my concern, he smiled but essentially waved it off. There wasn't much I could do since he tipped so extravagantly. I couldn't exactly tell him to stop drinking, now could I? Instead, I began watering down his drinks and comping a few so he would continue his weekly (sometimes daily) pilgrimages to Marion's.

He began confiding in me that I had always reminded him of his ex, and told me he was in love with me. The funny thing is, I knew he meant it. There wasn't a disingenuous bone in his body. The melancholy look on his face, even when he smiled, brought out the maternal side to me. It didn't lessen the attraction, but made it confusing and interesting. When after a year of this I told him that I was getting married, he looked crestfallen and angry at the same time.

"Are you sure?"

"Brian, aren't you happy for me?"

"Are you sure Kurt will make you happy?"

"Yes. You don't look very happy for me."

"I'm not."

A few months after my wedding, which he attended, he had had one too many Ketel Ones on the rocks when he said flat out, "Ty, let's cut the crap. When are we going to have our affair?" He was serious.

I wasn't. "Not ready yet, Brian. Maybe in a few years when the marriage gets stale," I said with a laugh. A mistress should always be as adoring as Brian.

Restaurant workers can't keep their hands off each other. In a restaurant, particularly behind the bar, it's downright incestuous. Drudging in a dark lounge setting, sexy music permeating the air, cigarette smoke fluttering into the red and gold lights, martini

glasses full of temptation . . . it's an atmosphere that invites intimacies. There is *nothing* that we don't tell each other. Everyone suffers a
sense of woe-is-me for having to work in a restaurant (*I'm really an
actress/writer/model/dancer, goddammit!*) and that cues the feeling
that misery seeks company. We eat and drink together. We have our
birthday parties in the restaurant together and bring our dates in to
impress them. There's a real comradery when we're in the weeds,
dealing with rude and hard-hearted customers, and just when we
think we'll burst, a fellow employee will bail us out. We transform
into a kind of family—albeit a dysfunctional one full of contempt
and jealousies, but with the kind of unconditional love our real families never gave us.

Then there's the proximity in which we work together. Because of
tight spaces we rub up against each other quite a lot. An infinitesimal
attraction turns into explosive lust and eventually everyone has to be
beaten off each other with a stick. Without exception the flame fiz-
zles, work suffers, and someone ends up quitting—usually the
female.

I once asked one of the Marion's owners if he'd ever had sex in the
restaurant. He looked at me as if I were crazy. "Of course. Haven't
you?"

"No. Of course not!" I protested.

"Of course you have, you hussy."

He'd been in the restaurant biz a long time and understood how
things worked. I've never met a bartender who hasn't delighted in a
rendezvous of some kind in his or her place of work. Because we tend
to have to close the place down, bartenders can exploit the situation.

Harry, one of the fill-in bartenders, was an incurable flirt and a
wild success with women—this despite the bald pate and compact
size, and the fact that he was living with a woman named Georgia
whom everyone in the restaurant adored. He candidly eyed and
teased beautiful women who came in and had them eating out of his
palm. His behavior also extended to the waitrons and bartendresses,
though I never thought anyone at work really bought into his mag-

netism. But when the catering crew showed up at 4 A.M. to prep a job one morning, there was Harry getting a blow job from Mona, a waitress who at the time was totally au naturel, doggie-style, on, appropriately, the aforementioned Kennedy Booth.

I myself can look back at booth number thirty-five and the coatcheck room with cheap and fond memories. Whenever diners would sit at that table, I would recall Julian, a screenwriter from Los Angeles who replayed with me a scene from *9½ Weeks* with vigorous, sadistic flair. He took humiliating his lovers to celestial heights. I never realized I was capable of being talked into crawling around in my skivvies barking like a dog for some guy's gratification. Like Kim Basinger, I was a submissive who couldn't release the compulsion.

But what could I do? By the time I threw the last lush out into the night, Julian had been waiting for me for at least four hours. We had shared a couple of shots of Lagavulin, our favorite single-malt, and I was feeling pretty foxy. The music was soothing and the room's fetor was aromatherapy for the lonely. The amber lights were low, the chairs were up on the tables, and the unmistakable stench of the night's vigor gave it all an erotic edge. We were the only two in the damn place and the catering crew wouldn't be in for a couple more hours. Physical exhaustion offers itself to some kind of release, and add to that an entire night of playing hard-to-get with customers!

It is well known that bartenders know the dirt before anyone else. We witness human intimacies so closely that it gives us an edge in predicting human behavior. We can detect the subtleties, much like the way we know the order in which customers should get served even if the bar is packed, the way we eavesdrop on their conversations even if we appear to be too busy to notice, the way we remember a customer's bad tip four years back; we just notice things succinctly.

I began suspecting that Harry and Mona were sleeping together long before the Kennedy Booth incident. I'd noted the many times they brushed up against each other during service, the "casual" glances they exchanged, and the way they smiled as they talked— the way only potential lovers do. Most of all, it was in the way they spoke to each other. Had they not been so giddily attracted to each other, the things they said could have been considered harassment.

"Your breasts look mighty lovely tonight, Mona."

"Yeah?" she asks, pushing them up for more cleavage.

He laughs. "What time did you get out last night?" he says, trying to conceal the fact that they saw each other after work.

"About three. Hey, do you want to get a drink after work?" she asks.

"Nah. I'm pretty tired tonight," he replies, again to convince us that they aren't going to hook up later. "Where were you going to go anyway?"

This is where she plants the spot for their rendezvous. "I was thinking of going to Balthazar, but I'm not sure. Maybe Shark Bar. I probably won't go out anyway."

Okay. From that conversation, I learned that they slept together the night before and that they're planning on hooking up later at Balthazar—but that's just where they'll meet. Just in case any of us who listened to this conversation shows up, they will actually be drinking at Shark Bar.

"You've been working out," she says, testing his flexed arm.

"Feel my butt. I've been working those."

She cups his bubble butt and squeals, "You've got the hardest little ass I ever felt."

At this point, it gets boring and I yawn. I've got bottles to restock so I get back to work.

The amount of dirty talk within the confines of a restaurant is profuse to the extreme. I know who's sleeping with whom (employers, coworkers, and customers), how many times, and what positions they enjoy. We talk in graphic detail and curse like truck drivers. The bartender that just put your gimlet down with such grace and charm just walked away to join the staff at the end of the bar to continue her conversation about her debauched date last night. "His cock was bent to the left and really left me with cramps, but he could go all night!"

"Did you get any oral?"

"Of course not, but he did demand his fucking blow job. Men are such assholes! I'll be right back," she says, noting a new patron. "Hi, what can I get you?" After the whiskey sour is shaken and delivered she returns and continues. "Anyway, as I was saying, he came like two fucking times and, for a change, I didn't have to fake it!"

The waitress chimes in, "I have to confess. I've faked every orgasm I've ever had."

The bartender flashes a look of shock and outrage as she prespears the olives. "You're fucking kidding me! Shit, I come at least four times—*every* time. You poor thing."

"That's amazing," the sulking waitress says. "Is there a secret?"

The bartender takes two more orders and starts mixing when she rejoins the fully alert waitress. "Get yourself a great vibrator and spend a weekend at home with the phone disconnected. In fact, I demand it!" she says, trailing off to pour two martinis. "No woman should be without multiple orgasms. With all the shit we take from men, it's the least thing they can do for us."

You get the idea. We're pigs like that.

And speaking of pigs, there's always the rest of the staff. The Mexican kitchen toadies were always referring to women as cunts and the men as fags; my employers consistently referred to me as a bitch, hussy, or whore. The finger-snapping gay waiters were especially relentless in their sex talk and we had a lot of laughs about who was a "top" and who was a "bottom."

Sometimes when I'd swoon at an attractive man entering the bar, my boss would cackle and say, "Forget it, bitch. He belongs to my church."

"How do you know he's queer?"

"Look at his shoes, *duh.* That's the dead giveaway."

"He's wearing loafers, so what?"

"No socks *and* it's got tassels. He's gay, whore."

The bastard was always right.

Marion's was the closest I ever came to working at a gay restaurant. Most of them are in Chelsea—land of homosexual cruising and drop-dead-gorgeous men—and they have, bar none, the best-tipping customers in New York. Despite the fact that I applied to several of them, I could never get hired. I realized that I'd have to be a hot, hairless man with abs sporting a guinea-T for days to get the job.

A confirmed homosexual climate meant that the banter was sexually charged at all times and usually side-splittingly hilarious. There is nothing funnier than a gay man on a roll. Indeed, I've learned a lot about men from my many homosexual friends and coworkers. No one can teach a woman how to please a man quite like a gay man. One of the managers at Marion's would teach the girls how a man really likes to take his blow job or how to find the proverbial G-spot. "Don't forget the rim job. Just lick it while he's coming and it brings it to another level!" Point taken.

I'll admit, sexual harassment also comes into play when there is an abundance of sexual angst permeating a space. I recall a mixer fresh out of college telling me about the time she was called into her new boss's office. Her innocent disposition was all too easy for him to abuse. When she showed up he was sitting at his desk with a barely concealed dick in hand, masturbating openly as he asked her the most mundane questions. She was so terrified that she just stood there, frozen, answering his queries ("So, how do you, uhhmm urrmmphh, like it here so far, Joan?") until he finished himself off into a bar towel. I asked her why she didn't just walk out that door.

"Are you crazy? I was making three hundred dollars a night!"

She remained at the job for two years until she met her future husband at the bar and eloped.

Luckily my employers were gay and I didn't have to endure any kind of casting-couch atmosphere, though we had our own kind of hell to contend with. Namely the kitchen.

I have never braved a more unventilated, hot, and oppressive environment than the Marion's kitchen. The back of the house is notoriously abusive toward anything in a skirt. Marion's employed a fleet of horny, mostly married Mexican men. Some of the staff just dealt with it, and at other times coffee mugs could be seen flying through the air or knives being wielded. I myself had to tolerate a good deal of macho harassment and touchy-feely cooks—and it took me about a year to figure out how to put a stop to it.

Our workers had no respect for American women, calling us every conceivable desecrating name in the book (*puta, prostituta, chocha, pendenja*). They believed American women were loose, unlike their virtuous wives, sisters, and daughters. I suppose they got this theory by watching too much American television back home in Puebla. By the same token, however, they did value a woman who stood up for herself, proving herself worthy of their respect. And in the restaurant kitchen, that meant someone had to get hurt.

In the beginning, I sincerely loathed my trips to the kitchen—the leering eyes always at my breasts, the whispered comments and chuckles, the brushing up against me as I passed through the tight space were absolute agony. During one of my jaunts to rejuvenate my glass rack, one of the cooks—I called him El Diabolo—handled my bum as I lifted the heavy bus pan. I gave a piercing shriek and jumped. Nearly dropping the glasses, I managed to salvage most of them when I slammed the pan hard back on the metal rack. I saw *red*. He must have noted my fury because he began hedging slowly back to his station, giggling apprehensively.

"Wha? *Whaaa?* I din do nuttin'! Why you look at me like daaaa?"

I grabbed a martini glass from the bus pan and flung it at him, missing him by a whisker. He eluded the torpedo and began laughing nervously. "You loco! Wha you doin'! You crazy *puta*!"

I stormed over to him and hollered at the top of my lungs straight in his face, "If you ever touch me again, if you even talk to me, if you even *look* at me, I am going to call your wife and tell her what you do at work! I am going to tell her that you touch all the girls here and

that you are sick! And after I tell your wife what a *pervertido* you are,
I am going to take a butter knife and cut your tiny penis off and
shove it up your ass! *Comprende?*"

He got it. He continued his rant, calling me a crazy whore, but
stayed clear of me the entire night. For weeks it was all-out war in
which we didn't speak, and if looks could kill! He attempted to torture me in his own small way by not making the food orders I placed
for myself during work hours. In return I refused to give him any
alcohol, though I lavished booze on the others. I began placing my
snack dupes as if they were for customers and got food for myself
that way. He had other cooks order drinks for him. After he finished
licking his macho wound I began noticing a shift. He started asking
me for advice, cracking G-rated jokes, and we actually became good
friends. I never saw that leer again. Mission accomplished!

If there's anything I don't understand, it's a waitress who invites
this kind of torture. It's hard enough going into a kitchen pumping
with testosterone and fearing for your life, but throwing them a bone
is just asking for it. I don't care if it's the way you like to pass the
time; there has to be a better way to survive the shift besides taunting
sex-starved kitchen help.

Maya really asked for it. Instead of ignoring or shirking the horny
lot, she would actually tease and taunt them. If El Diabolo asked for
a kiss, she would plant one on his cheek. If the dishwasher made a
comment about her ass, she would shimmy up against him. It got out
of hand one night when the sous chef made a play for her and got
physical. She acted quite victimized and came to me in tears, out-
raged. I didn't know that she had been flirting with disaster, and I
told off the sous chef. But then the dishwasher let me know what had
been going on, and I had to tell Maya she was on her own. I understand women's lib and I'm behind it one hundred percent, but when
you torture a guy for months—and one working in a 109-degree
kitchen at that—the situation becomes a ticking time bomb.

Lest I forget our customers . . . They rejoice in intimate behavior at the restaurant. Exhibitionism runs amok around drink three. It's not unusual to see dry humping against the bar, and I've even seen a woman climax this way.

With drink number one the customer gets pretty optimistic and begins checking himself out in the large round mirrors behind the bar. This always reminded me of roosters cocking their chests. A lot of hair adjusting and posing ensues. At the same time he's cruising the bar through the mirror so no one catches him in predatory mode—he's still not comfortable enough to approach anybody even if the prey has been spotted. He gulps down his drink and waves a dollar in the air to get my attention.

Drink number two brings on a lucidity that yields direct eye contact with actual females. The innocuous girls he's ferreted out give him a sly grin and that feeds the fuel. He's fumbling with the adrenaline rush to his brain (making him talk too much and check himself out in the mirrors further). He downs that drink, adjusts his crotch, and orders drink number three for encouragement.

Now he's feeling pretty good. He and his buddies are roughhousing and talking rather loudly about what they'd like to do to these girls. The young women are giggling loudly because they're on to the scheme. Their body language opens up: legs get uncrossed, positions subtly get turned towards the men, lips get moistened, hair gets twirled. There is the imperceptible consensus between the potential lovers, and a now truly buzzed Lothario goes in for the kill. Here are some well-known pickup lines I've heard:

"Excuse me, I was wondering if you believe in one-night stands?"

"I'm a fashion photographer. You should be a model!"

"Hi. You'll do just fine."

"I'm visiting. Could you give me directions to your apartment?"

"Do you have the time? [Girl gives the time.] No, the time to write down my number?"

"What are you doing tonight at three A.M.?"

"I thought *very fine* only came in a bottle!"

Night after night, that's how it goes. But one ordeal really topped them all, though it was the sequence of events—that familiar scene that takes place *every* time—that was so laughable.

An indie rock legend from the eighties pranced in with a myriad of East Village–type cronies and without delay began cruising the bar for drunk women. He walked up to a blonde and activated his empty wit and charm. Within fifteen minutes he was downing drink number three, and exploring her tonsils with his tongue. As I was mixing other patrons' cocktails, I had to ask them to please keep her hair out of my garnish dispenser since she was practically bent over the bar. After apologizing every time I pulled her tresses out of the olive dish, they escalated into a necking session that bordered on oral sex. Somebody yelled from down the bar, "Get a room!" The response was a raucous laughing fit from the other drinkers, who could not take their eyes off the pair. By now it was like watching porn.

Finally I thought they were going to vacate and fuck each other's brains out when the smell of something burning caught my attention. I was putting down an Angel martini when out of the corner of my eye a light flashed. He had bent the blonde right into a burning candle and her ringlets were aflame! I yelled, "Hey, you're on fire!" and swatted her head repeatedly with the nasty wet towel I used to wipe up the sticky bar. Bucking up and down, she wailed and realized what was happening. He started whacking her mane with his hands until the inferno was out.

You'd think the embarrassment would dampen the mood. She looked ridiculous—her hair in the back was singed to within three inches of her head while the sides were down to her overburdened breasts—and she was thanking me even though I'd smeared cigarette ash onto her face and her tresses were matted together from old Cosmo backfill. No problem, I told her and expected their departure. I'd had enough of the lap-dance and watching this jerk take advantage of a drunk girl. Much to my anxiety, he gave her a smooch to tell her everything was okay, which ignited a more passionate kiss and they were off again! This went on for another hour until last call came and I could legitimately throw them out with everyone else.

For pointing out that his date's hair was aflame and assisting in a safe outcome, you'd think he'd have left a decent tip. No such luck.

Dry humping and heavy necking is de rigueur at the bar, but outright fornication does transpire on occasion. There is always a lot of hanky-panky going on under dinner tables, but bar customers usually take their overwhelmed libidos to the bathrooms. One of the toilets at Marion's was rather narrow and cramped, with a small window onto the kitchen. It had a textural effect, so all you could see through it were vague silhouettes of people standing there taking a leak or pulling up their pants.

One cheeky pair at the bar were getting out of hand when the girl, straightening her skirt, said she was going to freshen up. She certainly needed to; her mascara was smeared like that of a character in some bad soap opera tear-fest and her lipstick was smudged all over her face. The man, zipping up, gave her another lingering kiss and an almost imperceptible wink that only I noticed. Bartenders calculate every tick because it so often means someone is trying to place an order. As I suspected, within two minutes Romeo was looking around to make sure no one noticed his beeline to the bathrooms.

Within five minutes, a waiter ran over to tell me that he couldn't get any food out because the whole kitchen staff was transfixed watching a couple having sex in the bathroom. I ambled over and the first thing I heard was the acrid and wild hysterics of the chef: *"Ay, Dios mio!"* There was a huddle of cooks peering into the window, and they were giggling away as the poivre sauce burned and the soups got cold. I squeezed myself in and, lo and behold, the couple were going at it with the verve of rabbits in springtime. She was sitting on the sink with her skirt pushed up, legs in the air, back arched, and he was impaling her while hammering his head into the mirror. The workers had turned off their radio so that they could eavesdrop on her unoriginal howls. "Yes, yes! Oh God, oh God!" Had I not been there, no doubt they'd have all been whacking off.

Upon returning—she first, then Romeo—he dropped a twenty on the bar and they bolted out of the place. I found this suspicious since people who fornicate in the restaurant tend to bask in the afterglow of their triumphs over a nightcap. I ran to the bathroom for clues.

The quick exodus was explained. The twenty-dollar tip wasn't going to compensate for the mirror that was crushed where Romeo had pounded his head, leaving the image of a spider's web and broken glass everywhere, or the sink, which was officially ripped out of the wall, hanging by a leaky pipe.

Ah, if restaurant bathrooms could talk!

pet peeve no. 7 ⟶

> Bartenders and customers alike really hate to see couples engaging in explicit foreplay. Regardless of what you think, it's not sexy. After zippers have been undone and bras have been removed, it's really time to take it to a hotel. Dry humping is not only rude, but it makes most of us lose our appetites, and that's just not good for business!

⟵

Once, while working at a Tribeca eatery, a friend of mine spied a gentleman eating with his girlfriend while discreetly eyeing another woman across the room. The woman returned his gaze openly and enthusiastically. The girlfriend was oblivious. The other woman began playing with her food—dribbling it on her chin, sucking on her fingers, enjoying her fourth Kir Royale. The man was clearly having a hard time keeping his eyes off her and managing his girlfriend as well. Casually the woman spread her legs under the table for him to see her remove her panties, which she put in her bag. He told his date he needed to use the rest room. My waiter friend watched the other woman reapply her lipstick and shimmy toward the toilets a moment later. Needless to say, the two had a wild five-minute romp on the sink and upon returning, the man resumed his dinner as if nothing had happened.

I can understand men behaving like cavemen, being led by their privates, but why are some women so dense? I never know what to make of them. I'll admit that I'm guilty of sometimes using my weapons to get what I want. But the day my man goes to the bathroom for a quickie with some chick at another table, *I'll know in a New York nano-second.* It's part of my artillery—that hypervigilant talent for observation that came with mixing.

- - - - - - - - - - - - - - -

The disillusionment I felt toward men took hold after observing the different methods they incorporated to snare gullible women. Trusting men became futile for me; after years of watching them manipulate us, I went almost three years without a date, depending solely on apathetic liaisons. Armor is not naturally clad by women, as trusting as we can be, but if all women saw what I've seen, they'd think twice about every word uttered by way of a man's mouth. I know what you're thinking, that I'm just as guilty of deception. But the way I see it, the setup isn't a secret: I'm your bartender, and I'm after your tip.

One particular regular, an attractive Ken-doll type, had a schtick he would use on his dates that made me want to quit my job every time he came in. Let me preface this by saying, in all the years that David drank at my bar, I never saw him with the same woman twice. When we first met, in my fourth year at Marion's, he attempted unsuccessfully to take me out—but I was on to him. He called me his "Turkish Delight" and said he found Islamic women "unbearably erotic." When he finally understood that I would never rendezvous with him, he transformed me into his accessory in crime.

Strutting in with a gorgeous woman on his arm was my signal to automatically prepare his Stoli Gibson and, without exception, he would take the liberty of ordering his date's cocktail, a French martini. Always. I'd begin chilling their glasses the second they sat down. As they got frosty, I'd pour the liquors and look to him for signs of when to start the show. The drop of dry vermouth would go *plop* when it hit his Stoli, and the fresh lime juice would make my mouth water as it laced her Ketel One Citroen. Then I would add a splash of pineapple juice to her mix. I'd shake his Gibson while the Roses lime juice infused her cocktail. Then I'd shake that. The onions would be speared and positioned by the time I'd begin straining the Gibson into the freezing cocktail glass. I'd bring that to him while my other hand would garnish her empty glass with an orange slice. I'd return to her with the mixed French martini and begin pouring. I'd tell her *not* to drink it yet. I'd get the Chambord and float a dollop of it so that it sank to the bottom like a bed of purple nectar, giving it a fancy, layered look. I'd think, *Damn, I'm good.* She'd giggle and with a "Cheers!" he'd award me with a devilish wink.

Whenever he ordered for his women, they would think it was chivalrous and gaze into his eyes adoringly. Then David would nod at me; that was my cue. I was to secretly run to the kitchen and tell them to get a chocolate cake ready with a candle on it. As per routine, I was to tell the staff that they needed to help me sing "Happy Birthday" to David's dimwit date. They would roll their eyes and ask if this was the same asshole they had to sing for every month. I would tell them yes and they would tell me to 86 the motherfucker. I would say I couldn't and we would all get ready.

David would cue me again with another wink and I would bring the cake out with a candle burning on top of it about an hour later. This step usually meant he was ready to make out. The staff and I had to circle around and we would half-heartedly begin singing to the girl; inevitably the whole bar crowd—and sometimes the dining customers—would join in.

At first the date would look baffled since it wasn't her birthday. When it would finally hit her that David arranged this dreamy gesture in her honor, she'd invariably feel celebrated and special. She'd blush and giggle like a teenage girl. By the time the song ended, she'd have given him a long, passionate kiss, misled into thinking he was in love with her.

I promised myself that before I resigned from Marion's I would tell

David's next victim what was about to transpire and advise her to run like the wind because the guy was a first-class cad. But I never did.

I performed the act one last time after I had given notice, going home that night feeling defeated. As a woman it was intense watching the dates' pretty faces overflowing with love and adoration, knowing by next month they'd have been dumped like the others. Plus, aiding in the ruse filled me with culpability every time.

But I'm just his bartender, I would tell myself. *I'm just doing my job.* After all, he *was* an excellent tipper.

In New York the mating dance will always have its games and I am as guilty as anyone for playing them. On this neurotic and wonderful island we're bombarded by beautiful people every day—there should be no loneliness. But the more people the city absorbs, the lonelier it seems. There are no cheat codes, get-out-of-jail or marked cards to beat the odds; we play to win but unfortunately it's all too rare in bar liaisons—because fantasies are, after all, fantasies. I never took a man seriously that I met at a bar, but then again, the one time I did I hit the lottery.

He turned out to be my husband.

The Rules:
How to Date the Bartender

I envy people who drink, at least they know what to blame everything on.

OSCAR LEVANT

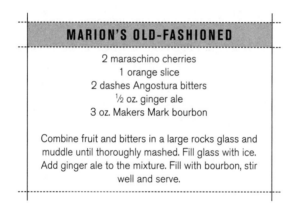

MARION'S OLD-FASHIONED

2 maraschino cherries
1 orange slice
2 dashes Angostura bitters
½ oz. ginger ale
3 oz. Makers Mark bourbon

Combine fruit and bitters in a large rocks glass and
muddle until thoroughly mashed. Fill glass with ice.
Add ginger ale to the mixture. Fill with bourbon, stir
well and serve.

What is it about bartenders that piques the carnal interest of their
customers? Bartenders and sex are a natural mix, or at least one
would think so. The pretty faces that come and visit, the come-ons
and dirty jokes all seem to lead to one thing: getting laid. A lot.

A mixer is behind a long bar with stools facing one way: toward
her. The "Platform" theory is in play. The stage is set, the spotlight is
shining. She's wearing something tight, something that demands
that you empty your wallet to prove your worthiness to her. Her hair
is slightly messy, in a good way, from all that shaking of cocktails and

jiggling about. The jazz in the jukebox has established a certain vibe, a brooding undercurrent that solicits teasing and reverie. You crave her but quickly divert your eyes every time they meet hers. She smiled at you when she made your drinks and listened to your anecdotes (at least nodding every so often, giving you the *impression* she gave a damn). You think she may be interested in you but you're a little tipsy so you can't be sure. You look at your watch and register that if you don't leave now you'll be a wreck at work tomorrow morning. Perhaps a sick day is in order. As the night plods on she's looking better and better. After drink number three, she is positively hot, dripping sex appeal like candle wax. You notice other men are giving her a lot of attention and she gives it back. You sense the undeniable twitch of competition and you want in on the action. You don't know why but you want to give her all your money. You think of her the whole way home and can't wait for her next shift. Suddenly you are one of her orphans, a die-hard regular.

There were many times, countless, actually, when a passing hunk would happen upon my bar and—after the waitrons and I cruised him mercilessly, sometimes to his obvious discomfort—I'd jump into action. If it was a slow night, I'd give him nearly all of my attention. It made the shift go by quicker, and even though I knew nothing would come of it, flirting with a stranger would often be the highlight of my whole evening.

I did have my own simmering crushes on certain regulars—hey, I'm human. Very often, I leaned in pretty close during exchanges with my customers, the nearness often igniting secret cravings. I wasn't invulnerable to the seductive atmosphere. At a bar, sexual tensions are positively tangible because I'm wearing a dress the size of a belt, my lips are glossy, the moody lighting and oscillating music are spellbinding and you've hit the unmistakable ledge of intoxication. Yeah, you're going to get a hard-on and maybe so am I, but I'm doing it for the money, not the sex. If you are attractive I may even brood about you for a few days after you've left—but that's about it.

Why didn't I date these gorgeous drifters who fortuitously came into my orbit? This may sound unfair and politically incorrect, but men after a few rounds are a pathetic and sometimes disturbing bunch to watch. It was disheartening when they were on the prowl, cruising for anything with a pulse. I'd even heard some tell their buddies that they were going to "nail this dog," or "beggars can't be choosers, ha-ha," then high-five them. Not to mention the adulterous men; there were plenty of those too. The bartender's distrustful outlook made a substantial impact on my psyche, labeling anyone of the male persuasion enemy number one. I'm not impenetrable; it got to me after a while. And I'm not exaggerating when I say I didn't believe in marriage—until I met my husband, Kurt.

I get the feeling that a lot of people believe that they haven't got a shot with their favorite mixer. Despite the illusion that we're beating admirers off with a bat, it's simply not true. The thing to understand is that people can be intimidated by us. It may look like everyone is enamored of us, but that doesn't mean that they all come on to us— most men don't have the mettle to do anything about their crushes. The bravest usually leave their numbers on napkins on their way out, but the rest skulk off with obvious lust and yearning.

I see it two ways. Either they think we get around so much that they wouldn't have a shot with us, or they think we're altogether unapproachable. After all, Manhattan has some of the rudest and most pretentious bartenders in the world. I often had a walk-in sit down for a drink and proceed to tell me that I was the nicest bartender he'd ever had in New York and how disappointed he was that he had just come from so-and-so's bar and the mixer was rude to him. "They didn't even say hi" was a common remark.

Try to grasp that it isn't part of the job description to welcome everyone with open arms, especially nonregulars. That takes time—

perhaps more than one visit for some mixers. At Marion's I had so many orphans that I had that "Mama Ty" attitude from opening till closing, but all bars aren't locals joints. Some are Eurotrash traps, hotel bars, nightclubs, truck stops, or places to go before heading to that Broadway show—not where regulars conglomerate and get to know the bartender. Don't take it so personally when you don't get star treatment—it's just the neutralizing wall that bartenders keep up as a form of protection. Some are too busy, others don't want to get hit on or have to deal with drunks. They just want to do their jobs and go home.

If you visited that same "stuck-up" bartender week after week, I guarantee you that she would remember you, say hello, and even buy you one on the house. Suddenly she's not so unapproachable anymore. Maybe you'd end up finding her rather charming. But your walking in cold never to return doesn't give the mixer much incentive to chat it up because, unless you're a totally insensitive sot, you're just going to leave the standard dollar tip per drink.

When I started mixing, I wasn't the most self-assured person in the world. My confidence was built through my bartending experiences. Maybe that's what people refer to as the "aloof" or "rude" bartender—that aura of self-esteem. I'm sure most mixers have undergone the same transformation that I have. When someone took the time to get to know me, listen to *me* for a change, I gave him all of me. I was the one he came to for help, and seeing the way I eased his load made me feel more consequential and valid.

I'll admit that I got cynical from the endless negative encounters, but it forced me to grow up. I didn't trust as easily as I once did, but the way I learned to judge someone's character so quickly continues to help me to this day. I don't have time or energy to waste on people who don't justify my friendship or love.

One day a friend, Stephen, whom I'd known when I was in high school, unexpectedly dropped by Marion's. He said he had met a guy

I went to school with and wanted to bring him by. I was apprehensive, being that our shared era was a dreary blur for me. I'd been incredibly unpopular and was considered mostly a loner. When he mentioned that his name was Alan, all I could recall was a reluctant, awkward boy with whom I shared homeroom.

As I was serving a few locals early one night the following week, Stephen literally skipped in, thrilled to be part of a reunion with Alan. My geeky sophomore year came flooding back the moment I saw Alan's face. He was older but still retained the quiet, repressed vibe he always had. He drank gin martinis and confessed that he had known he was gay throughout high school (I hadn't a clue). I told him that I was glad we could both be ourselves at last. Then he overwhelmed me with not-so-fascinating stories of what became of the few people I still remembered; most of them hadn't left Jersey. Those bratty kids who ostracized me and made me feel like an outcast alien were still living the monotonous suburban dream.

After his third cocktail, and feeling more lucid, he began describing what I was like during that period—even that was foggy. It made me incredibly sad to hear him characterize a hesitant girl who never said a word. Who dyed her hair black and painted pictures for everyone, winning the not-so-illustrious title of "class artist." The insecure girl who dreaded leaving school to go home to an existence of stern Islamic rules.

"You always looked so scared. You're so different now. A bartender, for chrissakes! I can't believe you're the same person," he said, genuinely surprised by what he saw.

I said, "Yeah, that life seems like a million years ago." It was.

A lot of the nightmares and fears I had as a spineless, frustrated Islamic Jersey girl had faded. For once, I wasn't afraid of anything. And my regulars were attracted to that.

Because of my situation, I had no choice but to get to know them, the orphans who frequented the place night after night, and sometimes it felt as if goodwill was being ramrodded down my throat.

These "friendships" could easily be misread—especially after a couple of Manhattans.

The camaraderie I had with my regulars could become confusing, with its vague innuendos and implications. There were those who I know wouldn't have had the same feelings about me had I been anything else but the bartender at Marion's. I went so far as to ask one guy who was intent on going out with me if he'd feel the same way if I were serving him jalapeno poppers at the Olive Garden. At first his reaction was incredulity, but within seconds, he answered, "No. I guess not." At least he was honest.

At a bar, image is everything. I used to think my favorite bartenders at Lucky Strike got the same attention as rock stars. It's one of the reasons I started mixing to begin with. Mixers tend to be hired, at least partially if not totally, on looks and are usually more outgoing and charismatic than servers—they have to be. We're commonly the first person a patron sees when she comes through the doors. A host or maître d' is often formal, but we're the first ones to ask, "Can I get you a drink while you wait for that table?" A waitress doesn't have to chitchat and will probably not serve that foxy burger eater from last night again for months, if at all. And if he comes back next week, he'll likely be seated in another server's station (unless she begs the host to seat him at one of her tables) so there is no real chance for a serendipitous relationship to blossom.

At Marion's, you get me and only me on my nights every time. If I think you're attractive, you'll be my toy for the night. If I find you disagreeable, I'm pretty much trapped into talking to you while I chain-smoke and attempt to find things to do at the other end of the bar.

A lot of people think their bartender is romantically interested in them. Just make sure you're not drunk every time you feel that way. If you're sober, you'll know for sure if it's just flirtation or the real deal. Personally, I think that when anyone meets a potential lover, it's best not to see him in a few key situations: (1) during two or more cocktails, (2) lit solely by candlelight (daylight makes all the difference), and (3) at work, when you're too busy to observe the warning signs and fine details. It's hard to take anyone seriously at the job when he's inebriated and I'm not. So if you're looking to date a bartender, be civil and try to be seen in some kind of light that will help her to see you as a human being and not just a sot with dollar signs tattooed to your head.

The rules are different for men and women mixers, but there are some things you should know. Most male bartenders get around and find it one of the perks of their job. They've got women throwing themselves at them all the time. If you're a raven-haired beauty with bee-stung lips with your eyes on Chad the mixer at your favorite watering hole, take a number. I've always found a looming risk at being behind the bar, trapped as we are, suspicious of the way men act after a few shots and generally having a hard time having faith in them. Bartendresses usually wield their feminine expertise on getting the almighty tip, not digits scribbled on matchbooks. Not the best vibe when perusing for a boyfriend.

All right, let's say you understand the essentials and are ready to romance that bartendress you've had a huge crush on for years. You've got to remember that we've heard and seen it all. Forget the insipid lines and corny come-ons. If you've been going to her bar for a long time and haven't disclosed your crush, then the first thing to do is be genuinely human—as in sensitive and modestly romantic. We don't see a lot of that. Don't babble away from nervousness—this isn't high school. Order a real man's drink, which means no apple, melon, or French martinis or anything else green, blue, or pink. The Cosmopolitan is forbidden. Look at her but never stare—and when you get into a conversation, try listening more. She is too often the one listening to everyone's life sagas and loves it when someone listens to hers for once. Give subtle clues: gentle eye contact, compliments that she may not have heard (which isn't easy if she's got lots of regulars), a show of genuine interest in her life, and a huge tip (never hurts). Nothing turns off a bartender like a tightwad. If none of these opens the doors to her cynical heart, I seriously doubt she will be swayed into going out with you. That, or she may not want to lose a regular she has nurtured patiently into a fine-paying grat week after week.

But you think you've got a good shot anyway. First off, understand that there are some basic turnoffs you should know about. If you're the jealous type, just walk away now and no one will get hurt. It's the number-one cause of disputes between bartenders and their lovers. After all, you'll want to hang out at your beloved's bar—it is one of the high points of dating the mixer. You enjoy watching her work, which gives you an infinite sense of pride in being her man. But you can't help but note that she's the center of attention. What with people clamoring for her attention, seeing her at her prettiest and telling her that she's the greatest—it can be hypnotizing to watch. As far as you're concerned, she's the most popular girl in the room, harkening back to your long-spent high school fantasy of going out with the head cheerleader. Control yourself and pass on bellyaching every time she talks to a male customer. I've been there and believe me, at first it's flattering, but within weeks it's just exasperating having to explain who every guy is that I'm friendly toward—plus it makes you seem distastefully insecure.

When we were still dating, my husband, Kurt, had a jealous bent to him. I thought it was a real hoot—at first. It was a new situation for me since I had never had a possessive boyfriend before. During one episode, early in our relationship, my boss at Marion's had tried to fix me up with an attractive physical trainer, Michael, he thought would be perfect for me. Even though I had told him that I was in a relationship, he went ahead and had the guy come and talk to me at the bar one night. I was concerned because Kurt was sitting at the other end of the bar and was watching my every move. Michael walked up to my work station and started telling me that he thought we should go out sometime. I looked over at Kurt, who was brooding and drowning himself in a shot of Knob Creek, pretending that he didn't care.

"I'm really sorry, but I can't. I just got into a great relationship," I explained. "Listen, this isn't a good time to talk because he's here and I don't want to make him uncomfortable."

"I totally understand. I thought it couldn't hurt to try," he said, and walked back to his table.

When I turned around, all I caught was the back of Kurt walking out the door onto Bowery and toward Little Italy—and he had *tipped* me. That was a low blow. When I finally got him on the phone after many attempts (not easy during a busy shift), he read me the riot act. I tried to explain what had happened but it took two days to get him to come around.

Look, flirting is part of the job. It's my number-one means of securing a decent tip. We serve a lot of people, therefore we bump into people all the time—hell, I've served thousands of people. When we're out for coffee, expect me to run into a couple of customers, and some of them might be attractive men. Try to think of flirting as a sexy uniform, something I have to wear. Or as a transaction between the customer and me. And if you can't, then don't go out with a bartender unless you're a masochist and enjoy turbulent relationships full of boring, melodramatic scenes.

Second, scheduling can be a royal pain. Are you a nine-to-fiver? That's not usually beneficial when dating a mixer unless she works the day shift. If she works on Friday and Saturday nights, expect to go it alone, or see your friends on these traditionally exciting date nights instead, because she's not going to give up $300-plus to go see a movie and eat popcorn with you whether you're the greatest lover she's ever had or not. And don't ask her to take those shifts off unless it's for your wedding, you're having major surgery, it's your grandmother's one-hundredth birthday party, or something else extra special. Your parents want to meet your special girl at a dinner party they're planning just for this occasion? Make it a Monday night. Your friends are hosting a brunch in honor of you making partner at your firm? We don't wake up for brunch. Breakfast dates? Forget it—we're in a deep coma until noon.

You're going to have to run a lot of bubble baths and give even more full-body massages. It's an unbelievably grueling job. For ages, Kurt thought my job was fraternizing and overseeing a big party every night. But when he came by one afternoon as I was setting up the bar, he was in for a rude awakening. Nothing is free, he realized—all the money I was earning was coming at a cost: my emotional well-being, safety, and utter physical exhaustion.

He was talking to me as I sprinted down the steps and literally hauled two full cases of Bass Ale up the stairs. "Here, let me help you," he said, grabbing a case. Then he brought up two crates full of alcohol and three bus tubs of ice cubes. Then he schlepped a couple of cases of wine, martini glasses, and ashtrays. By the time I was set up he was worn out, gasping for air—and I'm the smoker in the family. Sitting on a stool, slurping down a glass of Coke, he said, "You work fucking hard!"

Third, lovers have to understand that they need to back off when we have to act as bouncer. I never understood it when other patrons high-fived me when I manually ejected a violent drunk or vagrant. It's highly dangerous and I wished I didn't have to get in the face of some out-of-control maniac ready to slug me. Perhaps they never did because I was a female bartender, but most of the time I was shaken to the core. But I never allowed Kurt to help me even though sometimes he couldn't stop himself.

It wasn't easy for him, being my boyfriend, to get used to stepping aside when I had to cut someone off or throw him out; to watch me get into it with a drunk and not be allowed to defend me. But after he attempted to protect me the first time, I told him afterward that it was part of my job (even though I believed it shouldn't have been) and that I didn't want him getting involved. He respected that and most of the time, unless it got particularly ugly, he stayed out of my way.

Even though I appeared to be a lot tougher than most women, that I could handle myself with the worst of them, it didn't stop him from worrying about me—wondering if some horrible thing would befall me at the bar or after work when I was on my way home. When the other bartender, Casey, was mugged as he finished locking up the restaurant, Kurt began calling every night before I left and again when I got home. It's just another thing the boyfriend has to accept if he's going to go out with a mixer.

There are, of course, perks to dating the life of the party. She'll probably have loads of cash and a lot of free time to do fun things with you. You'll get to do things you never thought you would: have a groovier social life, meet the kinds of interesting people you never were exposed to before, indulge in and enjoy a vast nightlife, see more art than ever before (most bartenders are actors, but others are painters, dancers, writers) because they're likely a part of that scene, and be lavished with tons of free liquor and food whenever you dine out. You'll frequent her bar more and have a great place to hang out with your friends and be treated like royalty (for being her man) and be the envy of every male regular in the house.

Relationships with the bartender are challenging and require that the lover respect the intricacies of the job. It's not easy flirting relentlessly and freezing your ass off wearing next to nothing in the winter for the extra tips. Less flirting means less money. Less clothing means more money. Those are the rules of the job. But if we are given the freedom to do our jobs comfortably and sans drama, then the relationship will be one that's more fun than most standard ones ever could be. Trust me.

To Tip or Die in Manhattan

If you are drinking to forget, please pay before you begin.

SEEN IN A BAR

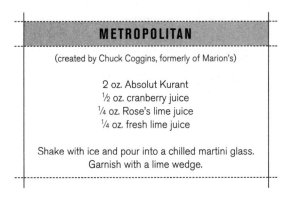

METROPOLITAN

(created by Chuck Coggins, formerly of Marion's)

2 oz. Absolut Kurant
½ oz. cranberry juice
¼ oz. Rose's lime juice
¼ oz. fresh lime juice

Shake with ice and pour into a chilled martini glass.
Garnish with a lime wedge.

For four years, I managed to keep my folks from visiting me at Mar-
ion's. The one time they made an appearance at the job was to view
my first and only "collection" of clothing, which was the focus of our
Fashion Brunch that month. Still trying to indulge my family, I considered it my last true effort in the industry. Fashion Brunch was an
event that the restaurant pulled off on the first Sunday of every
month, designed to promote and sell the creations of local designers.
It was always unique and entertaining for the diners—a genuine
New York experience. As soon as the diners were seated and served, a

bevy of models would emerge from the basement and sashay down the aisle between the tables. They would strut up the three steps, sometimes stopping to sip a diner's Mimosa on the way, to the elevated Sky Lounge—a looming platform at the back of the room that usually had two four-tops and two deuces flooded by spotlights. There they would strike a pose. The line of clothing was a financial disaster but I was extremely pleased that the show was packed to the gills. So was management.

I was hoping the display would make my parents proud. At the very least, I was trying to do something that showed I was on my way out of the restaurant business—a job they kept secret from the rest of the extended clan due to shame. Before they arrived I briefed all the waiters, owners, managers, and bartenders that I was *not* a bartender, should my parents ask: "Tell them I am a manager and a great one at that." No one could believe I had to go through such theatrics in my mid-twenties, but neither my parents nor Islam would exactly give its blessings to a woman shaking forbidden cocktails and wearing tiny dresses and enough makeup to make a streetwalker blush.

The show went off without a hitch, though when one of the models exposed a breast, my father's eyes seemed to pop out of his skull. My mother turned away in proper Islamic compunction. To their distress, the last model, clearly drunk, sashayed down the aisle with a bottle of Veuve Clicquot, got up on the platform, and finished off the champagne in a record two minutes flat and dry humped the male model she was accompanying. Typical Marion's fare but obviously new to my parents.

After the show I joined the folks for a quick omelette. I had downed three Bloody Marys earlier myself, trying to buffer the whole experience, and fought to keep from falling over. My mother asked if I was all right and I think I said, "I'll feel better after another drink." She squinted and asked, "What did you say?"

"Ah, I feel like I'm on the brink of a nervous breakdown. Just tired, Mom."

But my father was the one I really worried about. He and I had never gotten along and trying to please him had always been the challenge of my life. Even at my age, nothing I ever did made him proud, and as silly as it sounds, that agitated me. I was sure the show would validate me in his eyes.

In the Islamic tradition of treating women like crap, I grew up with a man who seemed to feel hostile toward my younger sisters and me. Custom also decreed that men should not show affection to their children, leaving us feeling rather inadequate and hungry for validation. It's probably why we dated so many unstable men.

My father hadn't said a word to me throughout the show and then throughout brunch. The anticipation of his reaction was devouring me and I couldn't keep from asking the dreaded question, "Well, Dad, what did you think?"

I got the same answer I got time and time again whenever I did something I thought would please the man. It was the same comeback I got when I bought my apartment at twenty-three, when I got the job at Bloomies and then at *Cosmo*, when my work made the papers, whenever I had poured my heart and soul into anything. He turned his head toward me and with his classic shrug muttered, "It was okay."

Bartending would be a great temporary job for me, or so I thought. I could do it for a few months, save some serious capital since the unemployment was running out, and proceed to look for the next gig that was going to come along any day. As the months turned into years, I was saving money like I never could in the past. For the first time in my life, I was able to conceive of going on a real vacation. It was intoxicating, that instant cash. I became a kind of somnambulist every Saturday night, lugging my tired bones home, mentally depleted, clothes stained with cranberry juice, stinking of cigarettes and cheap red wine—but in the beginning those were only minor inconveniences to put up with.

For some, meeting different people and sex was the true temptation of the mixing career. For me, the challenge of getting a drinker to part with the extra dollar (and they added up lightning-quick) became an exhilarating game that I controlled. Money, something I never had before, became a fierce lover—the seduction of the job.

Many a night I would take out the little metal box concealed under my radiator's cover, put the night's earnings in, and watch the sun come up. On the rare evening I would line up the C-notes by the thousands. And stare in utter disbelief. Just like an addict.

Screw the pat on the head from Dad.

pet peeve no. 8

> Who goes to a foreign country and doesn't find out the local customs? If you are visiting from overseas—England and France in particular—pick up a tourist guide. In the United States bartenders get a dollar per drink as a gratuity. Your nation's bartenders may be on generous salaries but we are not; we live almost exclusively on tips. Let's do something for international relations and break the nasty habit of bartenders cringing whenever they hear that cute accent of yours. You've been drinking watered-down cocktails long enough.

Milano's, a dive bar on Houston, is where my fellow mixers and I would commiserate after our punishing shifts. Twice a week we would meet to compare notes, tips, and horror stories. We liked it there because it didn't have a grain of attitude, the crowd were pure New Yorkers, it was open late, and the music was outstanding. In between listening to Rod Stewart's "Maggie May" and Sinatra's "My Way" on the superb antique jukebox, we would shirk VW Beetle–sized roaches, add to the butt-packed ashtrays, and down too many pints of Bass Ale with legendary barmaid Mary—sometimes until the sun would break, if she let us. The conversation would generally go like this:

"I had one projectile-vomit situation and one idiot who passed out into the peanuts, and I didn't even break two bills. All in all a crappy night," says Sheryl, who mixes in Tribeca.

Derek, from a pub in the Lower East Side, chimes in, "That's nothing I had two projectiles, one dry humper, and two groups of Brits. Top that."

I take a long drag of my Marlboro Light and say, "One projectile, one group of Frogs, two groups of suits, a frat-boy party, an ex-boyfriend, a group of vigilant antismokers, and a couple who decided to procreate on my bar. Now buy me another pint!"

We all would laugh and be regenerated (and drunk) by the time the morning beams peeked through the heavily blinded windows. Nothing sadder than hailing a cab while drunk at 7 A.M. But we needed that release only to sleep through a blur of a day until the next shift at 4 P.M.

One particular night it had come to our attention that we all had regulars who resented tipping us. John, from a gay bar in the West Village, said, "I've got this guy, Charlie, who tips a buck a drink, which is pretty good except that he makes a big deal about it every time. He can't just leave the damn dollar on the bar like everyone else! He's got to make it known to all at the bar that he's tipping me." He added, impersonating him, *"Here, John! Because you were so funny tonight, this is for you!* It's so fucking annoying!"

Carrie, from an East Village dive, jumped in, "I hate that! I've got a guy who makes me do cartwheels for every dollar he leaves. Last night he says that he won't tip me unless I make his drinks stronger. I told him he's going to get his drinks like everybody else. So he says that as a regular he deserves stronger drinks and that my tips are in jeopardy unless I do it. I told him to kiss my ass. Then he got the manager to lecture me. Can you believe it?"

Mine was a couple, Michael and Joanne, whom I actually considered friends—but they often came in with a clan that drank heavily and never paid the tab, taking way too much advantage of them. They frequented Marion's at least once a week, tipped profusely, but it was the way in which they left the grats that really annoyed me.

After many hours of suffering their bombastic and obnoxious friends and giving them a few rounds on the house, Michael would leave one to three twenty-dollar bills on the bar for me and plant a big smooch on my cheek on the way out. Then Joanne, his wife, would see the bills sitting on the bar and shake her head, implying that Michael was tipping too much. She would eventually submit to the amount and, to make me feel worse, would pick up the money and begin stuffing the bills into my hand in for all to see—except Michael. It would put me in the position of saying, "You don't have to leave so much." To which she would reply, "It's okay. I know it's a lot, but please take it." I would resist and she would keep jamming the money into my fist. I would relent and say thank you, like she was doing *me* some kind of favor.

I much preferred it when Michael would pull a Rat Pack move and slide the grat into my hand secretly so that Joanne wouldn't notice it at all. I wouldn't have to go through the theatrics of accepting the tip, which I utterly deserved after the four heinous hours of listening to their drunk comrades talk about their adulterous affairs and boring corporate lives.

Carrie went on, "I had a guy ask me why he should tip me at all, as if I'm a jerk for expecting it."

"He probably thinks we're all on salaries and it's a perk or something," John said. "Like we work at Starbucks! Even those guys get a check every week *and* benefits."

The conversation reminded me of two websites (www.stainedapron.com and www.bitterwaitress.com) I had run across where bartenders and waiters go to bitch about their experiences. They had guest books in which people who weren't in the business seethed at servers. I couldn't believe how much they resented tipping us!

I read comments like, "Do you know what *server* means? It means that your wretched existence is based on SERVING us. If you hate your lives so much, go get a GED or look for something else to do."

I read on: "Suppose I held my hand out every time I did my job. You are pitiful. Perhaps you should live in a commune of bartenders where they expect something for nothing. Or Somalia where they understand the importance of good service. Get a life!"

And: "You whine and bitch about how underpaid and undertipped you are. You make it seem as though you justify a 10% tip for doing your stupid job. Who else gets tipped for doing their job? When a police officer jumps in front of a bullet for someone does he ask for a gratuity?" or "If you don't like your job then perhaps you should have graduated high school. Perhaps you need a vocation change; I suspect that for you that is not a possibility. If you hate the world so much why don't you cleanse the gene pool a little and kill yourselves?"

The topic clearly deserves some thought.

I can't recall anyone in my life saying they wanted to be a bartender when they grew up. No one dreams of being a server, *period.* Most of us wish we were doing other things.

Most of the bartenders I know have beyond-excellent educations; I've even worked with Yale and Harvard graduates. I studied fashion design and worked in the industry but hated it. I studied acting for years after that. I made more money as a mixer than I ever did in the world that requires a diploma, apparently the only route to respect. It's just ignorant to say we serve drinks because we are uneducated.

People who have never served in a restaurant themselves invariably think we whine too much about the tipping situation. Listen, *everyone* whines about their job. I'll bet Bill Gates complains about his. But mine happens to take place in a public arena, and it's based on personal interactions. I'm sorry if you don't like hearing that I'm a real person with an opinion about the tip you just left.

Bartenders are a branch of the invisible people who make up society, like the mailman, cable guy, maid, meter reader, and the newspaper boy. People think of us as accessories to life, a necessary evil. The fact is, when you're in a restaurant and you want booze, you must go through us. I tell you when you've had enough and you don't like that. But who really appreciates the bitching of the gas pump attendant or the sanitation worker? When they go on strike, people do acknowledge their existence, but otherwise, they prefer us to stay in the background. And they would rather believe we're ingrates who should be ecstatic to serve them—well, how about a reality check?

The public needs to know that bartenders are not on salary and most of us are nonunion. Some establishments provide what's called a shift pay, which is a small amount of cash given to the bartender for coming in (usually $20 to $40). The rest of the take-home is in tips. The government and the restaurant/bar agree on what the worker usually makes in tips and on the set amount he/she should be taxed—so if a customer doesn't tip, we're taxed on it anyway. We are on the books but make well below minimum wage, something like $2.40 an hour, the lowest amount of any profession out there. I've received checks from Marion's to the tune of $14 for the week, though it depended on how many hours *they* clocked me for.

Before Marion's, when I worked uptown, making what the average bartender makes, *every* penny counted. The money I was going to take home depended on a multitude of variables: the weather, Lincoln Center openings, holidays, corporate parties. It wasn't a regulars joint, so the earnings weren't steady. If they couldn't book enough corporate parties that week, I could bring home $60 a night—if I was lucky. Say it rained—I couldn't pay the phone bill that week. No openings on Broadway meant I'd be broke and would have to eat at the restaurant for a couple of days. I never took home more than $50 from working brunch, so the restaurant added a $40 shift pay to make it worthwhile. Bartending isn't all fun and games, despite what it looks like. It's feast or famine, depending on the tips.

Seeing how our places of employment and the government compensate service workers, we are not "whining" without cause. We truly *depend* on gratuities to live. I was extremely fortunate to have landed a lucrative bar job, but many do not. Some bartenders take home a very modest amount of money while others land that dream bar gig. Male bartenders usually make considerably less than female bartenders. But all bartenders are taxed equally.

I would prefer it if the government and restaurant/bars worked it out so we were all given a dependable salary every week, but we're not holding our breath. Restaurant lobbyists have campaigned long and hard to ensure that you, the customer, will pay for the help not the proprietors. I would relish health-care and other benefits— things that are surely taken for granted in the real world. What about the lifers who have to look forward to working through retirement because they never had a 401K or stock options? Yes, we do have to be a little crazy to do this.

So why don't we quit and get "respectable," salaried jobs? Because bartenders are usually pursuing creative endeavors. We are the people who want more than the acceptable cubicle job and so we take that gamble. We sacrifice mental stability, self-respect, and in some cases our very safety to pursue that dream. I once asked a mixer/painter why he painted and he said, "Because I *have* to." That's usually true of most creative people, but they have to eat too. How else are we going to be able to take a month off (without pay) and work on an independent film and have a job to come home to? We're conscious of the fact that we live very shaky lives for our creative callings.

My family and friends reminded me of that every day.

pet peeve no. 9

By the way, the garnishes are not your appetizer while waiting for your table. Notice the cover on top of them—that's to keep your sneeze juices out of the lemons and limes and your fingers to yourself. We work hard to keep the garnish dispenser filled with fresh fruits, olives, and onions. They are part of the tools I use to make your drink attractive and taste better. So it's best to keep your little paws out of the condiments. I don't know if you washed your hands after the toilet, just brushed your hair, or if you just picked your nose. My hands are in disinfected water all night. It would never occur to me to show up at your job and just start removing your pens and stapler while you're attempting to work.

In the beginning, taverns were, for the most part, what they're viewed as today: a place where locals could congregate, exchange news and viewpoints, and invite neighborly rapport. But what were wanderers to do when they drifted through towns and couldn't find a watering hole in which to get drunk and enjoy easy women? In 1644, the Colonial Records of Connecticut charged "one sufficient inhabitant" in every hamlet to maintain a tavern, because "strangers were straitened" for want of diversion. The drifters continued whining to those in control until 1656, when they forced the General Court of Massachusetts to make towns liable for not sustaining a bar. Taverns were central to the heart and social dynamics of every early American village, and bartenders were close to being revered as attachés to the mayor. *Everyone* went to the bartender for money loans, advice, and matchmaking. They were trusted, valued, and, most of all, honored.

But would I have wanted to tend bar in a Puritanical singles joint? Hell, no. There were the strictest of rules, mostly to do with rampant drunkenness (punishable by forcing mixers to wear scarlet letters), and, worst of all, stockade humiliation (where in the middle of the night, the God-fearing Puritanical folks would come up from behind and do quite dishonorable things to your masculinity). Bartenders could be chastised similarly and pubs were often penalized by the rescinding of licenses and fines. Many ordinances were passed to keep booze from being sold to "devilish bloudy salvages," and in 1645, no one was allowed to drink for more than a half hour a day, *or else.* And if you were a completely dense dimwit, getting soused and fined over and over, you would eventually make it to the master list of drunkards that all landlords received. You were basically blacklisted from all vicinity pubs. Talk about getting 86'd!

And these watering holes were always part of a lodging situation. As the country expanded, more accommodations were needed for the ever-growing number of travelers who had to be fed and housed. Bars were not allowed to discriminate against transients, sitting all customers together at tables and, in turn, creating elusive cliques. Lodging was crowded too, often three to five beds to a room with men and women mingling in dirty conditions. So as the nation grew, barkeeps were making a killing!

Tipping has been around long before the Puritans decided to put bars in every town. One theory is that the word *tip* comes from England's ale houses from the dark ages, where scholars believe bartendering as a vocation began. When they wanted to promote faster service people left a tip, which stood for "to insure promptness." This is often disputed because acronyms were not a part of the English language until the 1920s.

According to Michael Lynn, associate professor of market and consumer behavior at the Cornell University School of Hotel Management, the most "neurotic and extroverted" countries tip the most and to the greatest quantity of different servers—and the United States blows every other civilized country away in that regard. Corresponding to his study on "tipology," he speculates that we are neurotics and are susceptible to guilt and generalized anxiety; Americans tip more because they sense guilt over status differences between themselves and the server. I say, God bless America.

In 1972, George Foster, professor emeritus of anthropology at UC Berkeley, looked at the origins of words meaning "gratuity" in many different tongues. He ascertained that the term resulted from "drink money," which pretty much sums up the notion that the custom began in establishments serving alcohol. He also claims that tipping began with a hope to avoid envy on the part of the server and to leave a little extra so that the server could have a drink at the patron's expense.

The theories go on and on. In any case, unless bartenders are union, their lives have centered on the tip for quite some time. To this day, the grat is often left to temper the feelings of servility, of the disparity between customers and the mixers who serve them. There's a hint of condescension attached to the custom. Yeah, there's prestige and history, and bars are still considered an integral part of society, but let's face it: we're working for tips, which can be demeaning and psychologically exhausting. When one has to depend on the kindness of drunks to survive, one gets mighty cranky.

In 1994, Linda Mancini, a talented actress and performance artist from New York, wrote and starred in a one-woman show called *Tip or Die*. It described with great wit the different facets and tumultuous nature of working in the service industry; the title eternally stirred the feelings of angst I carried with me whenever I was working. If I didn't break two hundred a night, I would get pretty irate—leading me to acquire that bitchy-New-York-bartender quality we all love to hate.

It took me years to realize that I never had to worry about making less than two bills a night at Marion's. I will admit that until then, when I'd been severely stiffed by a customer, I'd wish serious grisly harm upon him on his way home. There isn't a mixer who hasn't done the same, and if he says otherwise, he's lying.

All bartenders can ask is that if they hold up their end of the bargain as a professional, it would be nice if customers held up theirs via civil behavior and a decent tip. Alas, that is not always the case. Very often, civility gets thrown out the pub window once the alcohol starts flowing, making the mixer grumpy and ending up in a confrontational situation concluding in a 10 percent or worse tip—ultimately with the mixer getting taxed 18 percent anyway.

So, if you want a bartender who isn't miserable and in turn isn't going to take it out on you, there are a few simple insider rules to understand when you're drinking at a bar and want prompt service with a smile. The rules are common knowledge, though you'd be surprised how irrational people can be when they've had two or three Cosmos.

1. One dollar does not cover five drinks.
2. You better be leaving an unbelievably huge grat if you plan on hitting on me. (Especially if I hit on you back.)

3. If you didn't leave a tip for your last drink, I won't serve you until everyone else is taken care of—and then only maybe. It doesn't matter how long you've been standing there.

4. Are you telling me I need to do my laundry? Coins are not acceptable for tipping anymore unless they are accompanied by real, paper money. Bartenders hate to see coins left on the bar. See #3.

5. If your grat isn't strong, your next drink won't be either.

6. I don't care if you belong to the "Anti-Tipping Society" or other groups who walk around leaving cards that say they don't believe in gratuities and that my employer should pay me a salary. They should fill me in on how they feel about gratuities *before* they sit down, have me *slave* over them, tell me the saga that is their lives, then run like the *cheap asses* they are. I never forget a face.

7. If you tip heavy right off the bat, you'll be the first person we run to every time you come to the bar. It will get you stronger and better drinks and you'll always get a few on the house. That extra buck you drop goes a long way at a bar.

My wet dream is serving other bartenders. Fellow mixologists make it known right off that they are in the biz and that's code for "I'm going to tip the shit out of you so make it good." See #7. I know they're going to take care of me and I am certainly going to do anything they want short of bending over.

When I visit a bartender I always leave what's called "the Floating 20." For example, when I call on Brian, the bartender at Tom & Jerry's, another favorite bartender hangout, I always drop a twenty-dollar bill on the way out even if I've had a single beer or just water—and that's after I paid for the beer, though some bartenders let their own kind drink for free all night. Within the next few weeks he'll make an appearance at Marion's and drop a twenty for me as he walks out the door. That's the Floating 20, and considered common courtesy. I make his drinks stronger and better, he gets served first, and we always have a great time together. He'll also behave better than anyone else at the bar, because he knows the drill, making him the ideal patron of the night.

Good behavior is the other key in getting great service, though not to the extent that your large tip will get. Some customers don't use common sense at a bar, leaving me to believe that where alcohol is concerned, it's amateur night and incivility prevails. I don't tolerate lampshade-on-the-head antics. To throw a maniac out on his ass when he's behaved this way is just the right thing to do when normal people are trying to have a good time. I fully understand that I am a server, but that doesn't make me a punching bag for a patron's bad night.

People whistle for cabs. I hate it when drinkers whistle or scream my name to get me. For some bartenders, this is the number-one no-no.

It's also unbelievably audacious for everyone at the bar, not just me, when I finally get a customer's seven drinks together and he doesn't have his money ready. Pretty much the next five minutes is me standing there watching him fumble through his jacket for a wallet, then pull out the credit card for which we *all* have to wait another three minutes to clear, and then he has yet to sign the receipt. It's always the ones who fuss about how long they've waited who are never ready for the transaction.

Patrons sometimes think they're going to get really quick service when they wave a dollar bill in the air as I'm serving others. Okay, *so they have a dollar.* Why do they think I'm going to break the *Guinness Book* speed record to serve them? I've never understood the logic here. I am a professional and I've noted who came when and will serve accordingly. It's part of my job. Unless his last tip was horrendous or there's a mixer at the bar who needs looking after, the dollar waver will have to wait to be served in fair time.

To tell me that you want me to "make it strong" or "put a lot of liquor in it" leads me to think you're one of the *few* people who like their drinks heavy-handed. *No shit*—everyone wants his drink strong. It also implies that you think I make weak drinks. It's another way to actually *get* a weak drink.

On the same note, people shouldn't order a very sweet cocktail like a mango margarita and tell me they don't taste the alcohol. If they tasted the alcohol, it wouldn't have been made correctly. And if it's alcohol they wanted to taste, they shouldn't have ordered a patsy drink. Everything gets a heavy-handed four count at my bar, so if people complain, I assume they're already soused, they're going to be trouble, or they're a frat boy. My remedy is to put a little extra tequila in the straw so their next sip will give them a quick blast just to shut them up.

This leads me to the drinkers who make sure to add "not too much ice" to their order. A little hint: less ice just leaves more room for mixers. So unless you want your T&T to taste like tonic, don't request less ice. We don't pour to a line on the glass or shaker; I'm doing the four count that everyone gets.

The ever-expanding drink order has got to be one of my biggest gripes. A martini is ordered and when it's put down the customer will add a Cosmo. When that arrives she will (oh yeah!) apologetically order a couple of beers, and so on. I want to kill this person at this point but instead I will tell her that I already took another order and the next portion of hers will have to wait—see you in an hour.

Potential drinkers who wave incessantly as if they've been waiting hours and who, when I finally run over, give me a lingering, confused look *drive me to the brink*. When I say "What'll it be?" they don't have a clue. They seem lost and scared and have me at full attention until they finally ask me what drinks we have. It's a bar, so we pretty much make all of the contemporary drinks of our time. Flabbergasted, they'll move on to the beer list, which is even more exasperating because the beers are lined up on an overhang two feet from their faces. This behavior leads me to believe that they never got the attention they craved as children and when it arrives they don't know what to do with it. They need a *real* shrink—not a bartender.

The negotiators are classic, usually college students or underage drinkers who come in with quality fake ID cards and generally ask me what they can get for three dollars. When I say a Bud Light from the bodega across the street, they will take me to the bargaining table. We don't have a lowest-price guarantee; all prices are nonnegotiable—the boss says so. This behavior implies that they won't have enough money to tip me, so I am not very concerned about serving them anyway.

These people are usually novices at real drinking. Negotiators, when they come up with the money, will always order the sweetest drink possible (Amaretto, Midori, Malibu, and Kahlua comes to mind) or the proverbial Long Island Iced Tea. These kids wouldn't know single-malt scotch from Drano. They usually look very green and nervous so when I hear their order, it's my cue to card them. There is always one in the group who "forgot" his wallet. Huh? Who forgets his wallet on a night out with friends? Amateurs and twenty-year-olds who don't have quality fake identification. Leonardo DiCaprio was the only underage drinker I'd ever served knowingly (*three* Long Island Iced Teas and a Rolling Rock). Plus, he was a stellar tipper.

I haven't even started with the people who vomit at the bar, complain about every little thing (Can you turn the music down? Can you turn the music up? Are you sure this is Sapphire gin?), steal my tips that are lingering on the bar, think it's right to put out their cigarettes in their glass when there's an ashtray in front of them, pour candle wax on the bar (for me to scrape off at the end of the night) in order to make pretty pictures for their friend, do lines of coke in front of me, tell me I'm a bitch because I cut them off when they're clearly out of control, ask for glass after glass of Bowery sludge tap water (pull out the fiver and buy that bottle of good water, already!), steal my CDs from the manager's booth where the stereo is kept, and so on.

Still wondering why we can be so jaded?

Despite being one of the most entertaining jobs around, the intense amount of personal interaction lends itself to incidents where bartenders end up in argumentative situations with patrons. When these fires cannot be put out, despite every effort on the bartender or manager's part, the bartender inevitably gets stiffed. I experienced at least one highly charged altercation with a customer every week. I've been viciously screamed at, punched, spat on, kicked, had my hair pulled, and condemned for things I never did. After struggling to right the incidents, to no avail, I was left drained, embittered, and unjustly stiffed. Getting stiffed always proved the most personal.

It does seem, strangely enough, that certain people go out just to have a bad time. Doubtless, they are nine-to-fivers who have worked hard all week and are going to have a good time, goddamn it, NO MATTER WHO GETS IN THEIR WAY! Their anxieties and frustrations are boiling over and the slightest thing will set them off.

Acting like a civilized human being while drinking shouldn't be the exception, but the rule. There were too many times at Marion's when the staff and I would instantly turn to each other for support when a particular person walked in—and we're talking about regulars here, not walk-ins. We knew what the night held in store when this person decided to engage us with his or her company.

When Darren, a local activist, showed up at Marion's, everyone would pull straws not to have to serve him because he always left the worst tips and demanded the most service. He looked and smelled as if he hadn't showered in months and, up until my final day on the job, never once smiled. Peggy, an ex-Marion's waitress turned regular, couldn't leave the place until she was in tears, pontificating about her current ex-boyfriend. This after every one of the staff reminded her repeatedly how wonderful she was and that the cad didn't deserve her anyway—ultimately leading to more inebriated ranting. A relative of the owner came in and acted like *he* owned the place, bragging to his newest girlfriend that Marion was related to him too—then stiffed the hapless server who bent over backward for what seemed like all night. The arrival of Mark, a gorgeous radio personality, meant that he would drink a case of beer and finally pass out on the bar, but becoming inebriated so slowly that it caught you by surprise every time.

My personal favorite was Mac, a bitter writer who frequented the place so regularly that his presence was literally dreaded. He couldn't help but get into a frenzied argument with someone at the bar—usually a total stranger. Often he would drench me with the many reasons why Islam "is a dying religion," forcing me to defend it, which I never liked to do. Living an irreverent life wasn't easy to begin with, but then having to defend it felt hypocritical. Mac just needed to bitch. It always started out with me asking him to keep it down, since diners were always complaining about his haranguing voice sweeping through the room—I finally had to cut him off until his next visit, which was usually the next week. One would think (and hope) he'd be embarrassed by the scene, but it never stopped his weekly trips to Marion's.

I felt concern for many of these regulars and their situations, but once in a while I was just too absorbed with work or didn't have it in me to dole out compassion for those certain people who sucked my energy dry. My main wish was that they would come in and have a good time, not behave as if my bar were their living room and they'd gotten their hands on the remote. Or at least compensate us well for the grief they put us through. That's the bottom line, and ultimately a drinker's end of the deal.

Bartenders judge the book by its cover. I can tell a person's drink as she's walking through the doors. I'm not saying I'm right every time but more often than not, I'm dead on. Here's what I've observed: frat boys order Jagermeister and beer chasers; Anglos drink Kirs; African Americans and clubkids drink anything supersweet; gay men order martinis and Cosmopolitans; groups of women ask for either white wine or fruity martinis; the literary set request classic martinis or

Manhattans; bridge-and-tunnel drink Absolut and anything; young girls with bleached-blond hair love Malibu- and Amaretto- based drinks; Brooklyn types nurse bourbon and beer; Asian patrons try the wine list; bachelorette parties inevitably order Lemon Drop shots; European visitors request Cinzano on the rocks *every time* but Euro-trash prefer gimlets or Stoli shots; the swing-dance fanatics drink anything with an old-fashioned name, like the Gibson or Sidecar; and drinkers who just turned twenty-one consistently request Midori Sours. It goes on and on.

People generally think of their drink as an accessory, sort of like a handbag or hat. When you look at it that way, it's easy to ascertain a person's poison by what she's wearing or her hairstyle. *Everyone* is a type. I put so much concentration on the person's drink order that I often missed catching her name. Countless times I found myself on the streets of Manhattan with Marion's customers running after me, hollering my name, and all I could recall was their favorite cocktail. "Shit! Here comes Dewars on the rocks!" I'd say while ducking into an alley, hoping to avoid an embarrassing situation.

Patrons' behavior could be judged in the same manner. Very often, people stuck to their genre, behaving and tipping accordingly. I've observed many types but the following were the most conspicuous.

Suits are usually men who come in behaving like Rockefeller, bab-bling on about how much money they made from an inheritance or the stock market, how many women they screwed that week, and the incredible steak they had at Lugers. They always ask if they can smoke a cigar and drink martinis (to the point of inebriation, in which case the arrogance builds to a fever pitch). If you've seen the film *In the Company of Men,* you know what I'm talking about. They act like they're made of money. Until the tip.

Not only do people from Kentucky revere bourbon, but all South-ern Americans have an affinity for the stuff—Makers Mark being their favorite brand. Hundreds of Southern belles ordered mint juleps from me, though I never had the mint leaves to make one.

New Yorkers and drinkers from Los Angeles, in particular, are obsessed with the martini and its ever-expanding variations. More than the actual beverage, it's the glass that seems to have captured their hearts—they'll put *anything* into it. I've even had non-alcohol-drinking customers ask for their Sprite or Coca-Cola to be served in a martini glass and garnished with cherries or twists. Why should they be left out of the martini craze? In addition, parents have requested their child's Shirley Temple be served in the glass too, just to make things fun for the kid and high-maintenance for me. But I'm delighted to add, New Yorkers usually tip extra for the superfluous exertions they impose.

I—and every bartender I've ever met—shudder whenever I hear a British accent ordering a drink from me. The French one, a close second, applies as well. They're not malicious or bad people and you'd think those groovy accents would ensure that they are the sophisticated travelers they seem—but alas, not. There are some English drinkers who understandably don't tip since bartenders in the U.K. are on salary and would feel insulted by a tip—hard to believe. I know many a mixer who claims that they actually know our customs but pretend they hadn't a clue when confronted. I lean toward that theory.

Every time I've ever pointed an English hottie out to a waiter he'll systematically cringe and howl, "You've got to be kidding, *they're British!*" Nothing more unattractive to a service professional than a cheapskate. Unfortunately I'm one of those Yanks who find Brits unbearably attractive, and found myself the poorer for it every time.

What's more torturous than getting a root canal? Being the lone bartender for a large group of women, especially suits—which is a lot like swimming in a pool of drunken premenstrual liquid estrogen. There are two ways it can go: extremely angry or excessively needy, sometimes both. Clans of women almost always hate an attractive bartendress so their behavior borders on haughty and ostentatious, attempting to make her feel inferior. Or they're so insecure that they can't order a drink without the clique's approval. "Is this Chardonnay any good, Carol?" "I don't know. What do you think, Jane?" "I don't know. Ask Cheryl. She took a wine course once." "No, I didn't. Ask the bartender." I'm trying to sell it so *of course it's good.* At that moment it's the best damn wine we've ever had.

It's really annoying if the place has a martini menu and they all start ordering elaborate fruity cocktails, favoring Cosmos, apple and French martinis, and, without exception, never ask for the same drink twice. This eventually leads to wobbling, catty remarks, extra-loud laughing, the occasional catfight, and projectile vomiting. When they finally leave there's a 10 percent tip on the check, or 5 percent if it's a bachelorette party. Thank God we add an 18 percent grat on tables of six or more, or I'd seriously lose it.

Other comments that ensure that the tip will suck:

"Water with lemon."

"Cheers!"

"You're the best bartender I've ever had!"

"Do you have happy hour?"

"I just want you to know, I'm a *great* tipper!"

"We're splitting that beer."

"I'll have a Bud."

"Is it open bar?"

"Can we have separate checks?" (And there are eight people in the group.)

Another bad sign is when the gang begins to systematically sprint for the rest rooms when the tab is given and only one totally soused person is left to pay it. The drunk usually can't figure out a decent tip or redirects his resentment at me for leaving him with the bill. I've often remedied this dilemma by adding the "large party" gratuity to the tab, knowing he wouldn't see it. He would usually add a tip (10 percent or less, usually) to the one I already tacked on.

A stiff is imminent whenever I ask a person what he'd like and his comeback is something like, "What do you think I'll like?" To which I reply, "Let me just go get my crystal ball," and walk away.

I really hate it when the wives come back to the bar and take part of the tip back after their husband (and yes, it's always women), who is waiting for them outside "while they use the bathroom," leaves a decent one—there's a special place in hell for women like that. As far as I'm concerned, that's called *stealing*.

Joe and Terry were a couple I had to serve late, just before closing time, two or three times a month. I will never know how they always managed to catch me as I was restocking the bar and just about to cash out the register. They would waltz in from the dark street, always looking as if they'd been somewhere fancy. Terry would act as if she hadn't seen me in years and never failed in making me feel like a real cad when I told her I was in the process of closing; but after years of her begging to be let in, I would relent and serve them. Joe was a man's man: quiet, brooding, and faithful to his bizarre wife. He looked as if he had poker buddies and smoked cigars. When all was said and done, Terry would grab some of that tip when she thought I wasn't looking and jump into the cab Joe had waiting.

pet peeve no. 10

> Women who come in and can't seem to order for themselves. Unless you have laryngitis, are deaf, dumb, or mute, please answer me to my face when I ask you what you would like to drink. Don't turn your head and whisper your order into your boyfriend's ear. I already got his order.

Celebrities are never predictable. It is quite disillusioning when someone I really admire parks himself in front of me for a cocktail and leaves me with a subpar grat. I mean, most of these people are millionaires! It's also quite uplifting to someone like myself, who, as an actress for a time, is granted a great tip from someone I've seen on the big screen for years. It's a toss-up and it's fun to watch the dust settle when they leave, no matter which way it goes.

I'm not the star-struck type, having served hundreds of celebs, but there is one who remains fresh in my mind. One evening, back at the nightclub, I had a quiet moment before the throng of club hoppers arrived, so I was cutting lemon and lime wedges to garnish the drinks with and pass the time. The cutting board was piled high with beautifully cut lemons and limes that sent a citrus aroma wafting into the dank beer perma-smell I was accustomed to. I was in a zone when I heard, "I'll have a glass of water, please." When I looked up, Bruce Willis was standing in front of me with that goofy crooked smile and I *all but lost it.* The cutting board somehow flipped over. There were lemons and limes flying all over the place and one hit me in the eye. "Oh shit! I'm sorry. Damn! I'll get your water," I said.

He was quite amused and decent about the incident. I continued to apologize and he said it was okay, and even asked about my eye, which was bloodshot and tearing at that point. Smiling, he took his glass and walked off into the dark, luminous red and blue lights of the room as I began collecting all the fruit. When I lifted my still-stinging head I saw that he had left a tenner for the glass of water.

The last celebrity I served before my departure from Marion's was the Edge from U2—and boy was I (and most of my patrons) excited he was at my bar. I'd been listening to that band since my hair had its first perm! The first sign that all was not right was when he ordered a girly drink. I placed the melon martini in front of him and later bought another round for him and a friend. He left me a paltry two dollars. It was heartbreaking on many levels. I'd purchased every album of theirs since their inception, attended nearly every tour, and he left me two bucks! That one hurt.

Thankfully there are a lot of celebrities who make up for the stingy ones. Russell Simmons is a notoriously great tipper, though you couldn't pry that cell phone from his ear with a monkey wrench. Others include Charlie Watts, Pele, Robin Williams, Christy Turlington, John Travolta, Uma Thurman, the late great Jeff Buckley, Frank Sinatra, Howard Stern, Susan Sarandon and Tim Robbins, Bill Clinton and family, Tom Petty, Bernadette Peters, Joe Pesci, Bill Paxton, Jason Patric, Chris O'Donnell, Conan O'Brien, Stevie Nicks, Bill Murray, Shirley Manson (Garbage front woman), the guys from They Might Be Giants, Kyle MacLachlan, Jennifer Jason Leigh, Pierce Brosnan, Sean Penn, John Kennedy, Jr., Angelina Jolie, Holly Hunter,

Morgan Freeman, Johnny Depp, Courtney Cox, Kevin Costner, Patricia Arquette, Andre Agassi, Helena Bonham Carter, Gwyneth Paltrow, Jon Stewart, Tom Hanks, and Tim Allen.

pet peeve no. 11 ....➤

> People who say, with a wink, "I'm so sorry, but I don't have enough to tip
> you tonight. I'll get you next time, all right?" My answer to them is "No
> problem! My kids don't need to eat this week!"

◄...

Outside of show-biz folks, the greatest tippers are men who need to show off to prove something—usually the size of their, uh, wad. And what spells "big wad a' money" like the Mafia? These guys love to pull out the C-notes and drop one in front of their moll or hooker.

The nightclub I worked at over a decade ago was supposedly owned by the Mafia. Sprinkled between the models and celebrities I had to serve were an awful lot of men sporting dark polyester suits or disco shirts unbuttoned to the navel showing off a fantastic array of cheesy gold chains, fingers adorned with pinkie rings—*I shit you not.* They couldn't buy class but they sure could tip.

One sweaty evening when I was ten-deep serving cocktails in plastic cups, a short and clammy little man squeezed his way through the throng of drinkers. He had on his arm a Teutonic blonde with the most inflated breasts I'd ever seen. He told me his lady wanted cigarettes, to which I explained that the machine was by the toilets in the back.

"I don't wanna go to the back," he said, eyeballing my pack of Marlboro Lights. "Listen, Cookie, lemme have your pack, it doesn't matter how many you got. The lady wants 'em."

"I only have a couple left and that won't make it to closing. There is no amount of money you could give me to fork those over, sorry."

"I'll give you fifty bucks. I've had hookers give me blow jobs for less," he declared with a wink, pulling out "the wad."

"When you're down to six cigarettes, no contest. Sorry."

"You drive a hard bargain," he said, adding, "a hundred."

"Nope."

The "lady" was getting desperate as her nic fit clearly peaked. She began to twist him away.

"Five hundred dollars," he said, waving five C-notes in the smoky air as she took a lingering glance at her watch.

I howled, "Okay, okay! You can have them!"

Dumbfounded, I handed the six cigarettes in the box over to the little man as he planted five hundred smackers into my waiting palm.

"You're one expensive bitch."

"Thanks," I said, pocketing the bills. He smiled before he was dragged into the sweaty, pumping crowd.

We all have a price, don't we?

Pink Drinks and the Downfall of Culture

An alcoholic is anyone you don't like who drinks more than you do.
DYLAN THOMAS

COSMOPOLITAN
2½ oz. citrus vodka (preferably Ketel One Citroen)
½ oz. Triple Sec
Splash of fresh lime juice
Splash of Rose's lime juice
½ oz. cranberry juice for color
Shake well and strain into a chilled martini glass.
Garnish with a twist.

*Every shift ushers in sots who can't seem to veer away from the pre-*dictable array of insults and shock-value catchwords that make me want to yawn. Mondays I'm pelted with "You bitch!" and other clichéd taunts that are supposed to make me feel bad about cutting off late-night bar hoppers who come in soused to begin with. These strays are usually out-of-towners who got thrown out of Bowery Bar around the corner and thought we looked empty enough at 2 A.M. to accommodate their kind of business.

Tuesdays hit me with swing kids who like to come in for the deejay's Swing Night and who decide to stiff me after the fifteenth Cosmo because they can no longer see straight. I can count on the fedora-clad young'uns trying to get away with badly made ID cards and when I confront them, they casually ask why I'm "such a bitch."

Wednesdays are alcoholic-regulars night. This is the shift where I have to have talks with certain drinkers who have been in every night since Friday and ask if it would be a good idea to take a break. The acquaintance/drinker invariably tells me to mind my own business and asks why I'm being so cranky tonight. Then he'll disappear for months and I learn he's drinking at Jones Street Café around the corner.

Thursdays are always fun. We get a mix of out-of-towners and regulars who decide to get a jump-start on the weekend so it's amateur night all around. The occasional vomit to clean, a handful of Brits that stiff me, a bachelor party of frat boys to cut off, and an out-and-out fight where I have to throw out a drunk who threatens to come back and beat me up. Ooooh, I say, now I'm scared—now get the fuck out. And by the way, you're 86'd.

Fridays and Saturdays are nearly identical. The nights start out with a slew of geriatrics in for Marion's "Yellow Plate Special" that runs from 6 to 7 P.M. This crowd is simply mean. They come in at five and get pissed that we're not open yet, and when they wait at the bar, which they invariably do, they whine the whole hour nursing a glass of water about how the restaurant isn't open for their momentous cheap night out. The play they're about to see isn't for another two hours, so what's the problem? You're not a very nice girl, they say, and I roll my eyes. Not a regular in sight the whole night, just hundreds of bridge-and-tunnel types, Frogs and Brits, and the occasional drag queens making a martini stop before heading over to the trendy Bowery Bar, where they'll be accosted by inexperienced (but gorgeous) bartenders and a "doorman" who'll make them wait half an hour. I can count on ten "nonsmokers" who'll insist on bumming cigarettes from me all night without so much as a thank-you or tip (cigs are a luxury item these days!), at least six "You're a bitch"s, four cut-offs, two heaving rookies barely able to make it outside or to the toilet, three fake IDs, two dry-humpers who just won't go home, and a partridge in a pear tree.

Sundays I sleep all day and night.

From my perspective at the bar, I've come to the conclusion that my generation has been raised by wolves.

The nonprofit citizens' group Public Agenda can back me up on this. In April 2002, they published a famous study that claims rudeness and a basic lack of goodwill toward fellowmen is at an all-time high. One of their reasons is that when people have money they feel entitled to behaving like degenerate jerks. The more wealth this country acquires, the more technologically advanced we become, the more addicted we get to the toys that come with all this. These trinkets, like the cell phone, are indeed fun and are supposed to make us more efficient. They're fast, instant gratification embellished with glitter, pretty bells and whistles—and this trend has ultimately led us to an infatuation with pretty drinks like the Cosmopolitan. More on that later.

Rudeness has become a socially accepted attitude, according to Public Agenda's earlier, January 2002 nationwide survey of 2,013 adults called "Aggravating Circumstances: A Status Report on Rudeness in America." We're not talking about Emily Post's etiquette tips on eating with your mouth closed. The daily barrage of discourteous, greedy behavior occurs in the home, in the car, in the air, at the job, on television, in stores, and every other setting imaginable. Most of all, at bars.

The age of Starbucks has given birth to a generation of people who can't see past their own, self-magnified needs. It's a cultural predicament that is contagious, and accordingly, it feels like the norm. We're getting farther away from the mom-and-pop shops of neighborhood life, and it's slashing the sense of community, which we need to help us feel connected and to keep us from biting each other's heads off when something doesn't go our way. Politeness is going the way of the rotary phone—and this progressive, new "me-me-me" attitude is leading the way.

Two summers ago I was buying produce at the Amagansett farmers' market when I heard a familiar voice. Turning around with my basket of peaches and apricots, I spotted none other than Alec Baldwin rambling to himself. For a moment I thought he had gone mad since Kim cast him off. Bumping into people, distracted and oblivious, he kept on talking. I giggled and continued sniffing the fruits of summer. He wasn't exactly inconspicuous in the Hamptons; in fact, he is a sort of bombastic hometown mayor. He's *everywhere* and it wasn't the first time I'd spotted him.

He had the whole place wondering what he was doing. As it turned out he was wearing a new accessory: an earpiece that made his cell phone handless so that he could babble away and shop at the same time. It was just a few months before everyone, it seemed, had gotten hold of the item and also started walking around like zombies talking to what appeared to be themselves. I'll admit, it isn't exactly rude for Baldwin to walk around with a handless talking device while filling his fruit basket. But do we need to hear his conversation with his agent when we're trying to enjoy a quiet summer day at the farmers' market?

I can remember incalculable times when I had been swiftly summoned by a drinker during a heavy rush and I asked, "Hello, what'll it be?" only to receive a finger in the face that told me to *shush* as he continued babbling on his cell phone. I took particular care in making these tactless morons wait forever for their order and added a dollar to everything they drank. Do I feel guilty? No. Do two wrongs make a right? No. Am I contributing to the rudeness problem in America? Probably. As I said, rudeness *is* contagious, according to Public Agenda.

I once had a customer, Joe, come in with friends with what I thought was a laptop computer. Bad enough, but to my unrelenting mortification, it turned out to be a portable DVD player. He sat at a busy dark bar with his drink and watched *The Rock* while his friends had fun without him. And that wasn't the odd part—his friends didn't seem to mind! He and his companions thought nothing of ignoring each other for the sake of watching a film during their many rounds, or cutting each other off to accept an incoming call on their cell phones. Had a friend of mine brought a gizmo like that to our Saturday night out and proceeded to watch a movie (a lame one at that), I would have taken the thing and thrown it out onto the Bowery.

I did my drugs the old-fashioned way—in a bathroom stall away from anyone who might be offended. I've stopped plenty of people from lighting up their joints and cutting their coke at my bar—did it ever occur to anyone that that might be considered appalling to some? Not when there's booze to stoke that fire. It's bad enough to hear four cell phones go off in their separate, stale versions of Mozart melodies but then to have to listen to these unbelievably boring conversations is just another level of hell. "Cindy, you have to try the Cosmos here! Turn the TV off and get over here right away—I'm holding a stool for you!" Or, "She did what? I can't believe she dumped you! Wait, I'm ordering a drink. Miss, oh bartender—over here! Get me a French martini! [Back to the friend.] No, the Cosmo is *not* better than the French. How would you know anyway, you've never had one!" You wouldn't believe the verbal diarrhea I have had to listen to. I have really begun to appreciate restaurants and bars that ban cell phones altogether. Clearly people *are* getting pissed off and I'm one of them.

Still, the study claims that people today are unwilling to question a person's bad behavior. Not me. Of the hordes of people who ordered from me without so much as a "please" or "excuse me," my response was often "What's the magic word?" Were these people raised in dreadful orphanages or something? I had to treat adults like children in order to get the ounce of respect I always expected. Their expressions would change into one of a shy, scolded child and they would acknowledge with a "I'm sorry. May I please have a . . ." Hell,

I was working hard and I can't tell you how refreshing it was to hear those simple words, sometimes making the shift a totally uplifting experience.

Before the Cosmopolitan took over the world, I was officiating at a classic "martini bar"—my Marion's clientele didn't drink many beers or down shots, despite the proximity to NYU. (I agree with Björk, who says beer tastes like wood.) For the Bowery, I had a lot of cultivated drinkers. It was pretty much prime martinis, gin and tonics, Bollinis, and vodka and cranberrys. But gin and vodka martinis were our schtick. The occasional beer and glass of wine rounded out the catalog. In the winter, Manhattans sold well, and in the summer, vodka gimlets were all the rage. It was a chic crowd before my bar morphed into a daily blitz of *Friends*-watching amateurs.

I still remember the first time a customer ordered the pink potion from me at Marion's. It was around 1992. Her name was Julia and she was a writer for the trendy rag *Paper* magazine. I had started making the Cosmo when it was still in its infancy during my early days at the nightclub, but suddenly people were taking the drink seriously. Julia was a regular and normally drank vodka martinis, but she was going around tasting Cosmos at different spots downtown. A few months later, a friend told me to pick up a copy of the magazine because there was a mention of Marion's. When I found the list of hot New York bars in its pages, I saw that Julia had written that I made the best Cosmopolitans in town. It just takes the smallest mention in a magazine for a drink to gain popularity (*Esquire* magazine personally jump-started the resurgence of the Sidecar in one issue). That's when I saw the pink drink set in motion a frantic snowballing appetite for fruity cocktails in martini glasses and my crowd get frivolous.

Indeed there were frou-frou cocktails long before the Cosmo, though perhaps not as well known since this one's debut on *Sex and the City* and *One Life to Live*. Bartender Junno Lee of Junno's in Manhattan proposes that an Absolut vodka marketing team created the cocktail as a way to sell Absolut Citron. Those marketing geniuses do things like that. (Chuck at Marion's used the same philosophy to sell one of the newer enhanced vodkas. He invented the Metropolitan—identical to the Cosmo, only made with Absolut Kurant. We couldn't *give* it away when it first debuted. The most chronic complaint was that it tasted like Robitussin cough suppressant. Nevertheless, it caught on.)

Another theory is that in the early eighties the Cosmo was being served at the Fog City Diner in San Francisco. Soon after that, it could be had in New York at the Odeon. An ex-bartender of theirs appears to be taking credit for it, though when I e-mailed the Absolut people in Sweden, they didn't have a clue about it. Absolut Vodka often acknowledges bartenders who have created drinks with their product—a sort of certificate of authenticity. It doesn't really matter who came up with the pink elixir—but it was pure genius because it changed the way people drank forever.

Drinkers who insist on colorful cocktails in martini glasses tend to nip a lot more than the scotch or gin drinker. How can they not when they're guzzling the sweetest possible concoctions that usually taste like fruit juice? It used to be that my youngest customers drank the sweetest drinks and got intolerably drunk; but since the Cosmo there's no telling who we have to card or throw out. The drinks go down faster and the effects aren't often caught until it's too late. Plus these drinkers are always asking if there's any alcohol in the drink—order a real drink and maybe you'll taste the booze.

The "martini"—by this I mean in its pseudo form—became a force to be reckoned with when the film *Swingers* was released in 1996. Just down the street is a dance studio that became inundated with swing dancers galore, and guess where they came after flipping-my-gal-over-my-shoulder, in suspenders and fedora? You guessed it. They were *young*. And the real martini's sting was too strong. Someone had heard about a drink called the Cosmopolitan. It came in a martini glass, which matched their Rat Pack costumes perfectly. And it tasted like Hi-C cran-lime juice! That was the end of the real drinker. An era came to a close.

The martini glass was suddenly so in demand, cocktails that had long been out came back in full force, such as the Negroni, Gibson, and Sidecar. People ordered margaritas straight up more and more. If they still wanted the caché of ordering a classic martini but couldn't handle the vodka or gin, they ordered it "dirty," with a good dollop of olive juice. It *was* downright filthy inasmuch as I couldn't keep customers' grubby little fingers out of the olive dish, and had to eventually keep the juice in a separate container, away from their reach.

The young'uns wanted extra extra *extra* olives, to the point that they seemed to be garnishing them with vodka. Olives have gotten fancy too. Not only could you get the small standards, you could get pimento, tomolive, blue cheese stuffed, garlic stuffed, jalapeño stuffed, black olives, depending on where you were indulging. I had a lot more esteem for the martini drinker who sported a twist, since it's only an enhancement of the liquor's flavor, not a downright *affront*.

pet peeve no. 12 ───▶

> If you're of the male persuasion, don't order anything bright green, pink, or neon. It looks ridiculous, and you should be drinking like a man. I don't care what the trend is or what *The New York Times* says. There is nothing manly about Midori drinks or pink cocktails in martini glasses.

◀───

The classic martini made a comeback in the eighties and its followers were devout drinkers who worshiped its maker's technique as much as the drink itself. These were unaffected imbibers who led the way out of the polyester Screwdriver age. But in the nineties when the Cosmo emerged, drinking styles fueled a distinctive shift. The new drinkers are mostly concerned with their cocktail's enthralling colors, nonalcoholic taste, and uniqueness; drinks were more like an embellishment to their look than something to quaff with adults. These drinks have led to long waits—sometimes up to twenty minutes a drink—that make people testy, especially if a real drinker is waiting for a scotch or glass of wine and everyone else wants an evening equivalent to a Mardi Gras–scale production. Women have suddenly begun to *always* order these fruitier cocktails, and because of their smaller frames they get wasted faster—though that trend has been changing. More men are "eating quiche," so to speak, and, in turn, projectile vomiting and getting thrown out just as much.

There is nothing quite so disheartening for me as to see a rugged, hulky man swagger in, take a seat, and grab the girly-drink menu. Like two fingers putting out a candle. In the old days, I'd guess he was having a Manhattan or gin martini. These days, that chiseled face, five-o'clock shadow, and tussled mop of hair, a man who looked like he just rolled out of bed after fucking, is sitting here having a melon martini. I am sure my expression is a look of disbelief, then a grimace, as I turn around to make the cocktail. I made it *known* to him that I have no regard for him as a man. I hate to say it but it's true—I did this hundreds of times.

In the old days, as you got older, you would acquire a taste for the sauce. It was a rite of passage, not unlike slurping down your first oyster. Like cheeses that smelled like the most pungent of farts, or steak tartare, its rawness intermingling with spices and uncooked egg, making your mouth drool.

Maturity started with the proverbial beer, then vodka or gin, then rum, if you wanted to get stupid. (Bob Pollard, songwriter and lead singer of Guided by Voices, calls tequila *To'killya*, and drinking with that band is surely a death wish. "Another round of *To'killyas*," someone says as a guitarist passes out.) When you'd ventured most of the liquor groups you started rarifying your mediums: bourbon, single-malts, scotches, aperitifs, good wines, cordials, and the like. Sweetened drinks were for amateurs still acclimating to liquor. Remember your first sloe gin fizz? Or you may have started with SoCo shots with chasers, perhaps even the archaic Tom Collins, now making a revival. You thought single-malts tasted like gasoline, so subsequently you graduated from college and upgraded to the vodka cranberry or gin tonic. Finally you dropped the cranberry or tonic and downed your first real martini. You thought it was cool when James Bond ordered it. You liked to say, "Shaken not stirred"—which, by the way, irritates all bartenders. With the guys, you strived to be cool and had your first shot of Glenlivet, pretending it's been your poison for years. Someone coerces you to quaff their peaty-tasting Lagavulin and slowly you see the subtleties between the two. It grows on you, that taste of Scotland marsh. Just when you weren't looking you became a man.

There are some girly drinks that I find less grating than others when ordered by men. The gimlet, made with gin particularly, is one I regard as legitimate. It doesn't involve a lot of fruits and when made with a touch of fresh lime juice, it's divine. The pear martini is quite refreshing while still retaining a light but dynamic taste of alcohol. The same goes for the smoky martini. This is a splendid alternative for people who actually like single-malt scotch, though it's not for the faint of heart—you've got to *love* scotch to drink a smoky. For die-hard drunks there's always the Kamikaze straight up. It'll get you where you want to go—fast. The retro Negroni has fast made a respectable comeback with the help of the martini craze. It's a real drink, so those who are alcohol-challenged may want to shy away from this one. The Sidecar, like the Negroni, is a classic enjoying a healthy revival. It's basically a margarita but made with brandy and I prefer it without the sugared rim.

While some drinks are making a resurgence, it is sad to say that there are many outstanding cocktails that are fading away into our subconscious file called "liquor has-beens." The Rob Roy, once a great alternative to the Manhattan because of its use of sweet vermouth and bitters, has lost a lot of its fan base due to the obsession with fruity drinks. Another scotch drink that seems to be waning is the Rusty Nail—but if it's sweet you want, it can be done with this drink by candying the alcohol with more Drambuie. Every time the seventies comes back in vogue, I think the time-honored Harvey Wallbanger will reemerge. Alas, it has not. It was ordered from me four times in all the years I tended bar. Along with Harvey, believe it or not, the Screwdriver seems to be on its way out. I imagine it has a lot to do with the fact that it doesn't come in a martini glass and is too uncomplicated for today's youth. Pretty soon you won't be hearing anyone ordering a gin martini, scotch and soda, or even the suburban classic, Absolut and cranberry. They don't come in that stylish glass so consider their days numbered.

Cocktails I wish *would* disappear from the planet are primarily high-maintenance or those that get people toasted too fast: the Sazarac (a Southern fave of cheap, well, Southerners), Long Island Iced Tea (the college darling), the Old-Fashioned (I don't know a bartender who doesn't cringe when this is ordered because we have to "muddle" fruit before we add the booze), and anything that involves a blender (only people out to behave as juvenile as possible order these) or has the name "shooter" attached to it (no explanation necessary, I'm sure). Drinks with witless names should also be stricken from bartending bibles. Though there are too many to list, here are my most dreaded: WooWoo shot, Blow Job, Sex on the Beach, Buttery Nipple, Fuzzy Navel, Creamsicle, Screaming Orgasm, Jell-O shot, Toasted Almond, Tootsie Roll, and the Zombie. I'm getting the feeling that American drinkers are so sexually deprived that they need to drink their orgasm instead of actually have one.

Following the path of the Cosmopolitan's wild success, bartenders are fast formulating drinks with every type of extract and juice imaginable and adding to the never-ending list of lame drinks populating the recipe volumes. Drinks that had historically been served on ice are now being made straight up. In my final years at Marion's I was asked to serve whiskey sours straight up more and more. Same goes for the champagne cocktail, Mimosa, and Baybreeze. That glass has made a lot of people pretentious about drinking.

I'm not saying that the "market" doesn't deserve to be heard, that people who want to imbibe cocktails tasting of juices aren't important. But the days of a posh clientele admiring the making of a timeless martini, swanky or even down-and-out men finding a bat's squeak of masculinity in their gin or single-malt, or the novice experimenting with his first gin-tonic are over. Chances are the amateur is experimenting with an apple martini only to graduate to the melon; suave gentlemen are canvassing a menu for anything that doesn't scream *Sissy-Boy*—but can't find it. You can't exactly drown your sorrows in a raspberry-and-papaya-infused cocktail.

The New York Times recently published an article stating "the age of the celebrity bartender had arrived." While I'm tempted to agree, I take issue with their perspective on the subject. No, I'm not a *cocktail engineer*. I'm not a *bar chef*; I don't treat my bar like a kitchen. I won't be pulling out any guava/papaya/passionfruit puree, smashing mint leaves with my muddler, or stuffing goat's-anus paté into olives so you can experience something munificently absurd. My barback (a mixer's assistant) was not ever referred to as a *commis du bar*, as the article suggested; a recent Mexican immigrant, she could barely speak English, let alone French. These bar chefs are obsessed with ice cube density and obscure liqueurs to plop into their concoctions— slowly destroying the collective consciousness that stores centuries of alcohol reverence. When did bartending turn into a celebrity sport?

When the "cocktail menu" made its comeback.

Originating from the days of Prohibition, the speakeasy listed its classic mixed cocktails along with the wide array of alcohols it managed to sneak in. It was no small feat to stock an array of single-malts, bourbons, and sipping rums—and to have a choice was of great appeal. Secret tunnels and alleyways provided the link for the Mafia to deliver their goods, and the menus liked to show off their coup. When Prohibition ended the bars could stock anything they wanted, and the menu's relevance eventually faded.

When Dale DeGroff reinstated the cocktail menu at the Rainbow Room in the early nineties, the concept took off. Most of these menus are specialized for the place that they serve, thus exhibiting drinks that you can't get anywhere else—not bad marketing for the joint if you can get people addicted to the selections. When Stolichnaya couldn't keep up with the demand for flavored vodka, Smirnoff and Skyy made comebacks with citrus-enhanced varieties. Even Ketel One vodka, the once revered, underground—now hugely successful— brand came out with Ketel One Citroen, and who knows what's in development. A lot of the time, though, these cocktails are love 'em or hate 'em when you consider the bizarre combos that have been developed. It's virtually a tanked fruit juice bar: apple martini, pear martini, citrus martini, Stoli orange martini, melon martini, raspberry martini, etc. Cabana Boy Rum comes in pineapple/coconut, cherry/vanilla, lemon/lime, orange, raspberry, etc. As if rum weren't sweet enough. There are also the sophisticated fruity or just odd martinis: French martini, black martini, chocolate martini, blue martini, smoky martini, Mexican martini, sake martini, black truffle martini— huh? You get the idea. I keep hearing about ostentatious drinks that require a bar to stock things like lemongrass, plums, Swiss chocolates, peach purees, shiitake mushrooms, and century cordials to round things off. They're stuffing olives with everything but the kitchen sink and stations are starting to look more like a mad scientist's laboratory. The bars that are serving drinks with pricy ingredients are charging $25 (the truffle martini at Towne Restaurant) and up for a single cocktail. And these "beverage directors" are making stellar salaries *plus* tips and benefits.

I'm the genius who thought it would be cool to have a martini menu at Marion's. I guess I was trying to kiss the new manager's ass since she was on a firing rampage and I was worried I'd lose my job along with the colleagues I'd worked with for almost seven years.

The idea came from my jaunts to the bar Kurt and I frequented when we were dating, Bar & Books. They had a cocktail menu that featured a lot of classics; nothing too weird, just the tried-and-true with their own stamp. Their selection of cognac, aperitifs, and other top-shelf liqueurs was mind-boggling.

The management at Marion's loved the idea, bought a bunch of plastic stands for the bar, we came up with a slew of kooky drinks, and the rest is history. The cocktails on the list instantly began to outsell the mainstays we had made for years. I can't say I didn't regret it—I was working doubly hard yet making the same money, plus the crowd was getting irresponsible about their drinking. Casey, the other bartender, and I bitched and moaned about the added load, but it was going to happen anyway. Toward the end, not a single night passed that a drinker didn't ask to see our cocktail menu as if it were as required of a bar as a food menu is of a restaurant.

Sometimes I miss what the Bowery used to be, sans techno-apparatus, attitude, and waxed citizenry. I even miss the embittered and dusty derelicts and transients exteriors fully rigged with threats, tacky come-ons, bar tricks, and dirty jokes. Now *they* knew how to drink. God bless 'em.

Want to know how to make the easiest $150 of your life? Gary, an ex-Marion's bartender, had gotten himself into the alcohol focus-group loop and was recruiting all the other mixers he knew to join the club. Although they could be a really tedious stretch spent talking about liquors I'd never heard of, they were quick cash. I never spent more than twenty minutes at one and always made more than $100 a session.

One in particular really stood out. I was called to show up at an impressive building in midtown at the ungodly hour of ten-thirty in the morning—which for bartenders is the break of dawn. (A note to the marketing geniuses of the alcohol industry: bartenders don't really function until noon and then only after at least two cups of coffee. We're usually hungover or just plain wrecked from the night before.)

When I showed up, there were nine other nodding bartenders sitting around a small conference table chugging the free coffee for dear life and feasting on the doughnuts the suits had prepared. Marketing people love to get us loaded on caffeine and sugar as soon as possible to get us hyped for whatever crap they're trying to sell. I'm sure they get more positive results that way to impress their clients—and they probably figured *that* out at a focus-group session. Our bloodshot eyes were outshone only by their puffiness, and because we didn't have time to take showers, the body odor was palpable. I recognized only one other mixer and we nodded to each other in vague acknowledgment.

Plopping into the only seat left, the suit—so perky I imagined he was a cartoon—greeted us, had us sign in on a yellow-lined sheet attached to his clipboard, then introduced the poison we were going to try for him. It was a new flavored cognac. I wasn't sure if I heard him right.

"Did you say *flavored* cognac? Who would do such a thing?" I asked.

"Our client. [Pause] Any other questions before I begin pouring?" he said, grinning with his perfect Ken-doll teeth.

We looked at each other in repulsion. I could tell no one wanted to try the stuff but was feigning interest nevertheless. We were bartenders, for God's sake! Giving a mixer flavored cognac is like giving a four-star chef Velveeta cheese to work with. The only consolation for us was that at least it had alcohol content and could be considered hair of the dog. Coffee's good but *nothing* kicks a hangover like more of whatever destroyed you the night before.

We were given a moment to sip (some of us chugged) the passion-fruit- and then the cranberry-flavored cognac. A handful of the bartenders downed them like shots and lifted their glasses for more. Their eyes were coming alive. The suit enjoyed playing barman, and the cognac, so to speak, started flowing like Cuervo shots on a Friday night. We were told to describe our experience drinking this "nectar of the gods," as he called it. Some words that were thrown out were: zippy, tangy, fresh, nectary, thick, and interesting. I kept silent, hoping he'd forget I was there. Just give me my $100 and get me out of this cat-piss seminar, was all I could think. Mr. Suit finally got to me and asked to give him an adjective that described my "experience."

"Undrinkable."

"Why? Don't you find it refreshing?"

"No," I whispered. "It tastes like syrup to cook with. As a drink, it tastes like a mistake."

"Hmmm," he said, scribbling away on his clipboard. "Is that all?"

"No. I think it's a trend that shouldn't happen. I don't think we should be flavoring every liquor on earth. I mean, we're flavoring vodka, rum, and now cognac? What's next, papaya-flavored gin?"

"Flavored gin, huh? We have a gin client as well," he said, excitedly. "Do you think people might like that?"

"No," I muttered, shaking my head. "I can understand vodka and even rum. But cognac is sacred, and what they're doing is desecrating the religious tradition of cognac making." I looked around at the other bartenders, who were conspicuously silent. The only thing I could think of was that they didn't want out of the focus-group loop so they lied about *everything* for the easy cash.

"Thank you for your very candid opinion," he said, still smiling. "Here you go and have a nice day."

He handed me a small envelope containing the cash and held the door open. I ambled out, hoping to get home early enough to take a quick nap before my shift.

- - - - - - - - - - - - - - - -

The liquor industry markets to the general public in both obvious and manipulative ways. Dale DeGroff had suggested to the Hennessy people that they promote "Hennessy Sidecars." (When DeGroff talks, liquor companies listen.) The next thing you knew, Manhattan was plastered with billboards displaying a cartoon version of the cocktail—these days you have to put even cognac in a martini glass to sell it—and it worked.

Another technique they used to sell the Hennessy Sidecar was to pay grade-C models in halter tops and trendies to bar-hop and make a holy stink about the drink. They once came to Marion's on a warm evening. Here's how it went:

"Oh, miss! Can I have a Hennessy Sidecar? It's so yummy," Model A vociferates.

"*Mmmmmm.* This *HENNESSY Sidecar* is soooooo amazing," cries Model B. "I'll have one too!"

"I want one too. But only use Hennessy, please!"

"Me too! Me too!"

No one ever fell for it, though, and we watched in horror as attractive young women forced themselves to drink one after another, orgasmically, as if they were fucking the damn thing. Naturally, they were sauced after one too many and jiggled on to their next haunt. I can say one thing about Hennessy, though, and that is that they tipped *very* well.

But what troubles me most about the alcohol industry is its notorious, heavy-handed publicizing and endorsing of liquor-branded malt beverages targeted for African American youth. In densely populated black neighborhoods one cannot shake the looming billboards, liquor stores, and the unbelievable amounts of store window signage emphasizing glamorous black youths enjoying crappy booze in either a club or rap scenario. Or there's a scantily clad black woman humping a malt-liquor bottle. The sexual end of this advertising assault is just another angle that liquor companies have abused to entice black youth. For example, Smirnoff Ice is depicting provocative young African Americans enjoying hip-hop culture, blatantly attempting to appeal to young black people in both sexual and ethnic ways.

All of this is particularly distressing because black youths are at a much higher risk for developing heavy patterns of alcohol use due to environmental considerations (e.g., overexposure from the media, particularly hip-hop culture, and poverty in certain black neighborhoods) even though they tend to stall initiating alcohol use for a longer duration than other youth. They watch more television than other ethnic groups (six hours or more per day), a phenomenon linked to detrimental use of drugs and/or alcohol. African Americans as a group encounter greater levels of adverse health and social repercussions related to alcohol use.

In my neighborhood, the liquor billboards are quite dignified: white people lounging about, falling in love in between sips of whatever they're selling. In African-American neighborhoods, alcohol is sold via tits and ass and gangsta rap. It's sad for me, as a bartender, to see such irresponsible marketing of alcohol—especially when the suits are in full knowledge of the consequences. They destroy the very self-esteem of these neighborhoods, the future of these kids—and take their money anyway.

Henry Miller wrote: "You know, there isn't a thing in the world worth fighting for, except peace of mind." Liquor people, take note.

If the Cosmopolitan did one thing, it separated the boys from the men, girls from women. Real men don't walk into a bar with their buddies only to whip out their laptops—they know how to have a good time without the escapist trappings. They're in the here and now. Real men go outside to use their cell phone because their conversations are off-limits to outsiders and dedicated to the one they're speaking to, and they *know* how to listen.

Most of all, real men and women know how to drink. It's not part of their outfit, but a part of their inner glow. They grow up and master the art of cocktailing, they savor the concrete encounter of booze, and they're often substantially more responsible about the way they do it. I celebrate them—the real drinkers are the rare jewels in a mountain of fakes.

I know it sounds as if I see my martini glass as half empty, but I actually worry that we're raising a generation of people who will never learn how to appreciate the finer properties of alcohol. And in doing so, they will never value anything in life that isn't easy to swallow.

The Orphans

The hard part about being a bartender is figuring out
who is drunk and who is just stupid.

RICHARD BRAUNSTEIN

ROB ROY

2½ oz. scotch
¾ oz. Italian sweet vermouth
2 dashes Angostura bitters

Pour all ingredients over ice in a mixing glass and stir
as you would a martini. Strain into a chilled cocktail
glass. Garnish with a lemon twist.

Up until my fourth year at Marion's every night was capped with one
thought: *I can't believe I'm getting paid to do this!* The job was like
finding the illusive sanctuary from *Logan's Run*—Michael York running from his computerized bubble world where people are put to
death at thirty. Every shift was like going to a party where I was
meeting fascinating new people who thought about things that had
nothing to do with skirts, shoes, and sample sales. It was refreshing to
talk about art in all its forms, to see friends in downtown plays, to go
to galleries where my customers were showing their work, to attend

poetry readings—walk down the street, for fuck's sake, in the middle of the day! My days were filled with rediscovering Manhattan. My life had taken on a cultural sheen and I was loving it.

The city had facets I never noticed until then: afternoon jaunts to cafés with a journal and daydreams, empty movie theaters before the happy-hour crowd left their prisons, Gotti and his cronies standing outside the "club" on Mulberry Street with espressos and cigars in hand, Chinese children playing in the autumn air in the park across the street, Charles Street in April when the trees flaunt their blossoms. To be honest, I don't think I ever noticed a tree in Manhattan before Marion's came into my life.

It wasn't until the middle of my fourth year when I began to notice a dark stirring in my personality. The transition was subtle but snowballing into something I couldn't ignore. I think most of it had to do with the violent derelicts that I had to contend with almost nightly. Being the bouncer was something all the bartenders complained about, but management turned up their noses and virtually ignored our pleas. They knew how much money we were making and basically knew we couldn't quit. They handed us a bat and called it a day.

I still loved the Bowery's charming grimness, but hell, drug addicts are pretty scary when you ask them to leave a bar. Management even allowed them to use the rest rooms, unnerving customers and staff alike, but they never could deal with confrontation of any sort. So, it was up to me, every time, to throw the vagabonds out.

One night I'm pulling a crack addict off a hostess, the next I'm pounding the bathroom door down and dragging a passed-out wino or customer into the street. One homeless lunatic came back night after night until I finally grabbed him by the shirt collar and pants and flung him onto the cement. He managed to get up with his flailing gestures and bulging eyes, and came running toward me again. I stood there with my usual look of indifference as he came up pretty close. He arms were still thrashing wildly—was he drunk, or stoned, both?—and announced two inches from my nose, "I'm going to come back tonight and rape you!"

"Yeah, whatever. Fuck off."

But I watched my back for a few weeks after that.

That's when it started happening—the slow onset of something. My heartbeat never sounded so loud. The palpitations were so strong I began staying in and canceling plans because of them. Pretty soon I was running out of restaurants and movie theaters for air because of claustrophobia. Then, within weeks, agoraphobia was beginning to rear its ugly head, and leaving my bed became truly terrifying.

Most of my days were spent ordering books on anxiety disorders off the Internet and reading the Koran, praying like I never had before. I kept a journal that housed my frustrations, most of the pages asking *why me?* For the first time in my life, I was angry with God. Didn't I pray enough? Was it payback for serving alcohol to thousands? If it was, this was beyond cruel and unusual punishment. Why would He hijack my mind and turn me into a paralyzed Garboesque freak—a prisoner in my West Village studio? My body was changing too. The dark circles under my eyes were so pronounced I began wearing sunglasses every time I went out, and I lost sixteen pounds in a week and a half. Had anyone I'd known bumped into me they'd have thought I'd turned into a junkie.

I started calling the bodega across the street ahead of time with my order of a bagel with cream cheese, regular coffee, *The New York Times*, the *Post* (had to have my fluff), and a pack of Marlboro Lights so it'd be ready and waiting for me. Donning my dark glasses, I would run across the street, have the exact change ready, and literally make it out of there in fifteen seconds flat—and pray no one I knew saw me.

I knew I had crossed a psychological line when I went to rent a movie from Kim's Video, which was located on the ground floor of my building. Finding myself stuck in the Comedy section, my legs suddenly turned to mush and I had to sit down or I would have fallen. Trying to appear normal I grabbed two videos and crouched in the corner, feeling the sweat drip down my neck, pretending to read. When people walked by I acted as if I were mesmerized by Jim Carrey's *Ace Ventura, Pet Detective.*

When finally I got the gumption to get up, my vision blurred and the videos began throbbing, coming to life. The whole episode became crazy when the tapes on the shelves appeared to fly toward me, floating in the air as if in attack mode. I dropped the tapes and ran out as fast as I could. It was official—I had lost my mind.

My job at Marion's was only tolerable if I started the night with two secret Cuervo shots and a couple of Xanax, which I had with staff dinner. I poured the tequila in my Sprite, then maintained my high at a steady pace with Rolling Rocks, wine, or more shots throughout the shift.

Whatever insanity that was in my head accelerated on one particular Saturday afternoon, on the way to work. I passed out on Christopher Street in front of a friend's shop. Blowing it off, I proceeded to work, thinking the hot July day had given me heat exhaustion. I drank a lot of water that night but it happened again the following Saturday afternoon. That time I was in a cab and blacked out in the backseat, only to revive when we pulled up to Marion's curb. The following Saturday, I was once again in a taxi and could feel the lightheadedness coming on. At that point I secretly referred to this phenomenon as my "Saturday night fever." I popped a Xanax and told the driver that if I fainted he was to get my employer. Once again I blacked out. This kept happening for two months until one Saturday I went over the edge.

The blow dryer was blaring away when the fear began creeping up again, coursing through my veins, only more intense this time. It was almost becoming like a friend who visited every Saturday, only to become more and more menacing every week. In smooth, seamless surges my mind detached from my body until they no longer coexisted. My fingers went numb and the only thing I could hear were my heart's palpitations. Suddenly it was as if two hands were squeezing my throat, making it impossible to breath. Running back and forth, I desperately dove into my bed and pulled the covers over my head. All I could do was sob uncontrollably and just when I thought it couldn't get worse, it did.

I urinated on myself. I couldn't stop the agonizing tremors, and the sweat was pouring off of me until I couldn't tell where the urine started and the sweat stopped. I realized that if I didn't sprint to the bathroom I would defecate on myself too—but I was terrified to get out from under the covers. Making a dash for it, I made it in time. Removing all of my soaked clothing, naked, I called 911. I described what was happening to me in between hysterical sobs. The operator was cavalier, asking for me to calm down. She explained to me that I was having a panic attack but that they could get an ambulance over if I still wanted one.

A panic attack? A panic attack is a figure of speech, isn't it? I never imagined it was a real thing. I'd used the term a million times. "If he doesn't show up, I'm going to have a panic attack!" Or "If I don't get the audition, I'll have a panic attack!" Talk about self-fulfilling prophecies. Here I was actually *having* a goddamn panic attack!

I called work, got my shift covered, and made a cab driver speed through downtown New York to my doctor's office. My internist wrote out a hefty prescription for more Xanax and told me to try yoga. It wasn't the last time I was to run to his office because it happened again the following Saturday—but unfortunately my doctor was on holiday. His apathetic substitute gave me a prescription for Prozac and showed me the door. Clearly my hysterics were boring the office to tears.

You know that phrase about people "snapping"? Late in August as I got into my lonely bed, I took ten milligrams of Prozac, hoping once again for the elusive sanctuary I had once enjoyed. Looking up in my delusional state, eyes bloodshot and puffy, heart palpitating in familiar dread, I could see the guillotine's blade coming down hard, its shiny edge just inches from my neck when my mind finally snapped. I actually *heard* it.

That feverishly torrid month of August, that beautiful, sweat-dripping Manhattan summer evening, cloudless and starry with evacuated streets and empty taxis—people were in the Hamptons, of course—was the last August of my previous life. I had unwillingly crossed a threshold I didn't think I could ever return from.

pet peeve no. 13 ....➤

> My regulars are not a free drink repository and just because you think
> you are a scintillating conversationalist doesn't mean you can hit every
> one of them up for a drink.

Neil Simon once said, "There are two million interesting people in New York and only seventy-eight in Los Angeles." I'm tempted to presume that of those multitudes of Manhattan dwellers, a respectable percentage of them were regulars at Marion's—no, really.

Marion's is and always will be a locals joint. Most nights I could scan the packed bar and know I'd served every single customer at some point in my bartending life—some from a decade ago and others from the previous night. I can't tell you how many times a customer would come in and I'd say, "Hey, how are you doing? It's been a while."

And he'd reply, "I can't believe you remember me. I haven't been here in six years!"

Years feel like weeks when you've served thousands of people. Their faces were put away in the file cabinet of my mind, though undated. I would almost always remember people's drinks and that always impressed them. If I had remembered their birthday or astrological sign it wouldn't have touched them like knowing their poison.

Orphans usually fall into categories like everyone else. Call me bored at work, but I enjoyed putting customers into genres—and we all end up in one at a bar. Here's a tasting of the most prevalent types:

The Expert is the guy who knows a little bit about everything, but nothing substantial about anything. He's been there and done that and doesn't hesitate to tell you in minute detail about it—and, in doing so, bores everyone to tears. He will also eavesdrop on your private conversations just to put in his two cents. No one can clear the bar faster than this guy.

Our ultimate expert was Zane. This Brooklynized, bald-pated drummer in a floundering band worked at a grocery store to pay his bills; but from the daunting monologues that flowed from his mouth, you'd have thought he'd accomplished much more than that. The first few years with Zane weren't exactly taxing since he came in once a month or so. But my last three years were full of daily shifts spent closing the joint while pouring his Makers Mark shots, listening to his rhetoric, and even having him pull the restaurant's gate down when it was time to go home. I would do a lot of nodding as he rambled on about the state of America and complained about the music I was playing—not subjects that a bartender wants to discuss when she's trying to coax everyone out. I just considered him Marion's own Cliff Claven and mainly tried to ignore him.

He "advised" me on topics such as how to get rid of the fleas that attacked my new house in Long Island (burn sage and iron everything), how to use a Fischer Price Pixel 2000 film camera (I don't think he'd ever actually used one), how to get a mortgage (he's never owned a home in his life), and the proper way to brew your own beer (this I think he might have known a thing or two about).

Let me just say that Kurt, my husband and a novelist, is the most prolific reader I've ever met. It's his unbridled passion in life and I even recall him saying something to the effect of, "I'd kill myself if I was unable to read." He pores over both classics and contemporary writers, guilty pleasures as well as serious fiction. There are few writers he hasn't read. And if he hasn't, it just means he hasn't gotten to them yet. Often Kurt would come by Marion's to pick me up so we could go home together—and cringe whenever he saw Zane, alone as usual, gulping down his fourth double-shot Makers Mark.

I looked forward to Kurt's visits to Marion's and loved making his drinks (there's something about making your man a cocktail that just feels right). There were times when he'd glance in before entering just to make sure Zane was not sitting there wearing everyone out. Sometimes when Kurt had slinked in, thinking it was safe, Zane would pop out of one of the bathrooms before I could warn him. He would just smile, realizing he was trapped, and would toughen up for the ambush, sometimes even humoring the lush.

One night Kurt came in with a good friend and they got into a romantic discussion about their favorite writers. The friend, a film-maker, was going on about DeLillo, and Kurt was enrapturing him with stories of his own heroes: Fitzgerald, Hemingway, Roth, and Salter. Zane had zeroed in on the tête-à-tête and crammed himself in between the two men for a literary ménage à trois.

"Have you ever read anything by Rick Bragggggggg?" slurred Zane, as if he'd been in on the conversation from the start.

Kurt shook his head and smiled, realizing he had been bull's-eyed. "No, never read his stuff."

Zane's mouth dropped to the floor and he shot a look of utter dis-gust and shock. "*You're* a writer and you've never read Rick Braaaaaaggg? He blows Fitzgerald out of the water! What kind of writer are you that you've never read Rick Braaaaggg? Jeeeeeez!"

"If Rick Bragg is as good as Fitzgerald and Hemingway, then I'll have to look into it," Kurt said with good-natured skepticism, and went back to a private chat with his buddy. Zane continued a glori-fied tirade of Rick Bragg (who, as it turned out, was a perfectly fine writer, but *really...*) and Kurt was compelled to defend his heroes to a drunken know-it-all until I finally dropped the night's receipts and we could go home.

A lot of "experts" seem to lead solitary lives, often depending on bar culture for support and even love. From the years of bantering with Zane, I learned that he'd been in love with his best friend's wife and when the couple separated, he managed to ask her out. After a decade of unrequited love, his affair with her lasted for what seemed like a New York second. Not unusual for him. In fact, he'd confessed to me that he made falling in love with married and committed women an unintentional habit. "Don't take this the wrong way, Zane," I said, "but it sounds like the classic problem with commitment when you're going after women you can't have."

"Yeah, I know," he said, downing his drink. "I've known that for a long time."

When finally he opened himself up to date women other than his buddies' girlfriends and wives, they were so young that I had to force myself to card them. I didn't want to, being a friend of Zane's, but I had no choice. One of them was so blatantly underaged she was forced to nurse a Coke all night, and the rest were conspicuously twenty-one years old on the nose. These inexperienced girls were just naive enough for Zane to come off as an intellectual, instead of the know-it-all dilettante we knew him to be.

Then there is the Snacker to deal with. Every bartender knows one. She's the whiner who parks herself next to your garnish dispenser whether she's already ordered from the menu or just drinking. You've never actually caught her filching the olives but you know she goes to town every time you turn your back. You can't miss the pits and maraschino cherry stems piling up in front of her and she constantly begs you to refill the snack dish a minimum of seven times— or worse, pumps you for the free bread meant for diners.

These Snackers aren't necessarily cheap, though most of mine didn't understand the concept of tipping adequately for all the extra services they required. Running for bread every five to ten minutes isn't an easy task when you're saddled with a crowd that's five deep plus a full dining room. They're also the ones who will say things like "Would you mind if I tipped you next time? I'm a little short." And that usually comes *after* they've eaten the house bare. To top it all off, they tend to conveniently forget about tipping me "next time," putting me in the impossible position of asking for it.

Anna-Lee, a perfectly nice girl, came in at least once a week to work me with serving full-on dinners at the bar. Of course, these jaunts were always when I was so slammed that my effort at making her dining experience pleasant could not possibly come off. So in between my making fifteen laborious cocktails Anna-Lee would mouth "menu" and I would have to fling it to her from my station and tackle writing down a food order with one hand while shaking a martini with the other. Then, after running the order to the kitchen, at the far end of the restaurant, I would have to sprint all the way back to face a phalanx of angry waitrons waiting for their drinks to be made—not to mention my own irate drinkers who'd been waiting for their orders to be filled. But I couldn't get to any of them until I put the first basket of bread, a napkin, and silverware down for Anna-Lee, who was on her second Bombay martini—and which came only after the Knob Creek Manhattan she'd already inhaled.

Then it starts. Within a minute her bread disappears and the olive pits are piling up. When I'm not looking, two cherry stems make the stack. I am alerted that the Pepperidge Farms goldfish we stock as bar snacks are out and could I refill it—for the third time. Many more olives later (which I have to restock out of a heavy, huge jar), a waiter finally delivers her appetizer.

She wants another martini. "Oh, and can I get more bread, too?"

"Yeah, when I finish with some of these orders," I bark. Instead I beg a waitron to get it for me, which she does and that allows me to finish five more cocktails.

"Ty, more goldfish? Would you mind too much? I know you're busy," she begs.

At this point I despise her and the woman who brought her into this world. I get her the goddamned goldfish and her entrée arrives, but not before my olives are out again.

"Anna-Lee, these are garnishes. If you want another appetizer just tell me."

"I'm sorry, Ty. Maybe you're right. Can I see the menu again?" she asks ominously, and I propel it at her like a missile and get back to the drink-making.

Because of Anna-Lee, I asked management if we could stop food service at the bar on Fridays and Saturdays—which they did. And nothing gave me more pleasure than letting Anna-Lee in on our new policy.

Now the Name-Dropper is a lot like the Expert, only his stories can be really entertaining. He's the one who seems to know every celebrity who's ever walked the planet. He can't help letting you know that his girlfriend was doing drugs with some rock star the night before, or regale you with his long-winded tales of trysts with young ingenues while visiting Hollywood. It usually went like so: "Last week in London I was getting myself a drink and chatting with Jen and Brad at Madonna's house when Rose McGowan virtually *threw* herself at me. The next day she took me to brunch and her he/she-specie ex-boyfriend Marilyn was actually jealous of me, can you believe it? When I got back to New York, Brett and Candace came over quite unexpectedly and *we painted the town.* The following night I had a fabulous bottle of Burgundy at Tribeca Grill that Bob, you know, as in DeNiro, recommended. Ugh—now I have to fly to Paris to interview Polanski. He's *so* yesterday. I'm just not into it but my friend Catherine will be there too and she's wild. She's a Getty, you know. Would you mind getting me another Cosmo?"

Our Name-Dropper, Peter, was incredibly charming, intelligent, and very handsome, but the bragging just got hilarious after a while. He came from a respectable family from the suburbs of Detroit. It's funny how people from suburban families go a little crazy when they hit it big in the city. As a successful journalist, he was so impressed with the life he had made that he needed to keep reminding everyone, and apparently himself, about it. All the parties he went to, the famous shoulders he rubbed, exotic trips, and beautiful women that made up his daily life must have made the boy feel fabulous. And what better way to declare his good fortune than to broadcast all of the famous people he mingled with to a media-crazed society?

Peter had a hard time staying faithful to his girlfriends, what with all the Hollywood darlings throwing themselves at him. I'll never know how many of his tales were true. Every woman he became involved with was "the one," though usually by the sixth month he was actively betraying her. On one Marion's trip, he even went so far as to tell me that the woman he was with was just a colleague from work, then he hid himself in the crowd while buffing her tonsils with his tongue. The very next week he came in drunk, rambling on about how much he loved his girlfriend and complaining that she didn't "get" him. When I would mention the coworker, he would act like I, too, was misunderstanding him. I didn't know how two hours of French-kissing could be misread, but I would nod in agreement anyway.

I'm his bartender, not his mother. What was there to say when he happily lived in his drama-charged bubble world? One day he might actually meet "the one" but she'll be the girl who couldn't give a shit about the superfluous crap his life seems to be made of.

The Big Spender acts like Donald Trump by buying the bar a round of drinks every time. He's an incurable show-off and repeatedly tells his friends and total strangers that I'm his favorite bartender. Whispering like a tennis-match announcer, he'll describe to his friends how I make his drink in fine detail as I'm preparing it. (*"She puts only one drop of vermouth in, then she shakes exactly fifteen times, then she pours it into the glass which she has chilled for a minimum of ten minutes, then…"*) The tab will come to $78, for which he'll whip out eighty dollars and tell me to keep the change. Oh Happy Day!

Jeremy loved to talk about his killings on the stock market. On a good day he'd prance in with his bimbo-du-jour, already soused, and proceed to buy all the other regulars a cocktail. The whole first year I served Jeremy was spent in ire that he didn't know how to tip, but he'd come in so often that I didn't know how to break it to him. Plus he seemed like a nice guy without a malicious bone in his body.

"Cisco prevailed today! Who needs a drink?" he'll say, putting a twenty on the bar. Of course everyone wants one so I am put to work in a panicked state. He'll have his Ketel One martini in two giant swigs and everyone else orders the most expensive and arduous drinks they can think of (usually Long Island Iced Teas, Belvedere and Greygoose martinis, and Knob Creek Old-Fashioneds).

When I drop the tab he flinches. "Sorry, Jeremy, that's what happens when you buy everyone a drink. Maybe Cisco can pay for them," I say, trying to pacify him.

"No problem," he says, whipping out a bunch of twenties. The three twenties are sitting on the tray and I finally find the nerve to say something.

"Uh, Jeremy, the tab is fifty-eight dollars."

"You can keep the rest," he says, now sucking face with his lady. After a year of this I began adding a dollar for every drink and made my tip that way. He was too drunk to care, plus who wants to interrupt a cheap drunk in the middle of foreplay? Not me.

Which brings us to the Whiner. This is the pain in the ass who can't stop complaining about her miserable life. Everything that came out of Gail's mouth was a sob story and, after her second or third Stoli Gibson, her night out would invariably climax with a round of uncontrollable wailing. Some of her dilemmas: the boyfriend dumped her, someone stole her car, her ex-boyfriend has a new flame, her hairstylist fucked up her hair, she got locked out of her apartment, kidney stones, her mother railed at her about not being married, the IRS is auditing her—just to name a few. We're not talking particularly unique life experiences, and though they were a drag, they were just the standard gamut of trials we all have to slog through. But for Gail, a broken nail was grounds for a lengthy bar monologue.

The Babbler is the customer who doesn't notice my bar is six deep, I'm serving a full dining room, and there's a Hawaiian theme this month, so currently I'm blending mango daiquiris, carding the NYU crowd, and answering the phone because the hostess is in the bathroom. The Babbler starts by saying she has to tell you *this one story* and proceeds to drown you in verbal diarrhea. She's oblivious that you've tuned out twenty minutes ago. If I'm lucky, I can match her up with people of her own ilk sitting at the bar, and hope they end up great friends for the night. Ordinarily I indulge her stories, but once in a great while, I just can't manage it. Secretly I often think to myself, "Please get yourself a friend."

There was an orphan couple I served, Joe and Evelyn, who were on the verge of separating. After a few years they were coming in individually to talk about the other, which always made me uncomfortable. I'm not a marriage counselor! Toward the end Joe was clearly becoming strangely drawn to me and his monologues were getting longer, more intense every time. He didn't seem to care that I was at work. As far as he could tell, we were alone in a café somewhere on a date.

The last time I saw Joe at Marion's was on a congested Friday night. I had just cut someone off, so I was edgy to begin with, but when I saw him walk through the doors I thought I'd lose it. Trying to remain calm, I let him drone on until I thought I would burst.

"Have you ever been to India?" he asked after babbling on for half an hour.

"Uh, Joe, I really can't talk. I'm a little crazed right now," I said matter-of-factly. He looked genuinely dazed and hurt.

"Oh, am I *bothering* you?"

Unable to reply, I ran to answer the ringing phone, which was my duty when the hostess was seating people. Now Joe thought I was ignoring him, and it was obvious that he was getting more upset when I jumped back into my frenetic pace of mixing.

"I said, am I bothering you?" he asked again.

That's when I lost it. "Joe, I'm a little busy right now. Can't you see that?"

"I didn't realize you couldn't talk," he said miffed.

I barked back, "You've got to be blind not to see how fried and busy I am! No offense, Joe, but I'm at work. I really can't have this conversation right now."

He hollered, "Fine!" He threw a fiver down for a tip and stormed out.

The Owner's Shadow is the one who acts like he owns the place because he's your boss's closest friend or lover, or is related to him so he thinks he can browbeat and, sometimes, spy on the staff. He drinks more than anyone you've ever seen because he drinks for free, and at these prices, he can afford to come in every night, often with friends in tow.

My employers gave us a short list of people we were never to charge and the name at the top was Carol. My first three years was spent serving her and her sidekick, Phil, who came in every single shift for gallons of free vodka and appetizers. Carol would go so far as to tell the chef how to change things to suit her, get her own bread whenever she was waiting on line for the bathroom (which was near the bread station), and tell the owner if any of us was behaving badly. I was required to make her cocktails strong, filling the entire glass to the top with Stoli and squeezing a couple of limes into it for flavor. We're talking three or four shots of booze per drink, and she probably had four to six of those *every* night. I actually pitied her liver. The other bartenders and I would joke that we should just chill the bottle of Stoli and serve it to her with a straw to save time.

Phil tagged along for the free booze, of course, and I think I saw them fall in love with each other, though they could never admit it. They sure argued like a married couple. In some ways I thought they were comfortable in their loneliness, and the companionship that they gave each other was enough to get them through the blue periods.

Still, they both claimed they were looking for love like every other lonely lush that came in. They were both constantly asking me to fix them up with people, though nothing ever materialized even after I had made numerous phone calls on their behalf. I didn't understand why they couldn't see that finding a true soul mate would be impossible if they continued spending every evening at a bar getting wasted. In all my years at Marion's, they never had a relationship with anyone else.

I was very irritated with them the first couple of years; I don't even want to see my husband as much as I had to see those two. But I learned to love them like so many of my other die-hard regulars. They lent me a shoulder to lean on more than once and I enjoyed helping them out if I could. Toward the end, Carol realized that her life would go nowhere unless she stopped drinking—and she did. I wouldn't have believed it had I not seen it for myself.

The Floorshow! Here's the guy everyone loves. He's the twisted bar patsy and people flock around to buy him drinks just to see what he'll do or say next. Most of his stories are made up, and everything he says is for shock value. His antics are legendary even though he comes off as the fool. When he's truly honest with himself he knows how pathetic he appears. Secretly, he's a very lonely and disappointed guy who plays the puppet just to get the attention he never got as a kid. I always buy this guy a pity drink.

We had a couple of Floorshows at Marion's, but Bailey took the cake. This guy came in so often he took phone calls at the restaurant. The first night I met him he left a fifty-dollar tip, so he made quite the impression since all he had were two Cosmos. Whenever he was trying to impress a girl he would order a Dewars and soda, his "manly drink," but when he really just wanted to be himself he asked, sheepishly, for the pink drink.

"No date tonight, Bailey?" I'd ask, placing his Cosmo down in front of him.

"No, but it's the manly drink tomorrow. I've been stalking a gal from my swing class and we're going to have drinks here before-hand," he'd say excitedly.

"Is she pretty?"

"Nah. She's fat and incredibly ugly. She's not you, Ty, that's for sure. I'm embarrassed to have you meet her, but I gotta get laid." He said this strictly to get a rise out of me.

"Bullshit," I'd reply, laughing. "I don't believe you'd date someone you weren't attracted to."

His response was "Oh, poor Ty. You are so naive."

Sure enough the following day he came in with a very large lady who was decked out in forties gear, shoulder pads, veiled hat, fake mole, and all. He gave me a look that implied, *You see?* and smiled in his infamously depraved way. He said, "I believe you know what I'll be having."

"A Cosmo it is!" I said to stifle him before he blew his date.

"Now, Ty, you know I don't drink sissy drinks! I have hair on my chest and everything."

I smirked and put down his scotch, mouthing "asshole" when I got back to my station. He just winked at me as he put his arm around his fleshy date.

He was notorious at regaling the other regulars with tales about his junkets with transvestite prostitutes, hermaphrodites, and married women. Or how he was beat up at this or that club by angry boyfriends and husbands. He would confess how deeply I wounded him by getting married because he had been "in love" with me from day one. He would add that he still enjoys whacking off to me and that gets him "through the tough spots." Even though I was sure that it was meant for shock value, the idea still made the hair on the back of my neck stand up.

Late in the night the staff liked to play a tape that featured Marilyn Monroe singing "Let Me Entertain You"—and this was all a drunken Bailey needed to start trouble. He was on his fifth Cosmopolitan one night when he declared, "Ty, I want to strip for you!"

"Oh please, Bailey, I just ate," I said with a fake yawn.

"Come on, Ty. Dare me. Please! Dare me!"

"Even if I did dare you, you wouldn't do it, so shut up," I asserted and went back to mixing for the smattering of drinkers left at the bar.

"Dare me, dare me, dare me!" he said, gyrating in a grotesque and bizarre way.

"Fine. I dare you. But if you're going to strip, you'd better do it all the way. None of this Hanes-briefs bullshit," I said, turning up the volume to ten on the stereo.

And up went Bailey onto the bar, kicking a few candles and ashtrays as he ascended. His performance was so believable that I was convinced he'd worked at a strip club or two in his day. His shirt came flying off and landed on my head as his paunch jiggled uncontrollably over his unzipped pants. I still didn't believe he would go through with it, but was terrified that he would.

Marilyn Monroe continued on to the sexy final verse when Bailey's socks were slid off and his pants went shimmying down. All that was left on his compact frame were the well-known Hanes briefs that all men seem to wear and the unmistakable *bump*. "Okay, Bailey! I believe you, and now you're going to stop! I'm going to lose my dinner here!" I pleaded and pleaded, but he'd gone too far to stop. He looked right at me and licked his fingers to give himself two tittie-twisters, then slid one hand down his briefs. Crouching down he whispered, "How much do you want it, Ty?"

"Not much, Bailey. Please stop! You've made your point. I'm actually nauseous!"

"Tell me you want me and I'll stop," he said, exposing his pimply bum.

"No. Please don't. *Gross*. I can't handle this." Finally I decided to give in. "Okay! Okay! I want you, you warped freak! Stop!"

He slowly turned around and gave himself one more tittie-twister before the briefs were eased down and "little Bailey" was slinging side to side and up and down as if jumping on an invisible trampoline. It was as if I were looking straight at a gruesome train wreck, and I couldn't turn my eyes away. I was frozen, transfixed and repulsed, but I couldn't move. Little Bailey was tiny, a little turtle of a thing in a snug shell, flailing around as if afraid of the lights. I felt bad for it and wanted it to withdraw. As Bailey gave me one final giant thrust, the song mercifully ended.

The entire restaurant was stupefied and silent. Calmly Bailey pulled up his Hanes and slid off the bar. In a state of shock, all I could think was "I just saw Bailey's penis. I'm blinded. I can't see. I just saw Bailey's penis."

He located his socks and pulled them on, then slipped on his shoes and gathered his clothes in a large clump. In complete silence, he walked out the door. Through the front windows I could see him at the curb hailing a cab. Before getting in he flashed me a look. It wasn't the face I had become accustomed to, the devilish spark that was his unquestionable trademark. Before getting into his taxi, exposed save for the armful of underpants, socks, and shoes, his expression was one of sadness and self-loathing. He was making some point, trying to tell me something—whatever that spectacle was supposed to be all about. I'll never forget that look as long as I live.

Lotharios who use Marion's to intoxicate and hook their dates are not usually my choice customers, but Max threw me for a loop one night. He was a handsome young actor who came in with a different ravishing woman at least once a week. The staff and I couldn't believe the number of women he maneuvered into dates. He was surely attractive—but he certainly wasn't all that! We had a rating system for the girls from one through ten and most of them managed high scores of eight and nine. Only once did he come in with a five and even she was very pretty. I finally got the balls to ask him how the hell was he meeting all of these gorgeous women. He begrudgingly confessed, after one too many pink drinks, that the Internet was the answer to his sexual prayers.

"Wow! Do you ever date any of them twice?" I asked, truly curious since he had never brought one back a second time.

He gave me a quick smile and said, "Ty, there are a lot of beautiful women in Manhattan. Why not enjoy them?" Hey, I wasn't judging him. I just had never seen anyone score quite like Max.

Late one evening, after the bulk of drinkers had made their exodus, Max walked in alone. I hadn't seen Max solo *ever*, so I figured he was waiting for a date. I made his usual without being told and placed it in front of him. "So where's the babe?" I asked eagerly.

He downed the drink and picked up his head. His eyes were so full of tears that I thought he might burst. I was taken aback. Quickly I went around the bar and put my hand on his shoulder. "What's up?"

"My dad died last night," he slurred after a short pause. When he finally let me in on his tragic event, he pulled me into a long embrace, and his eyes finally gave way to the stream of tears. I realized he had already begun drinking elsewhere.

I don't know what it feels like to lose a loving father, but to see a vibrant, sleek guy like Max fall apart in my arms showed me something I hadn't considered about my customers in a long time: that they may be drunks, derelicts, Casanovas, and oddballs, but they're human all of the time. It was a wake-up call.

It's like the story Gary, a mentor and veteran Marion's mixer, once told me about a "typical" episode at a bar he once worked at. One day an orphan of his came by for lunch—which generally consisted of three or four Dewars on the rocks—when Gary noticed the fellow looked worse than usual. When Gary asked him what the problem was, the man said his daughter had tried to commit suicide the previous night and he didn't know what to do.

"I wanted to say, Put the drink down, go home, and deal with this. It's your daughter, for God's sake,' " he said, looking down, shaking his head. "But you don't say these things. I'm there to pour."

I've seen more customers go through divorces than I care to mention, teaching me lessons in maintaining relationships. The effects it had on their children were heartbreaking to hear about— how the kids had to be shared, and how they'd rather be with them at that moment than at the bar with me. Time with their kids that they took for granted for so long. The losses of family members to suicide or AIDS or drunk driving—the latter giving me a twinge of guilt—were also abundant. So many regulars had come in after funerals that I felt like a part of the mourning process. I got to know these souls through drunken stories told to me while I poured. After a few cocktails, it usually transformed the melancholy jaunt into a few hours of remembrance. Of the good times with their lost friend.

Alcohol is a great way to soften the blows of life. Many people have told me that they wished they could "stop the pain" for a little while—and what better way than a few hours of the numbing effects of alcohol? I'm not saying that it was the answer to their problems, or that the sting would disappear. It's just that a different mood within a different atmosphere—albeit doctored—can be a wonderful escapist tool. And it's better than drinking alone at home, where there is no one around to listen to the venting that is needed for the release to take place. That's when healing can start, but not without a safe place to open up in. That's where I came in.

After the World Trade Center fell, I was flooded by a group of regulars who worked in the buildings and survived. At Marion's the haunting stench of burnt steel, plastic, and only God-knows-what couldn't be ignored; nevertheless for months they came by in their black suits after funerals to get wasted. I was happy to oblige and thrilled that they'd made it out alive, though a few of them were seriously shell-shocked. And I was proud that they chose Marion's to gather at after such grief-stricken days. One girl told me of getting laid for the first time in months the night before the tragedy and ended up arriving late to work because of it, missing the catastrophe altogether. "I would have been in my office," she interjected, bringing humor to the sad moment. "I owe that guy the blow job of his life!"

I have been a phantom friend to countless people. People would call me at the bar early and say something like "I just got fired. Will you be there tonight?" Or, "I can't decide what to do about my girl-friend. Will you have time to talk tonight?" They want someone objective to talk to, someone who will make them feel better. Part of it is an illusion—it's really the booze that makes them feel good. But the other element is that I'm usually able to attend to them and their issues. Bartenders make great listeners—we're paid to be. When you have listened to people's problems for such a long time, it's easy to be open and not judge. Solace is sometimes hard to come by in Manhattan, a city rumbling with so much excitement that it's hard to slow down and really deal with what is bothering you. After more than a decade of listening to people talk about the peaks and valleys of their lives, I've gotten good at counseling. Compassion is something I always tried to give open-heartedly.

It's easy to forget that people aren't *really* the mere types I ascribe them to be. Shit happens and then that glimmer of humanity peeks through the dark lights, booze, and debauchery. As Gary said, we're here to pour. But in doing our job, it's nice to know we can dull the pain for a while, if that's what the customer needs. In a world of instant gratification, alcohol and an ear go a long way for the misbegotten.

Desperation is something mixers see all the time because alcohol loosens up those feelings that are eating us up, allowing them to flow, sometimes out of control. At times people are so angry after a few drinks that it's evident that their rants of "the music is too loud" or "this drink stinks" are concealing the real culprit: the divorce, the death in the family, the pink slip he got today.

We all need a remedy for the overwrought feelings that can consume us, something to soften the edges. Who knows why we're not all drug addicts and alcoholics. Maybe we are temporarily, when we need to be—and I'm something of a part-time pusher. Some of us need to be anesthetized more than others. I'm not proud of pouring the booze down a dejected guy's throat, but hell, if it gets him through the night I'll happily oblige.

pet peeve no. 14 ⟶

> The one thing I can't stand is a whining pansy. If you have a grievance about me or the service I just gave you, don't run to my boss or manager like a big crybaby. Before it comes to that, act like a grown-up and try to talk to me about it. Bartenders are reasonable people who don't like to get into it with customers and we'd love to resolve the issue, too. It's silly when customers report to the boss when they don't get their way; I've apologized when given the chance and altered my performance to accommodate the disgruntled patron the next time around.

◀

In all my years at Marion's, I couldn't have imagined a more opportunistic place to work. When I was acting I met so many fellow actors, directors, and playwrights that I got myself cast regularly in independent films and plays. I met Frank, whom I started a theater company with, when he was sitting across from me swigging one of the Stoli martinis he'd have every night.

When my husband finished writing his first novel (while waiting tables) he didn't know what to do with it. He'd just spent two and a half years spilling his guts but he had no contacts. I'd worked in publishing and had a lot of friends who were in the business. I promised him that I would do everything in my power to get it published.

I had a regular, whom I was slowly getting to know, who drank the respectable Sapphire gimlet two times a week. Doug would come in with different people every time, mostly on business, though I couldn't guess what business that might be. One early evening, while placing his drink before him, I overheard him discussing a book he was excited about. I was genuinely interested, being a bookworm myself, and asked what it was. Doug explained that it was an unpublished manuscript by a client of his. He revealed that he was a literary agent.

I found myself in a quandary. Did I just pour his drinks and forget the question I was dying to ask: Would he take a look at Kurt's manuscript? I wondered if it was an inappropriate direction to take in our relationship. As an actor, I knew how protective performers could be of their agents, sometimes refusing to give you their name for fear that they will be used as a reference if you called them. Agents are hard to come by, of course, more precious than gold. Plus, I didn't want to lose a great regular.

I concluded that my allegiance was to my husband, that I had to help him no matter what the consequences were. Besides, I'd promised. The worst that could happen, I speculated, was that Doug would say no and would never come back to Marion's. Or he'd return, but there would be a new awkwardness to overcome. So I went for it.

"Doug, this is really hard for me to do," I began. "I was wondering if I could ask you a question and please be up front with me if you think it's out of line."

He flashed his wide smile and said, "Sure, Ty, anything."

"I never told you that my husband, Kurt, is a writer. He just finished his first novel," I explained.

He smiled, knowing instantly what I was going to inquire. But I have got to say this for Doug; he didn't have that condescending bent New Yorkers tend to have when they're asked for favors. In fact, he looked sincerely happy to give it a skim, telling me he'd read at least three chapters. Doug was with an editor from a major publishing house who also requested to see the book (in the past few months and through gimlets, the three of us had become friends). I think I thanked them about a hundred times that night.

The following week, Doug dropped in with our editor friend to kick back a few drinks, talk publishing, and pick up Kurt's manuscript. I gave it to them full-length since I thought that the real juice of the story started soon after the first three chapters, and took the chance that, like me, they wouldn't be able to put it down. They indulged me happily and put the pages away into their briefcases. That night, after work, Kurt and I left for Long Island for the weekend to relax and brood over the possibilities. We wondered if his book, *Lit Life*, might be able to free us from the restaurant business. By Sunday afternoon Doug called. For the first time, he sounded serious—all business. I wasn't sure if that was a good thing or not. Kurt stood by, pacing anxiously, listening in on our talk.

"I loved *Lit Life*. I couldn't put it down," he said. "Can Kurt come by my office tomorrow to talk?"

"Really?" I asked, giving Kurt a thumbs-up. "That's great! Of course he'll be there. Just say when and where."

I never saw Kurt so elated. At the meeting Doug was all trade, asking Kurt to sign a binder and claiming he could sell *Lit Life* in three weeks. Not ten days later, and like that quintessential New York story that never seems to happen to you, Random House bought the novel.

On any given night there are powerful people nursing their cocktails across from me. I've served writers, actors, painters, publishers, rock stars, playwrights, and God knows who else. It's a wonderful way to network with people who share your passions, whether they're computer geeks, graphic artists, fashion designers, or makeup artists. *Everyone drinks.* (And even people who don't drink enjoy patronizing bars—the fascinating people, loud music, and engaging vibe shouldn't be missed just because alcohol is forbidden to them. I really respected those nondrinkers who still frequent bars, so much so that I always took special care in making their sodas and nonalcoholic cocktails beautiful to look at and great-tasting. Everyone, especially those who've had a hard time with liquor, deserves to be served with respect. And nondrinkers for their sacrifice.)

Most of my colleagues became very attached to certain regulars. It's inevitable when so much time is spent together in a drunken haze. The atmosphere lends itself to intoxicated infatuations. Stanley, an actor/singer and our senior manager, was one of the most loving and funniest people I've ever known. His comic timing was unsurpassed (except perhaps by the now-professional actress Amy Sedaris, who worked at Marion's for years). People couldn't get enough of him. There certainly was a lot to love: all three-hundred-plus pounds of him, the warm smile, and the refreshing demeanor that could charm anyone out of his pants—*literally*. The staff loved working with him and would often cringe when the other manager was on; the vibe was so markedly distinct when he was on duty.

He had a certain way of captivating celebrities so that they frequently became regulars. A tale that epitomizes this talent involved the mercurial Drew Barrymore.

An exceptionally bitchy waitress we used to have was having a hard time dealing with Ms. Barrymore. A significantly frustrated actress, this waitress had most of the staff terrified of her and often requested any shift she wasn't working—that's how offensive she had become in her stymied life. She began grumbling that Drew was being a "total bitch" and how dare she send back her entrée to the chef! I, on the other hand, had met Drew at the bar and thought she was sweet as punch. The waitress was simply a ticking bomb and we were readying ourselves for her to "accidentally" spill red wine or cold water all over the petite actress. Stanley and I were worried, and he quickly had her replaced at the table so that there would be no unnecessary conflicts. Next thing you know, he and Drew were talking for what seemed like hours at the bar. Soon she was a regular and they even had dinner in Los Angeles when he went out to visit his mother. This was not out of the ordinary for him.

Everyone loved Stanley, but none more than the orphans. When he became obsessed with a customer, and that was often, it was because he was secretly in love with him. Then again, Stanley was in love with the world; anytime a gorgeous Puerto Rican man (he loved Latin men, surprise, surprise) walked by his eyes would be glued to the door. A spicy Spaniard was in for the Yellow Plate Special with his girlfriend? He got them a round—who cared if he was straight? A handsome, raven-haired hottie in a guinea-T was walking his dog across the street? Stanley was *on it,* eyes locked in from the restaurant's front window. He didn't miss a beat.

When Paul, a small, cherub-faced (and straight) fellow, started coming in, Stanley was hooked. His eyes would glow and he'd whisper to me, "I'm in love!" the second Paul came in through the doors. He'd jump up and down like a lovesick teenager, which is strange when you consider the man's girth. Upon first meeting, he chatted Paul up and within a week Paul was a die-hard regular. They were hanging out at Stanley's, who happened to live in my building in the West Village. It didn't matter that Paul was straight—the love was clearly reciprocated. It was that impossible not to fall for Stanley. Hell, if I were a gay man I'd be in love with him.

Everyone who worked at Marion's had at least one Paul they could dream about. Mine fluctuated by the year. I, too, had a crush on Paul, then Sam and Neil. Toward the end there were Simon and Alex. By the time I had met Kurt I'd had it with silly crushes on regulars I had no intention of dating. But it sure was fun.

Other characters that kept Marion's on a notably eccentric plane were the drag queens. There was a group of five men who came by for a monthly visit who turned quite a lot of heads. They were six-feet-tall, middle-aged married men with paunches who left the wives at home to paint the town red. Their look was top-of-the-line Westchester-mode housewives' clothing, accessorized with size 12 Fayva vinyl pumps and tacky wigs. We're talking dowdy to the extreme, as in Bea Arthur and the Golden Girls. Clearly they were balding orthodontists and accountants who liked to have a little fun when they left Scarsdale and the teenage kids behind to visit the big bad city. They were so unbelievably unattractive that everyone—and I mean even the most freakish of our customers—couldn't believe their audacity. They weren't homosexuals, in fact one of them had a crush on our manager Andrea, who was not at all amused. It disturbed her to the core, so much so that she couldn't stop bringing up her boyfriend, hoping to dash the transvestite's hope. They cracked me up. Nothing says New York quite like a bunch of straight dentists transforming themselves into a band of homely women to get their kicks.

Kiki and Herb were definitely very intriguing. They were a kitschy drag cabaret duo who often performed at Marion's and who took entertainment to the levels of pathetic and glamorous at the same time. Kiki's character is a sixty-year-old, liquored-up, has-been lounge singer with a deranged bent. Her sidekick and accompanyist is the polyester-clad Herb who plays her gay "friend," and is the tipsy foil to Kiki's bombast. They do incredibly demented versions of songs like "Love Is a Battlefield" by Pat Benatar, "Paranoid Android" by Radiohead, and "Open Arms" by Journey. She'll also sing songs by Bruce Springsteen, Peaches, Nirvana, and Prince—so you can't say she's totally out of date even if she looks like Carol Burnett half the time. Sprinkled in between songs you can enjoy Kiki's slurred, drunken monologues about her life, loves, and even political stances. One famous line of theirs is "Between the AIDS and the Alzheimer's, we don't have a fan over forty." Kiki and Herb even played at one of our Christmas parties, though I bolted because Kiki's drunken shrieking/singing was driving me insane. She's the kind of gal who will, in the middle of an "inebriated" performance, get up on your table, eat your food, break your dishes, and then tell you off because you spoke in the middle of her song. She has quite the temper, and her fans love her for it. But on the other hand, she'll also sing you the corniest of love songs if she thinks you need a hug; just don't expect her to hit the right notes. And get this, Alizé crap-flavored cognac sponsored a national tour of theirs.

But the jewel of the bunch was the fabulous crackpot dubbed Miss Julia Wonder, who allowed me once to be a part of her cabaret show. Because of her stature and husky build, folks presumed she was actually a he in a big blond wig and a tacky blue suit with the demeanor of Ann Richards, the ex-governor of Texas. Her name was actually Colleen and in real life she was a genuine woman. She played a man playing a woman. It's hard to explain, and it succeeded in perplexing everyone. Diners and drinkers alike were taken by surprise, and were always drawn deeply into her theater. As a matter of fact, one of her acts at Marion's was "Julia Wonder for President," which she kept up until the elections in 1996 were over. I can't remember now what her slogan was, but Stanley and I got to run as her vice presidents. She was the kind of gal who'd put on a bake sale to win votes and called herself a real "people person." Needless to say, we didn't beat Clinton, but we had a magnificent time in our attempt.

Regulars gave me so much more than the steady income I came to depend on. Besides the many headaches, they overwhelmingly provided me comfort when my own sagas unfolded, like when my grandmother died or when my relationships ended. I hadn't seen most of these drinkers in daylight; as I said, we were phantom friends, never to share so much as a brunch or a phone call together. But when regulars came in predictably week after week, I found I could rely on them as much as they could count on me. As much as their leaving a tip was part of the transaction/relationship, my part was being there for them in their hour of need. What was surprising, though, was that I sometimes got back twofold what I doled out.

There were many times in the decade at Marion's where I felt I had hit bottom. When I was plagued by my panic attacks, many of my regulars confessed to the same torment and gave me the kind of ear only someone who really understood could give. When depression hit, it was the same thing. We discussed the different types of meds to try, names of therapists and new breakthroughs they'd heard of. A couple of them even brought me clipped articles on the subject and directed me to great websites. The bliss of going to my job, my home away from home, to be surrounded by people who loved me, who seemed to care and listened to *my* sob stories for a change, made situations seem much less troubling and depressing.

I was grateful to them that July, the orphans who were spending glorious days in a sunless bar being served by a mixer with as many troubles as they had. They seemed eager to offer me their support on those beautiful cloudless days, as people were using the last of their vacation time and students were enjoying lazy afternoons at the beach before school started. I was being saved by my regulars—I was experiencing life again. Thanks to the orphans, my following that wouldn't quit, Mama Ty was back.

That wasn't supposed to be part of the deal, but it turned into the best part of the job.

After I quit bartending for good, people kept telling me that I was going to miss "the life." I had only heard that expression before in reference to ex-convicts and drug addicts attempting to lead a clean existence—as if bartending was so addictive that it would forever be a temptation. In retrospect, it is apropos, having been *freed* for some time now, that I always referred to my life of booze as being "behind bars." And for a long while when people asked me if I missed it yet, I'd truthfully respond with a sure-footed no. That world was behind me—I'd done my time and paid my dues to society.

But if someone asked me that question now, almost a year later, my response wouldn't be so quick. I'd have to think about all the things that bartending has meant for me: a lifesaving move out of my oppressive life in fashion, autonomy to be the creative person I had always felt I was, enough money to stop agonizing about bills every month and even take a much-needed vacation, and most of all, an intimate way to meet incredible people. It's more than a job. It's a makeshift community fueled by the lucid effects of alcohol and a familiar atmosphere. My regulars were supportive, at times loving, inspiring, and a lot of the time totally insane and draining. They were my extended family, who would listen to my darkest secrets— just as I had done for them. As with any adviser—a clergyman, shrink, hairdresser, close aunt—a lot of trust is given and taken. Friendships rise from the ashes of despair and loneliness, whether you work in a bar or not; it's just more intense when the booze magnifies these acute emotions, which seem to flow like shots at a strip joint. With me it was a safe place to unravel.

Yeah, I miss my regulars.

At the Kahiki Lounge

I envy people who drink, at least they know what to blame everything on.

OSCAR LEVANT

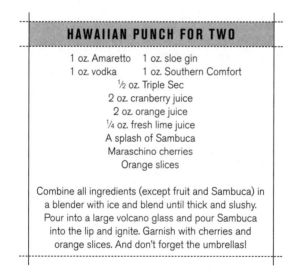

HAWAIIAN PUNCH FOR TWO

1 oz. Amaretto   1 oz. sloe gin
1 oz. vodka   1 oz. Southern Comfort
½ oz. Triple Sec
2 oz. cranberry juice
2 oz. orange juice
¼ oz. fresh lime juice
A splash of Sambuca
Maraschino cherries
Orange slices

Combine all ingredients (except fruit and Sambuca) in
a blender with ice and blend until thick and slushy.
Pour into a large volcano glass and pour Sambuca
into the lip and ignite. Garnish with cherries and
orange slices. And don't forget the umbrellas!

The alarm clock rings and with my eyes still sealed shut I push the snooze button, wishing with all my heart that I could muster up the energy to throw it out the window and into the bustling traffic of Mulberry Street. Popping a lid open, I see that it's two o'clock—in the afternoon. That means I have been subconsciously swatting the clock since eleven this morning, every nine snoozing minutes. That makes twenty times that I've heard the alarm and fallen back into a deep sleep. Pathetic, I think. What kind of life is this?

I hear the television mumbling in the living room. Kurt's watched *Charlie Rose* and is on to CNN by now. He's probably already gotten me my morning essentials: Starbucks' grande vanilla latte and the *New York Post.* I have an hour and a half to get ready before I go out the door and walk to Marion's in the sweltering heat. Apropos, since Marion's has transformed itself into the "world famous" Kahiki Lounge, a riff on a tiki restaurant in Ohio, which they pull off every August until Labor Day.

The very thought of Kahiki Lounge fills me with so much dread that I resist getting out of bed. It's impossible not to recall the previous night because my hair still has someone's piña colada juices stuck to it and I smell like an ashtray. That compels me to light my first cigarette. On the chest of drawers lies the Betsey Johnson floral halter-dress I wore the night before. In the daylight I can see the juice stains hobnobbing with the floral print, altering the pattern dramatically. I bought the frock the first year I worked Kahiki Lounge and nine years later it's still the one that works best for the sticky explosions that are inevitable when working with blenders. I lay in bed, smoking and dreading the shift, wondering if I'm going to need a hit of Xanax to get through it all.

Will I have time to shower? If only I could wake up earlier, I would have more in my life other than Marion's and sleeping. I contemplate all the great things that New York offers that I'm not doing because of the exhaustive bartending necessitated by the Kahiki Lounge's luau-obsessed patrons. Kurt pops his head into the bedroom, rolls his eyes at my smoking before breakfast, and shuts the door. Finally I force myself to get up and into the shower.

With my hair dried, I begin adding the embellishments that will transform me from the bitter, groggy New York crank into a flirty, slightly slutty Hawaiian hula-babe. I've been so wrecked after shifts that I haven't had time to do the laundry so, reluctantly, I shimmy back into the Betsey Johnson number. The next thing that goes on is a layer of glitter cream, on the face and shoulders, which will give me an ethereal quality in the candlelight. My hair is looking too proper pulled up, so I loosen it a bit, tresses falling all around, trying to capture that sexy "just got out of bed" look—not exactly a stretch. Then, I pin at least fifteen flowers all around so that I resemble a kind of fairy from *A Midsummer Night's Dream*. The makeup is heavier than usual—more sparkly eyeshadow, lip gloss, and blusher. Now I look more like a naughty fairy who'd do it with you in the bathroom. That's the impression I'm going for, so I check the clock and realize it's three o'clock. I swallow hard. I have half an hour to go.

When I step into the living room, Kurt smiles and raises an eyebrow. "I like this look," he says, groping me. We fool around a little and I have to pull myself back together before I can do anything else. In fifteen minutes, I fix my hair, drink the latte, read Page 6 and the horoscopes, and head out with a lump in my throat and my heart beating fast. The anticipatory anxiety is substantial.

August in Manhattan is merciless. It's ninety-four degrees outside and my makeup feels like it is coming loose from the surfacing perspiration. I pop into my local bodega and the guys give me a quizzical look. "Going to work?" the Egyptian man asks. I nod, thinking they probably suspect that I'm a stripper or a hooker. Purchasing a bottle of water that I wish I could pour all over myself, I drink the whole thing by the time I hit the corner.

The long walk to work gives me a chance to goof off. On East Fourth Street I pop into Other Music and buy the new Ron Sexsmith album and a copy of *Alternative Press* magazine. I realize I'm only one block away from the Kahiki Lounge and the luau from hell. Passing Bowery Bar, I peer in. They're slow, a couple of waiters wiping their brows, sipping water and lingering on the patio. The lush spring-flowering wisteria is still blooming in the suffocating heat on top of their garden's obnoxious enclosing wall that encompasses half the block. Turning right on the Bowery, I see Marion's awning and José, in his kitchen whites, sweeping the sidewalk. He sees me and flashes a big smile.

"Ty, you look beautiful! *Mucha bonita!*" he says.

"*Gracias, señor,*" I say, giving him my daily kiss and hug. We're both sweating so much that the droplets that have formed on our noses and chins intermingle. "Are they all here?" I ask.

"*Sí,* Ty. Da bosses downstairs with Stanley and Andrea. Dey say busy tonight," says José, with the same look of dread I woke up with. "I been here since one, Ty. I so tired."

"You work too much, José. You working tonight, too?"

"*Sí.* Need money, Ty. Need money for my little boy," he says joyfully at the thought of his son.

I start heading in but I give him a last agreeing smile and say, "I know, José. I know."

The thunderous air conditioner is droning on, though it barely cracks the heat. I think of how the body heat is going to bring the temperature up when the place packs in. People in the front of the bar and in the dining room will complain about how hot it is, and the couple of urchins sitting under the air conditioner will beg me to turn it off. The diners will win.

The "early" waitress, Maeve, is putting the final touches on the tables. The candles that she carries on a large, round tray are illuminating her Raphaelite features—with her red curls sparkling and her alabaster skin glowing, she looks like a hauntingly beautiful apparition. She's wearing a cheesy kimono-type dress, pink with giant red and green flowers printed on it. "Hey, Ty!" she says. "Bring any music?"

"Of course," I say, slipping a cassette into the stereo.

Appropriately enough, the first song, "Alone, Stinking and Unafraid" by Lexo & the Leapers (aka Bob Pollard of Guided by Voices), comes on and suddenly the room has a lot more energy. The tunes we listened to as we set up were imperative to our sanity, especially during Kahiki Lounge. We were forced to listen to the "Kahiki Tapes" during the night, mostly ten versions of "Rock-a-Hula Baby" and lots of Don Ho—much to our *and* the customers' distress. There's just so much luau music anyone can listen to before snapping. It took a ton of lo-fi rock and grunge music to eradicate the maddening hum of ukelele undertones from my mind at the end of the night—and by Labor Day I'd be ready to assassinate Don Ho. The waiters appreciated my effort to balance things out.

The bar is a wreck from the night before and there is an infestation of fruit flies everywhere, which I attempt to shoo away to no avail. If they were bees I'd be dead right now. Despite my having scrubbed the surface of the bar, it's still gluey and someone stupidly attempted to design a "Pollock" with candle wax. I scrape it off using a tip tray and pour vodka over the bar. Pure, cheap alcohol is the only thing that gets it sparkling clean. Then I pull all the extras out and place them in their spots: fruit dispenser, rubber mats, napkin holders, candles, tiki crunch mix (which replaces the usual Pepperidge Farms goldfish crackers), matches, and standing Kahiki drink menus. The two blenders are still sitting on the bar and I forgot to empty one last night. It's still got a funky margarita in it with fruit flies darting furiously around the lid. I put that in the bus tub I also forgot to bring to the dishwasher (still brimming with gooey, sticky tiki glasses). Kahiki Lounge is so manually exhausting that it's impossible to function at a hundred percent at three o'clock in the morning.

Next I grab a pen and scan the bar for what I will need from the liquor room. On the back of a dupe pad (the checks that I write food orders on), I jot down in almost-illegible handwriting: *6 bottles of rum, 5 bottles of tequila, 5 bottles of Roses lime juice, two bottles of vodka, two bottles of gin, one bottle of bourbon.* Now comes the good stuff that was used up the previous night: four bottles of Bacardi rum, one bottle each of Belvedere and Greygoose and two bottles of Stoli and Ketel One vodka. I see we have plenty of Absolut. The "Hawaiian Punch for Two" was a hit, so I also put down three bottles of sloe gin, two bottles of Amaretto, and one bottle of Southern Comfort. The beer bin looks full except that we're going to need a case of Rolling Rock and Corona. The Bass Ale doesn't do as well in the summer, no dark ales do. Also noting some miscellany items, I add limes, lemons, oranges, plastic olive spears, maraschino cherries, and two boxes of paper umbrellas to the

list. Everyone wants goddamn umbrellas with their drink during Kahiki
Lounge, even if it's just water with lemon. With the list, I hop downstairs.

Unlocking the liquor room, I realize how tired I am. I sit on a case
of wine to collect myself and look around. We're out of a lot because
our liquor distributor is away on vacation—usually for a month during the summer. I'm low on Amaretto, sloe gin, and house rum so I
call our sister restaurant to see if they've got any and if they wouldn't
mind sending someone over with it, which they do. Locating three
plastic crates, I fill them up with the necessities and prepare myself to
lug them all up the perilous stairs in my filthy but glamorous outfit
and makeup that's already melting away. On my way up, I hear the
imposing ice machine, located next to the liquor room, burp out rab-
bles of cubed ice. I'll need extra loads of it because everyone will want
frozen drinks, of course. I brace myself and lift the first container,
which feels like a ton. Holding my breath, I gallop quickly up the
stairs and launch it onto the bar with a heave-ho. Putting everything
away, I run back down. The next crate isn't as bad since I'm loosening
up. By the third I'm ambling even though my back is beginning to
spasm. I finish up the lugging with three more containers of heavy
ice, and with everything put away, I light a cigarette and sit on a stool.

Looking around I can almost hear the crowd that will fill the space
in a few short hours. The theme from *Hawaii Five-0* will be blaring,
waiters will be catapulting Pupu platters aflame at diners who will
be squealing with joy at all the fantasy, wearing their free leis. If
Stanley is working, he'll be chafing under his sarong, complaining
about how much his feet hurt. If Andrea's on tonight, she'll be running around like a chicken without a head, overflowing glamorously
out of an incredibly loud sixties floral gown with the most gigantic
plastic gardenia you've ever seen in her red hair. She'll coerce me into
wearing more plastic flowers, maybe even some of her gaudy plastic
rings. *Anything* for a look, she says.

The original Kahiki Supper Club, a twenty-thousand-square-foot
restaurant built in 1962, was located in Columbus, Ohio, a hot spot

that one of our owners frequented for years while on visits to see friends. The club was placed on the National Registry of Historic Places for its "rich Polynesian culture, architectural design and influence on national and local restaurant history." Kahiki, which means "sail to Tahiti," was a tiki wonderland featuring war chants and steel drum melodies that traveled through cozy bamboo huts. The high point was the famous cascading waterfalls punctuated by giant tiki gods that showered rainfall every half hour. I can think of very few bars or restaurants that utilize such theatrics as those of the Kahiki Supper Club—Marion's being the only one.

The usual fifties shabby-chic is still apparent under the explosion of tiki-ware. The largest tables (#1, the Kennedy Booth, and #10) are under gigantic thatch roofs dressed up with stuffed plastic parrots hanging from the center on their perches. One of them is dangling lopsided, prepared to nosedive into someone's frozen daiquiri. The other side of the room, where the two-top orange booths (tables 31 through 36) are lined up against the wall, is also covered by an elongated version of the straw roof, edged with a chintzy multicolored plastic lantern light set.

The first year we had a two-foot waterfall in the middle of the room (between tables 21 through 25) that regurgitated two gallons of tap water, but we quickly realized it was also mangling the goldfish we threw in. And it became apparent that it was in the way of the frenzy, so it didn't last very long.

Instead of the usual clear glass votives we used low-boy candles in red and blue, the kinds you find in seafood shacks. Scattered all over the room, including the bar, are paper and plastic palm trees, plastic totem poles, head-bobbin' hula girls, plastic fish tied in nets, gardenias, leis, grass skirts, coconut bras, and other silly island accessories. It looks garish and cheap in the sunshine coming in through the front windows, but it takes on a kitschy island charm at night. And believe me when I say New Yorkers love nothing more than a tiki theme.

My cigarette break is over and I dart to the kitchen. *"Hola! Hola!"* hollers El Diabolo and Nico from behind the "window," which is where food is placed under heating lamps for pickup by waiters. They're frantically prepping for the luau-du-jour, but manage to marginally focus attention on my look. *"Te quero!"* I smile at them and call them both *puta*, fill two bus tubs with glasses, and restock the shelves with them. Next I cut two plastic containers full of limes, lemons, and oranges and squeeze twenty more limes for the fresh juice that all the martini-ish drinks and margaritas require.

Giving the bar a thorough run-through, I come to the conclusion that I'm ready to rock and light another cigarette, anticipating staff dinner. The "early" waiter will set the table for dinner, which usually comes to around seven people, including the hostess, kitchen staff, and any loitering owners or managers. (The "early" waiter is the waitron that comes in to open the dining room and leaves around eleven. The "late" server comes in at 7 P.M. and closes the restaurant with the bartender. The "runner" just delivers food and mercifully doesn't have to mingle with customers.) Staff dinner is usually potluck during Kahiki Lounge. Toward the end of my time at Marion's, the higher-ups had gotten cheap and we were given a lot of leftovers from their catering jobs (crusty crabcakes, old and rubbery calamari, stuffed mushrooms, bagels, and cold pastas—definitely not the feasts of the early years), and Kahiki salads and entrees that didn't quite satisfy anyone. I personally can't make it through a night with only chicken wings and two coconut shrimp to tide me over when I'm going to work till I ache. We often ordered off the menu at around eleven to get us through the rest of the night. At least that privilege hadn't been cut—yet.

It's almost five-fifteen and still no dinner. My stomach is growling and I'm light-headed so I dash to the kitchen and start yelling at the chef. My boss had become so obsessed with money that he no longer allows us the leisurely hour for staff dinner. He wants the doors open to the public at five-forty-five, leaving us with around half an hour to wolf down our pliant calamari and cold french fries if we are running late—which is often the case in setting up the dining room and bar for the luau's extra acrobatics.

Sometimes twenty minutes into dinner, one of my bosses would have already unlocked the front door. Scarfing down whatever, I'd run up to find the bar lined with geriatrics waiting for their Yellow Plate Special or waters with lemon all around.

Nico says, "Okay! Okay! Here, take calamari to table." He hands me a huge bowl of Kahiki's Dragon Calamari, which is tossed with arugula, grilled veggies, and feta cheese mixed in a sherry vinaigrette. The Pupu platter is the most popular item on the menu, which we get bits of for staff dinner. It consists of spicy chicken wings, glazed ribs, coconut-dipped shrimp, and crispy spring rolls, served aflame like some Hawaiian nightmare. He also shoves a bowl of french fries to take as well—a staple of all staff dinners. Maeve is carrying dinner plates and the entrées, some kind of papaya salad and vegetable dumplings. All in all not the worst staff dinner I've ever seen.

There isn't a whole lot of banter going on, just isn't time. The luau fanatics are piling up at the door, still just black silhouettes in front of the blaring sunshine. They're fanning themselves, probably hoping our air conditioner kicks ass. They're in for a rude awakening.

Maeve is poking through the papayas and eventually settles on the grilled vegetables. I will only eat the veggie dumplings—they're the only thing that doesn't have that distinct "Marion's" taste. (As in all restaurants, after working in a place as long as I have, everything tastes the same. They use the same sauces, oils, vinegars, and spices so that all the dishes eventually become the same blob of food. Sometimes I'll even grab a Big Mac before work, just for variety's sake.) We can hear Andrea's distinctive footsteps, as if she's pulling herself up the stairs by the rails. By the sound of her drawn-out skidding, she's already tired. When she saunters over, Nico says, "French fries."

"Don't mind if I do," she says, shoving José over and sitting on the edge of the banquette. Not one to pass up french fries, she goes to town on them.

"You hosting tonight?" I ask.

"Yes, and it's gonna be a wild night!" she screams at the top of her lungs, tossing her head back. I blow an eardrum and roll my eyes. I had been hoping for Stanley to be on, but alas, it is going to be a longer night than I had originally thought. Andrea's in one of her signature vintage negligees that comes with a floor-length robe and she has a gigantic plastic hibiscus in her curls. She hands me some leis to wear on my wrists. They'll itch all night, get sticky from the blender drinks, but I nod. They'll come off by seven.

The owner ambles up the steps, three at a time, and looks out the door, then at his watch. "Hurry up, people! We've got people at the door to feed! Chop chop! Time is money!" he says, clapping to speed us along. Before anyone can finish his dinner, he unlocks the door and lets in a throng of people who take over the bar. "It'll only be a minute," he tells them.

I swallow the last dumpling and nearly gag and run to the bar. Everyone seems to be examining the drink menus and giggling at the Hawaiian artifacts all around them. They have that look in their eyes, that it's going to be a magical night after all. Suddenly all eyes are on me and I smile back. Turning around, I put on my lipstick and gloss, fix my hair and say, "Can I get anyone a drink?"

Andrea is taking dinner tables, so half the group leaves without a word and the other half look at me desperately. They can't decide if they want the mango margarita or the banana daiquiri. I tell them to go for a real drink, a gimlet perhaps. They say things like, "But I want an umbrella!" or "That sounds too strong." I'll put the god-damn umbrella in even a real drink, but that wouldn't be as fun for them I suppose. Everyone settles on frozen margaritas (one mango, two strawberry, and one blueberry) and a piña colada. I make a huge batch of margaritas using well tequila even though the menu says Cuervo Gold (I figure why waste the good stuff only to throw fake-tasting syrups into it) and pour the flavored goop into the tiki glasses first. Then I top them with the white-liquored slush and watch the colors intermingle gracefully, like sand art. Some of the glasses are shaped like totem poles, others are geisha girls, coconuts, and pineap-ples. I top everything with a lime and maraschino cherry speared by an umbrella. The crowd squeals in delight when I present the drinks. I sprint to make the piña colada for the one poor souse who is left to wait while everyone else is well into their luau revelry. The drink's not exactly fresh, so it doesn't take a lot of time—not one coconut is harmed in the process. Within a minute, the ice has thoroughly crushed the rum and piña colada–flavored goop into a white substance that I pour into a geisha girl and I hand to the ecstatic patron with two umbrellas, for having waited longer. The check comes to forty dollars and a gentleman hands me his Amex card. When they've been seated at their table, I check the grat. It appears that there's a two-dollar tip waiting for me at the end of the night from the crowd who so deliriously jumped for joy at their elaborately decorated, high-maintenance drinks, for whom I had to inhale my last vegetable dumpling at dinner. It's going to be a very long night indeed.

Maeve comes over and hands me three drink dupes for her tables when the late waiter arrives. Donna bolts to the basement to get into her Kahiki dress and is ready to serve by the time the drinks are ready to go out. As usual she's wearing tattered and filthy sneakers with her grass skirt and coconut bra—only in New York, kids. She puts in the first of twenty pens that will accumulate in her big hair during the course of the night and takes one of the tables off Maeve's hands, serving them their frozen margaritas and one Cosmopolitan. Maeve runs over, having forgotten her order. She was too busy getting the Pupu platters together. "Kahiki hell—I'm already in the weeds and it's not even six-thirty!" she grumbles, placing her assorted frozen margaritas and piña colada onto her tray.

"I know what you mean, Maeve," I say, as I catch four separate groups of people trailing in and taking up all the stools at the bar. They all start passing the Kahiki drink menu around while I light yet another cigarette. I look over at the socially retarded Andrea, and she's flirting with some incredibly average-looking guy wearing a glaringly obvious wedding band. She pulls one of the leis out of the box and places it around the customer's head, making him look ridiculous. "You've officially gotten laid at Marion's," she says, bursting into a hysterical fit of laughter. "Get it? Laid, *leid?*" The poor guy looks uncomfortable, and when he gawks over at me, I shrug my shoulders. "Can't save you, buddy. *That's* my boss" is what my expression shoots back to him. When his wife shows up, they're both seated.

Donna hurries over and drops two more drink dupes and runs back to the kitchen. I see that one table wants a Hawaiian Punch for Two and I get busy while my new drinkers peruse the drink menu. Pulling out the huge bowl with a ceramic volcano in the middle, I splash Sambuca in where the lava would come out. In the ice-filled blender, measuring by sight, I pour in Amaretto, Southern Comfort, vodka, and sloe gin. As it's boisterously blending away, I funnel in Roses lime, cranberry, and orange juice and a large squirt of the fresh lime I squeezed earlier. It's turning into a thick, red slushy and grows so much that it touches the blender's lid. Now everyone is watching in curiosity, asking themselves what this Hawaiian nectar could be that goes into that enormous bowl. I pour the slush into the vessel and when the Sambuca is lit, the thing looks like a volcano about to erupt. There's a collective gasp. It doesn't take much to impress this lot.

Donna, with five pens already buried with the flowers in her hair, bustles over and takes it away, though one of the umbrellas catches fire before hitting the table. Occupational hazard indeed, but the table loves every minute of it. Her other customers want a Cosmopolitan and two white wines—finally an easy order to fill. When she's out of the way, I'm ready for my own drinkers, who have been waiting patiently. Out of breath, I bolt over. "What'll it be?" I ask.

"Three Hawaiian Punches for Two!" they all chime in, thoroughly sold on the heavy-handed, ruby-red, and hazardous cocktail. Andrea passes around leis making the same joke. "You've all gotten laid at Marion's. Ha ha ha!" I wince at the drunkenness that will follow suit and get to work. The vibe has been set and I look at the clock, which blinks seven o'clock. Seven hours to go.

Hilary, another waitress, walks in with her famous grimace

already forming. She checks her watch and smiles at me, shaking her head. She looks weary, probably coming straight over from her *New York Times* day job. I take a guess that she was called in by Andrea based on the growing reservations. "Shots later?" I ask her, wiping my hands of the sticky syrups.

"Definitely," she mutters, running down to the basement to change into a ridiculous costume.

Within an hour I am drowning in a sea of lushes on their third frozen drink, leis up to their chins and swaying in tandem to Elvis's "Blue Hawaii." Donna has switched to runner position and Hilary has picked up her already rowdy tables. She's in a frumpy floral number three sizes too big that Andrea picked up at a thrift store. Her hair is in a mess of a ponytail with a single phony gardenia sticking out of the rubber band holding the blond bob together. I have three table orders up, two still being made, making for a total of twelve frozen drinks to be made. My own bar crowd is waving money, scanning the menu, and begging me to serve food. It's Thursday night so I have no choice but to feed them so I take two Pupu platter orders and a Dragon Calamari for the bar. Then I finish up the table orders and run the food order back to the kitchen.

Coming in from the dark abyss of Kahiki Lounge, the kitchen's bright light is blinding. "Ordering," I yell as I place the food orders on the strip for the chef. "Ay! More Pupu? Pupu Pupu Pupu! Crazy Pupu gringos!" yells El Diabolo from behind the window. He looks miserable with his whites covered in sauces; one hand flips a fish while the other sprinkles spices onto a chicken breast. Donna picks up the dishes that are prepared and darts out. Maeve scrambles in and screams, "Ordering." El Diabolo hesitantly looks it over and shakes his head. "Pupu Pupu Pupu!"

I am adjusting to the lights, listening to the blasting Mexican music that El Diabolo brings in—hey, anything but Don Ho is fine with me tonight. I sit on a stool and take a breather, terrified to go back to the bar. Picking on a chicken wing that is up for a customer, I hear Hilary say, "Ty, I have two drink orders up. I also need a mai tai and another frozen margarita for table ten—they found a bunch of dead fruit flies in it."

"Got it," I say, jumping up and dashing to the bar with a chicken bone in my mouth. When I finish Hilary's order I pan the bar and two drunks are in a kissing frenzy, her right breast having popped out of her tube top. Hilary comes over and says, "Does she have a clue that her boob is out in the open?"

"Who cares," I say, looking at the brown eye–like dot staring at me. One of my regulars, Ryan, slowly makes himself visible amid the insanity. He says something but I can't make out anything because both blenders are roaring like Mack trucks.

"Hey, Ryan! Wanna drink?" I scream. He nods. "The usual?" He sheepishly nods again with a wide grin. I make his Ketel One on the rocks and hand it to him. He disappears into the mob and holds up the wall across from me by the picture of Burt Reynolds. Andrea spots him and "leis" him, much to his delight. He always got a kick out of her antics no matter how inane.

"Two piña coladas and a strawberry margarita," says a new customer, probably the only sober luau patron at the moment. Not for long, I think. "And can I get a bunch of maraschino cherries in one of the piña coladas?"

"Sure," I say as I run to empty the blenders for the waitresses' orders. Then, after the piña coladas and margarita are served, I cash in the leid man and run to the basement. I've run out of rum and had to make the last order on the weak side. They won't notice because the drinks are so sweet that it doesn't make much of a difference. Pulling up five bottles and holding them precariously on top of one another and under my arms, I hop up the steps and get back to work. The man comes back to me and says he'd like another piña colada, but stronger this time. "No problem," I say, smiling—my jig is up. Turning around I reapply my lipstick, which has lost its sheen, and start on his drink as two other drinkers wave dollar bills in my face.

"Please don't do that," I say. "You almost smacked me. I'll be right with you."

"Oh, sorry. Just trying to get your attention," one of them says.

Donna, who got stuck taking a drink order, screams, "Ordering." And scurries away. I see it's for one of Hilary's tables. A group of girls are fanning themselves and begging me to turn on the air conditioner. When I tell them it's on full blast, they gasp at each other. "We're sweating like pigs over here!" one girl cries.

"Imagine how I feel," I say, completing my customer's stronger frozen cocktail, embellishing it with cherries and extra umbrellas. When I place it in front of him, he brandishes a gleaming smile.

"Eight dollars," I say.

"I like your dress. Say, you want to get a drink later?" he says shyly. If only you could smell it you'd run like hell, I think to myself. It hadn't occurred to me that there was an attraction vibe going on, so I'm taken aback. I take his money and return with his change. "Sorry, I can't really talk right now," I say. "I'm married anyway."

"Oh, I'm sorry," he says. "I didn't think the wedding band was real. I heard bartenders wear them to scare away guys like me."

"Didn't work though, did it?" I say with a glossy smile. He's cute, I think, but so are a million guys in New York.

He takes a big slurp of his piña colada, pops a cherry in his mouth, and smiles. "So, is it real?"

"I'm afraid so," I say, taking the next drink order. As I'm filling the blenders with cubes, he motions me over. I move in while I wait for the blender to finish annihilating the ice.

"So . . . are you happily married?" he asks with a sly grin.

"Incredibly, thanks," I declare and move on, ignoring him from that point forth.

Hilary ambles over and whispers in my ear, "Shots. I need shots."

I make the girls vodka gimlets as Andrea walks to the kitchen, and the three of us down them as if our lives depend on it. "Now go back to work," I say.

It's so busy that I start taking tabs in record numbers. When I have time, I write them down and place the tickets in between bottles behind me, in front of wherever the drinker is standing. If there just isn't any time, I keep all the drinks in the file cabinet of my mind. Keeping track of a throng of people isn't easy, but after the first four years or so, it becomes an intense game of memorization. When things slow down I dart to the tabs and by memory add on all the cocktails the guests have finished and take more orders.

Soon Donna runs over with the Pupu platters and the order of calamari. Everyone stares at the flames licking the smoky air as if in a trance. I place them in front of the patrons and suddenly everyone at the bar wants dinner menus. Grimacing, I hurl them at the customers and proceed to make dining-room cocktails. El Diabolo is going to kill me when I walk in there with more Pupu platter orders.

I get four orders of Hawaiian Punches for Two and fill both blenders with ice and get the volcano bowls ready with Sambuca. As the drinks are blending, I light another cigarette. Looking down at my ashtray I notice there are five cigarettes that have burned down to the filter, leaving long sticks of fag ash from the barely smoked butts. After two drags I'm back to work filling bowls and decorating drinks, so that the sixth burns down unsmoked as well. A wobbly drinker comes over and asks to bum a cigarette. I hand her one, light it, and get back to working. The Esquivel and Martin Denny music is starting to get to me, and I'd do anything for Iggy Pop at that point. A few customers have asked where the wonderful tunes of Marion's have gone—to which I systematically reply: "I beg you, talk to the redheaded manager with the three leis around her neck." The wobbler comes back three more times for OPCs (other people's cigarettes), her favorite brand it seems, until I tell her to go buy a pack. She informs me that she doesn't smoke. "Only when I drink."

"That's one expensive habit *not* to have," I say, handing her another one. "Last one, then you'll have to mooch elsewhere." She agrees, drops a dollar, and goes away. At least she tipped.

Scanning the bar I see there are piles of money accumulating. I gather all the bills and I count the singles before I put them into my tip jar. Not bad—$36 by eight o'clock and when I check the gratuities on the charges I took, I see that there is an additional $47 so far coming my way at the end of the night. I take a guess that I'll plausibly break three hundred, the usual for a busy Kahiki Thursday night.

By ten o'clock my feet are starting to ache so much it feels as if my arches will collapse. I've run up and down the stairs twice to replenish the tequila and rum, and the ice an additional three times. Piña colada, daiquiri, and margarita slush has bonded between my toes through the sandals. I always believed my look shouldn't end at my waist just because people can't see below it, so I wear nice shoes. But my heels are sticking to the soles, making squishy sounds with every step. If people only knew.

The bar is filling up with fans of the live entertainment, which tonight is the Pontani Sisters. They are hard to describe, but try to imagine three *exceptionally* busty, heavily tattooed gals doing burlesque practically naked, wearing the most gorgeously ridiculous costumes imaginable. Think Ziegfeld Follies, the Cotton Club, and go-go dancers and you'll get only the tiniest glimpse of what I'm talking about. As people nibble at their Co-Co Loco shrimp and lick Hoisin chicken-wing juices off their sticky fingers, they can ogle the wild sisters jiggling to "Mambo Italiano" or a very sexy version of a French can-can. After each number, they run to the basement, change getups, and do their next routine. I can tell by the look of the crowd that they are wondering how the hell they're going to describe this scene to people at work tomorrow.

Hilary yells, "Ordering," and drops a huge dupe for six frozen atrocities, then Maeve stops by to bum a cigarette and watch the show. It's not easy serving and taking orders while there's a trio of bra-clad, tattooed girls doing an erotic and boisterous version of the can-can in the aisles of the dining room. The Pontanis slink out of the coat-check room and jump into the next song with headdresses so high they skim the lighting fixtures. Each Pontani is wearing a larger-than-life cutout pate of Dean Martin, Sammy Davis, Jr., and Frank Sinatra strategically placed within their feathered chapeaus. Their tattooed arms, backs, and chests are so extreme that they would make the hardest of Hells Angels proud.

One poor sot decides to go for it and lunges at Andrea Pontani in an attempt to dance with her. Without missing a dance step, blinking, or losing her panoramic grin, she smacks him so hard I can hear it all the way at the bar. He falls back into his seat, confused but chortling through his inebriation, and gets pats from his drunken chums for giving it a go. These girls do *not* fuck around. I get their margaritas ready because they are going to need it.

It was a nice respite from Don Ho's "Tiny Bubbles," and I'm grateful for their interludes. When they've concluded, they transform into their street clothes and race to the bar for their drinks. Everyone tells them how fabulous they are and they absorb it all with the pristine allure of cute schoolgirls. The rummy who went for Andrea during her number careens to the bar and tries to remedy his earlier behavior. "Shorry 'bout thaa. I wash just drawn in baa yrrr amazing prrrformance," he slurs, getting in too close.

Andrea takes a swig of her margarita and looks him square in the eyes. "If you ever do that again, I will rip your fucking dick off." She turns and fades into a circle of friends while her "sisters" follow suit. The drunk skulks back to his table.

It's Hilary again. "Shots, we need more shots."

I had just finished a batch of frozen strawberry margaritas and have quite a lot left over in the blender. I pour out three small drinks and wait for Maeve to strut over. Donna, the good girl, only drinks at the end of her shift. When Maeve arrives, I say, "Kahiki sucks—up yours!" We clink our rocks glasses and down our drinks in one fell swoop and hustle back to work. I'm feeling a nice buzz and notice a new drinker motioning me over. "What'll it be?" I ask.

"I'll have a shot of Knob Creek," the looker says with some kind of accent.

"My kinda guy. I haven't made a real drink since this madness started."

"I don't like frozen drinks. It's been a long day," he broods.

"I totally understand," I say, handing him the drink. "Nine dollars, please."

When I give him the change, he says to hit him again. When I place the bourbon in front of him, I ask if he'd like to run a tab instead. "No, I have to leave. But thanks." He hands me a twenty and tells me to keep the change. I thank him and he vanishes outside the doors to a city that thankfully has nothing more to do with Hawaii. When I go back to pick up his empty glass, his business card is sitting on the napkin. On it he has written: "If ever you're in Sydney, give me a call." He signed it "Mark." Best not to have Kurt find it, so I throw it in with the trash. In the old days, for kicks I kept a box full of matchbooks, napkins, and business cards with digits scribbled in drunken handwriting asking for dates and rendezvous never to be made. These days they all end up in the garbage can.

By eleven-thirty my right foot is numb and I can actually smell myself—there is just no deodorant that can tackle Kahiki Lounge. The crush of drinkers and diners has dwindled down to a manageable level and we're all a little intoxicated. The girls and I have all had another shot of margaritas and are actually enjoying ourselves for the first time tonight. Maeve is getting ready to leave, having come in early to set up, and is sipping on a Bombay Sapphire gimlet I've prepared as her parting drink. Hilary's boyfriend has arrived and is assisting her by folding dinner napkins so that she will be good to go earlier. Donna is still running food frantically for the last orders since the kitchen is going to close shortly.

The bar crowd is pretty tame now and the dining room is only half full. They're mostly regulars and people I haven't seen in a while. Ryan is still standing against the wall, nursing his Ketel One on the rocks, talking with other regulars. We've been giving each other loving looks throughout the absurdity. I'm still blending drinks but there are more martinis being ordered since the out-of-towners and luau enthusiasts have deported to a venue somewhere else in Manhattan. I light the first cigarette I can actually smoke down to the filter since six o'clock.

The stride I hit by midnight is the one I revel in the most. Overdue but inevitable, it's when I can actually feel the end of the shift creeping up. My entire body throbs from hunger and overuse, but the endorphins have kicked in from the acrobatics of the night and all I can focus on is the making of cocktails and small talk in stream-of-consciousness mode with my customers. "Yeah, it was hot today." "That'll be sixteen dollars." "Haven't seen you in a while. How are things?" "Here's your change. Have a nice night." "We don't take Diner's Club, sorry." It's the usual chitchat that I spew nightly that I don't even need to think to repeat. When the pace is compliant, the clientele civil enough, the bosses nowhere to be seen, and I'm tipsy, the job becomes a kind of lukewarm therapy that compels time to fly. I become a robot, an android that performs in a sort of peaceful way, content and grounded.

I look around and notice that there are no customers who need drinks or waitresses shrieking "Ordering" at me, and it makes me feel conspicuously inactive. Deciding to break down the bar, I begin compiling the list for the following day. Instead of leaving the tasks for the following shift, I determine that it'll just be easier to shlep everything upstairs now instead of when I come in tomorrow, when I'll be too wrecked to do such heavy lifting. I'll need to completely replenish the Rolling Rock, Amstel Light, and Corona, so a case of each is required. My inventory of rum, tequila, and vodka has dwindled again, so four of each go on the list. The tubs of flavored syrups are skimpy so one strawberry, one mango, and a piña colada are scribbled down along with a box of umbrellas and four bottles of Roses lime juice. The Hawaiian Punch was a smash hit, making sloe gin, Amaretto, and Southern Comfort imperative. Tomorrow I'll need to call the other restaurant for that stuff, since we were low to begin with on those, and leave a note for Andrea to order it from the supplier pronto. The liquor stock dwindles faster than usual during theme months. I head through the coat-check room and down the stairs and start filling crates with bottles. After replacing those items, I trot down the steps with my numb right foot and look at the list. I'm a little dizzy and apprehensive about lugging the beer cases up the flight.

I take a case of Rolling Rock and place it above the case of Corona and look at them. Thinking at first it would be easier to make extra trips and carry them one at a time, I change my mind and decide that I want to avoid a second uphill jaunt. I take in a giant swig of air and heave both cases until my arms are fully flexed and my legs lumbering under the weight. Walking up slowly, I shove a few people out of the way and make it through the small opening of the bar. The blokes I had prodded don't mind when they see the tonnage I'm carrying. I hear one of them whisper, "Holy shit, those can't be full! No way!" I realize I've never worked this hard in my life.

I begin emptying the cases into the metal beer bin. Lighting a cigarette, I take a long, lingering drag and anticipate the next load. Maeve asks me how I'm doing and I answer her with a blank look. "That bad, huh?" I nod in response.

Hilary runs over with an order for two piña coladas and a blueberry margarita. "I know, I know. They're relentless," she says piteously.

"I remember a few years ago, Pauline threw the one blender we had down the stairs and said it had broken," I say nostalgically. "Those were the days. It was so much fun to tell the luau nuts that we didn't have frozen drinks!" Hilary and I consider it with longing smiles.

When she withdraws with her tray of frozen cocktails, I hustle myself down the steps for the rest of the crates. Completely out of breath and hunched over in back pain, it takes me ten minutes to finish restocking the bar. Scanning the space I can taste the freedom, as half of the drinkers have vanished. Maeve left while I was in the basement and Donna is walking out the door. "Wait up, Donna," I say, walking over to her. My hand goes into her mane of hair and I begin extracting pens. She stands in front of me like a sheepish little girl, and I count them as they emerge. "Just twelve pens? That's not too bad," I say, kissing her good night. "See you next week."

Hilary is busy breaking down the dining room, flipping empty chairs and placing them on tables around the remaining diners, and filling bus tubs with folded napkins, courtesy of her helpful boyfriend. I tell her to do last call and she informs me that all of her checks are on the tables and that she's ready to leave whenever I am. Andrea is heard coming up the stairs and when she appears she's changed into leggings and a baby T.

"Another fabulous night, girls! Great job!" she yells as she walks out the door and into a waiting taxi. Hilary and I roll our bleary eyes and look at the clock, which says two-fifteen.

I holler, "Last call for alcohol!" And as usual three drunken Bowery Bar rejects come staggering through the doors as if on cue. "Sorry, boys, just did last call."

"Great! We'll have three Buds then," says the one with an AC/DC T-shirt.

Hilary looks at me as if to say, "Please get rid of them."

"We don't carry *Bud*," I say. "Plus all the beer is warm—I just restocked them."

"We don't care, anything," says the one with a ponytail.

"Sorry, guys, we're closed. Try Bowery Bar around the corner," I say.

"We just came from there! This is supposed to be the city that never sleeps!" cries Mr. AC/DC.

"The city may never sleep, but I do. Gotta go! Bye!"

They curse a little, shoot me a few dirty looks (at which I smile back), and fume on their way out. The two remaining drinkers at the bar thank me and stroll out into the darkness.

With the restaurant empty, Hilary darts to lock the door, just making it before a group of six starts pounding on it. They turn and walk away when I flip on the lights so bright the place looks like a Hawaiian cafeteria. I put in my cassette and listen to the song "Needle in the Hay" by Elliott Smith and begin the ritualistic job of counting out my tips. Hilary begins the job of splitting up the waiters' tips that are still in their jar and hands me the 10 percent that the wait staff owes me for making their diners' drinks. That comes to $56; my credit card grats come to $109 and the cash in the jar figures $205. Tallying my earnings for the night, the grand total comes to $370.

Because I didn't have a busboy for my first nine years at Marion's, I had no one to tip out at the end of the night, unique in most places. The night's haul is pretty great for the summer, when everyone is supposedly in the Hamptons.

Hilary goes back to fooling around with her man while I calculate the earnings for the restaurant, bundle up the money, and start the last leg of my night. "Get a hotel!" I say, heading for the offices, where I drop the cash and credit card receipts into the safe. Grabbing my handbag, I take a hard look at myself in the mirror the Pontani Sisters use when changing. Plastic flowers are dangling all over my head as they've come loose in the frenzy of the job. My mascara has smudged to the point that my eyes have a kohl look to them and the lipstick has bled into my skin, giving me a crazy person's twisted expression when I smile. The Betsey Johnson dress is soaked with blueberry syrup and God knows what else, and my toes are sticking to each other from all the drinks that have splashed onto my feet. Pulling the flowers off, I dislodge everything holding my hair up and it all tussles down over my shoulders. My scalp feels a release that startles me. Taking a napkin, I try to remove my makeup, but the stubborn glitter won't come off. When I check the mirror, I still look insane.

Hilary and her boyfriend are still kissing when I get back upstairs. She has turned the lights and air conditioner off, and put the gate locks on the bar. I realize I almost forgot to bring the bus tub of dirty tiki glasses and half-filled blenders to the kitchen and run them to the empty dishwasher. José will have to deal with it when he gets in tomorrow, I think. Hilary is anxiously waiting and when we get ouside, we pull the gate down and lock Marion's down for the night. Giving her a hug of support, I ask, "Working tomorrow?"

"At the *Times* at nine A.M.," she conveys with a pout.

"I don't know how you do that," I say, hailing a cab.

"Me neither," she says, vanishing down the Bowery.

When I get home, Kurt is drinking a beer and reading a book in his favorite leather chair. He offers a smile. "How was your night?"

"Another soul sucker," I manage to say. It's a term I use to describe particularly grueling nights. My ears are buzzing so loud that I have to strain to hear Kurt speak. In the taxi home, the shock of sitting in repose made the aches even more severe. I'm in my thirties and I'm working like some kind of animal, is what I think. It feels as if my soul has been sucked out and I'm just an empty shell of a human being. Plunking down into the sofa, I actually want to cry.

It hasn't been long enough for me to look back on Kahiki Lounge and lovingly recall how great it was. It has yet to give me that warm, fuzzy feeling that other elements of Marion's gives me. I'm sure it will some day. All jobs have hellish days, and for many mixers most days are. But Marion's in August was incomparable to any other bartending experience I've ever seen or heard of. You just plow through and try not to take it home with you—which is nearly impossible.

Kurt comes over, gives my sunken head a kiss, and suggests a shower. I jump in and stand idle, leaning against the wall for a long time under the hot blast of water. Kahiki Lounge washes off my skin into a muddy hue that twirls down the drain through a tiny whirlpool. When finally I am under my quilt in the calm of my bed, I shut my eyes and pray I won't have one of those nightmares where my shift continues and I wake up even more exhausted than before I fell asleep (referred to as "in-the-weeds dreams"). I tend to have these more during Kahiki Lounge than at any other time. The sounds of my night refuse to dissipate: "Ordering!" "Three piña coladas and a Hawaiian Punch for Two!" "Pupu Pupu Pupu!" And the buzzing of the blenders merge with the commotion of the local drunks on Mulberry Street below until I'm finally lulled to sleep.

There's a Fly in My Martini

Candy is dandy, but liquor is quicker.

OGDEN NASH

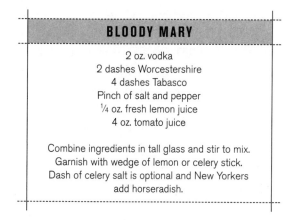

BLOODY MARY

2 oz. vodka
2 dashes Worcestershire
4 dashes Tabasco
Pinch of salt and pepper
¼ oz. fresh lemon juice
4 oz. tomato juice

Combine ingredients in tall glass and stir to mix.
Garnish with wedge of lemon or celery stick.
Dash of celery salt is optional and New Yorkers
add horseradish.

When Kurt and I finally tied the knot, I thought I could symbolically cut the proverbial guilt-ridden cord that linked my parents and me. Everything about the wedding was a nightmare—in fact, to this day I still consider it one of the worst days of my life. Kurt, on the other hand, thought it was a beautiful day that everyone thoroughly enjoyed. It was supposed to have been my dream day, the moment I was supposed to have waited for all my life. Yeah, right.

The groom did everything he could, short of a body transplant, to merit acceptance from my folks, going so far as to convert to Islam. I could ask no more of him. I mean, did they really expect someone like me to marry an old-fashioned Turkish-Muslim man, macho and mustached? The very thought of that was both hilarious and frightening. I had thought since my sister had married an Islam-converted American, they'd be used to the news by now. No such luck. When I went to see my mother at work and sat her down to tell her the news, she burst into tears and begged me not to go through with it. I told her it was happening and that nothing could stop us. The poor woman got shingles the following week from the stress of the news. My father refused to talk to me, which was actually fine, except he forbade my sisters to also. They protested and told him to get over it.

We had arranged a ceremony just for them at a mosque near where my sister lived in Montvale, New Jersey, hoping they'd appreciate the effort. They didn't show up—though my mother sent a cherished *abaya* through an aunt for me to wear. I figured that a reunion would happen in the near future and that their absence was more for show.

They couldn't exactly accept Kurt and his gentile ways in front of the clan, now could they? The rest of my family—cousins, uncles, aunts—and good friends came to witness this unusual ceremony with many wishes of luck and love. It was an English-spoken, truly spiritual observance that I will cherish always. To see Kurt sitting next to me, his entire WASPy family behind us, gave me bittersweet feelings of missing my own parents. Two months later we planned a big wedding with a judge in Manhattan.

Marriage wasn't something I ever aspired to. In fact, when I was growing up, my mother used to beg me to consider it until we'd end up in a screaming match with her in tears and me hollering, "Mom—I'm never getting married! Accept it!" I never had those secret bridal fantasies I was supposed to have—the outrageous wedding gowns, bridesmaids in orange taffeta, cheesy songs. My dream ceremony would have been Kurt and me at a beach with a judge and ten close family members and friends—then heading to the closest bar to get wasted before the honeymoon. With Kurt being an only child, his family encouraged a shindig to remember. And so, in wanting to please them, I put my own desires on hold and did what I do best: do as I'm told. After all, they potentially could be all the family I had left after this wedding phase was over.

The owners of Marion's offered to provide the food through their catering business, Marion's-a-Go-Go, as their wedding gift—a service they generously provided all their soon-to-be united employees. That sure took a load off my mind. I had sold my apartment to move in with Kurt and was paying for the celebration with some of the proceeds. My fluffy wedding gown was handmade by a wedding-dress-maker friend, Pura, at cost. Nearly everything was donated or amounted to very little so that we were able to pull off a wedding for sixty people. And we saved a little cash for a wild honeymoon in Cozumel, Mexico.

When the day approached, I felt ugly and depressed. My hair had been shellacked to keep it up and looked ridiculous; Pauline, an ex-Marion's waitress, was taking the photos as her wedding gift, and I was sweating so much I could hardly breathe. It was early May and the first truly warm day of the year. I took a peek down from the steps of the wedding space and spotted family members and friends clamoring in the front to get a good view of the ceremony. I went trembling back to prepare myself, mopping perspiration off my overly made-up face. Kurt and I were already married in the eyes of Allah, but this show had to go on despite my reservations.

My sister Reyhan prowled up to wish me luck and gave me a warning that would change the whole day. "Mom and Dad are here."

"What? What the hell are they doing here?" I said, hyperventilating.

"You invited them," she reminded me.

"I didn't think they'd actually come! They don't show up for my Muslim ceremony but they come to this nonreligious fiasco? That doesn't make sense," I cried. It took everything in me not to cancel the whole thing. Kurt noticed my meltdown and tried to calm me down, but when I heard the wedding processional fill the air, I knew

I couldn't turn back. It was our cue. My sister scurried down before I burst into tears.

Gerri, my oldest friend with whom I had worked at Bloomingdale's, was my maid of honor. When I looked down the death march of steps, I could see her smiling up at me from her post like a tiny angel. Kurt's two best friends, Guillermo and Francis, were beaming in their spots as dual best men, ready to give their crazy bachelor buddy away—the first of their group. Francis's sister, Francine, was standing at the altar, a judge and a friend, ready to joint us in holy goddamn matrimony. I wanted to run but I put on the suffocating veil instead. Kurt took my hand into his arm and, quivering uncontrollably, I plastered on my famous fake grin and walked down the steps with my soon-to-be husband.

Walking as slowly as I could, I scanned the crowd under the smothering veil. My mother was sitting in the front with a timid smile on her face next to my aunt, Asiye, who I couldn't believe had showed up. My nephew, Deniz, was on his father's knee, and Ariel, his sister, was on Reyhan's lap. I caught our comedienne friend, Reno, enwrapped in her girlfriend's arms and Marx was smiling wide. Marion's owners looked especially proud (did they still consider me a kind of lost daughter like in the old days?). Stanley and the Marion's crowd were huddled together with tears in their eyes. And there was Pauline, shooting away like the madwoman she is.

Suddenly my eyes focused on the spot where I was to stand. Directly behind it was none other than the man who had threatened all my life that if I were to ever marry anyone but a Turkish-Muslim man, he would destroy us both. Two feet away! I tightened my grip on Kurt's arm and figured if he was going to do it, it wouldn't be in front of everyone in that room. But my mind couldn't erase all the threats of my childhood.

The music ended and we were in our places, ready to seal the deal. Everything after that was a big, dizzying blur. Francine, our judge, said something about love and partnership, and our wedding party began reading poems we had let them choose. I couldn't make anything out over my heart palpitations, until something finally cut through the throbbing. It was a familiar deep, rhythmic gasping that got louder as the service progressed. Quickly I realized it was my father's breathing—I'd know it anywhere. During the entire reading of the poems, all I could hear was the inhale, then the exhale of my father's constricted passages. Slowly they became one—the gasps and my palpitations. I was trying to make out what Gerri was saying, but I couldn't get past the sweating and decided to remove the damn veil. My niece, Ariel, who was four at the time, came over and started tugging on my dress. It helped that I could focus on the little girl, as it took my mind off the disaster I was living. But it didn't alleviate the snowballing feeling of panic taking over my entire being.

Suddenly I couldn't breathe and clutched Kurt's shoulder. He looked at me in a cocked way. The experience was getting to be too much: the breathing, the flutters, the sweating, the goddamn wedding! I wasn't feeling well and needed more support. Once again I looked to Kurt, who tightened his grip on my hand. Gerri finished her poem and Guillermo was next when I pulled Kurt close and whispered in his ear, "Stop the wedding. I can't do this."

"Just wait two minutes, honey. Just two minutes."

I nodded and tried to focus on the poem. Francine and Gerri looked confused, and I smiled at them in hopes that they didn't realize I was having a full-blown panic attack. My shoulders were going numb (a telltale sign from my days of anxiety attacks). I lured Kurt close again and whispered, "You have to stop this. I can't breathe . . . I can't . . ."

Everything went black.

When I awoke, my sister was slapping my face, and I came to with the realization that I had ruined my own wedding. When I got up from the sofa I was lying on, I noticed someone had mercifully switched on the air conditioner, making it a lot easier to breathe in the sweltering room. I slowly lugged myself and the fluffy dress up and walked over to my poor fiancé, who had no idea what to do. "Let's have a wedding," I said, grabbing his hand, and the entire room exploded in applause.

The poems were reread in lightning speed and Francine retold the monologue about love and friendship. Stanley sang the song "This Is One of Those Moments," from the soundtrack of *Yentl*—his a cappella flawless and memorable. At last our vows were exchanged, our rings slipped on, and all was right with the world when I looked into my husband's eyes and kissed him for the first time as his wife.

I turned around and looked at my Marion's family, who were immersed in tears, smiles, and laughter. I realized that they knew more about me than my own parents, and with that knowledge, they understood how important this day was for me. That my mixing career at Marion's, the job that my family was forever in the dark about, had been my first step toward independence.

I then looked into my father's heartsick eyes and realized we were all human (fucked up and badly damaged, at best). At that moment, I absolved him for everything and cleansed myself of my consuming past. Because despite everything, we're family. And I needed to grow up.

pet peeve no. 15 --➤

I'll pay you to go away if you put your cigarettes out in my martini glasses or in the candles.

◄--

After Casey, the other bartender whom I considered part of the "old crew" (who were mostly fired when Marion's hired a corporate general manager), left, Spike, one of the waiters we had worked with for a decade, came by for a visit shortly before I retired. He bent over the bar and tagged me. Howling he said, "You're it! You're the last one. You're the loser!"

The owners were endlessly ordering us to pursue our outside lives, whatever those métiers were, but I always found it to feel more like a nudge, a diplomatic tactic designed to drive us out of the jobs we wouldn't leave unless firmly pushed. After my wedding, my bosses got into the habit of asking me when I was going to get "knocked up already?" I knew they wanted me to leave—after all, ten years is a virtually unheard of stretch for a bartender to tend at one bar.

I was the matriarch—the one who had been there the longest, the one with all the war stories. All you had to do was look at my hands to know I had been there and done that. I couldn't help but absorb the comment by Spike because he was right. I was the loser, the last one standing.

I woke up with that thought on my last day at Marion's. The morning of December 21, 2001, started out beautiful, though my mind was whirling with memories. The wintry sun flooded the room and the childless park across the street was gently dusted with snow from the previous night. I awoke much like I always did—at twelve-thirty in the afternoon. Turning over, there was my husband with his signature quirky smile on his face, knee bent and hand resting blithely on his chest. I was the early riser in the family.

I went to my closet. On certain shifts my wardrobe had a glamorous sheen about it—thanks to the bar's red and gold lighting. But on that last day I took a long, hard look at my clothes and didn't like what I saw. There wasn't so much as a belt that didn't have a glaring blemish. Cigarette-burn holes, wine and cranberry juice stains, hems falling apart, sweat stains, perforations from getting skirts caught on the fridge handle. Hose with too many punctures to count, arch supports piled high in the sock bin, dozens of pairs of socks I'd darned because of damage caused by standing on my exhausted feet too long. And even after washing them, you could still smell the persistent stench of beer in the fibers. I'd been buying ten- and twenty-dollar dresses for ten years, with the knowledge that they would last a few months at best. Here was the proof—*I had nothing to wear in the real world.*

There was no going back. That realization paralyzed me every day since I'd given notice. My employers had hired a new bartender (*the bitch!* I thought irrationally), my husband and I were moving to the country the following month—he to write his second novel, and I was going to be a mommy! I was four months pregnant with our first child and having a formidable time withstanding the aches and pains during the ten-hour shifts. My ever-expanding belly was propelling forward and threatening to get in the way. Customers were asking if I was expecting, and I *worked* those maternity grats. Pregnancy tippage was quite fertile indeed! The community really wanted to lend a helping hand—and I'm not talking about regulars here. The public tipped as if they were on a relief mission to help fund my baby. What was I—some kind of destitute unmarried teenager with nowhere to go? But I didn't begrudge a penny of it; after all, I was soon forsaking the finest-paying job I'd ever had.

At least my hands now stood a chance. During my years of working, they always had that lingering itch only those of bartenders and restaurant dishwashers seem to have, thanks to the industrial-strength detergents we were made to use. I was usually rather proud of my hardworking utensils, but at that moment in bed, examining my chipped nails and knobby knuckles, I felt ashamed. I wished they weren't so rough and cracking. After working in the dark bastions of a bar for so long, life on the outside appeared to be more polished than I remembered.

It was no wonder I didn't have polite hands. Every night, there were the twenty or so bottles of wine I had to uncork, beer bottles imploding from heat compression, acids from the lemons and limes I had to wedge, cocktails that needed shaking—those many chores that kept my right wrist in a chronic state of carpel tunnel. I thought of the withered and arthritic hands of my own mother—a seamstress for thirty-plus years. Now I was dreading that same fate.

My hands had definitely seen better days. They were covered with scabs, nicks, blisters, calluses, scars, and a brownish hue in the spot where I held my cigarette. Four times I'd gotten stitches for a bar accident. Once the juicer, which you have to use your whole body weight over when squeezing limes, had cut out a chunk of my right thumb. Another time an absentminded construction worker left his welding iron atop the bar turned *on* which scorched my left pointer into a blistered pulp (I worked in nerve-racking pain that night by rubber-banding an ice cube into the finger of a rubber glove over the burn—and replacing the cube every five minutes because the pain was excruciating once it melted). I never screamed so loud in my life as when I made contact with the tip of that iron.

My hair had caught fire three times lighting candles, once singing my eyelashes right off. My back had gone out at least ten times from lugging two, sometimes three cases of beer at a time up the steps— much to my customers' awe. I'd even fallen down the steps a couple of times, once hitting my head on the concrete wall, though thankfully there was no blood. Sometimes when pulling liquor bottles out of the cases, I'd find a shattered one, jagged edge up, had deeply punctured my hand (leaving me to work with an open wound no Band-Aid could ever enclose). I won't tell you where I've seen my blood splash into—believe me, you don't want to know. Let's just say that I'm grateful that the Cosmo is a pink drink on those busy nights I can't stop working for anything, least of all an inopportune gash.

Yeah, my hands have history, but hell, I'm a girl. No amount of nail polish would color them pretty—and it would take a year for the ladylike softness to return. They were so dry I had to use a professional-strength Eucerin lotion to keep my skin from flaking off in slabs. They were in the detergent every minute since I hand-washed the martini glasses, which never went to the kitchen (they broke too easily in transit), or when I rinsed out my mixing glasses, strainer, and other utensils for the next drink.

There are mixers who have serious issues with warts because when you put an open cut into water or on a glass with the virus adhered to it, you get them. I also heard about a kind of scurvy you could develop from immersing your hands in dirty water all night, too. At least I was spared this. But I won't get into feet. Let's just say I still don't wear open-toed shoes.

Maryanne was the bartender I had replaced at Marion's and she was the one I trailed when I first started. "Trailing" is when you follow a mixer around for a couple of hours to see how the place works. That afternoon I had showed up at an empty restaurant, save for the bustling kitchen staff prepping for the night. The redheaded spitfire of a gal was going to show me how the place operated in what felt like five minutes. Clearly she wanted to get on with her day, so moving at lightning speed, she illustrated how to stock the bar.

Grabbing an empty box, she said, "Find one of these and fill it up with the alcohol you need. This is where the booze is kept." She took me downstairs to the stocked shelves, which had at least two of everything. The shelves were lined with amber- and jewel-toned bottles of scotch, bourbon, and liqueurs, and the pure incandescence of gin and vodka sparkled in the harsh fluorescent lighting. The least-used liquors—Drambuie, Chartreuse Green and Yellow, Galliano—were in the back, coated thickly with dust.

She stuffed the box with the liquors she deemed necessary by checking a list in her hand, and then we sprinted up the stairs to the bar to drop it off. Swiftly heading back down, she located a crate. We trotted into the walk-in refrigerator and she began throwing fistfuls of limes, lemons, and oranges into it. Then we marched to the back of the basement and she filled the rest of the crate with a giant jar of olives, a container of kosher salt, and cans of juices. After dropping that off at the bar we headed back down the steps for the beer. With a heave-ho she hauled a case of Rolling Rock up and I followed her, panting and out of breath, with a case of Bass Ale. Then I assisted in putting everything away. Sprinting to the kitchen, she pointed to a jumbo silver ice machine, which was busy burping out frozen blocks of ice, and filled a bus tub with cubes while I grabbed another and crammed it to the top with glasses. As I refurbished those items, she started cutting fruit. "Why don't you go downstairs and check things out for yourself? Get a feel for the place."

I assumed she needed some space to work so I steered myself back down the treacherous flight of stairs. Really able, for the first time, to take my time in the space, I scanned the belly of the beast. I was jolted by a tipsy mouse loping slowly toward the offices. Apparently the exterminator had been there. Mice act like drunken sots after a nibble of the poison. It was dreadful at first, to see two glue traps with half-dead mice clinging to both life and the epoxy, their eyes frightened yet defiant. The other glue traps were overwhelmed by dead roaches. It doesn't matter how many restaurants and bars you work at, you never get used to the sight of vermin and roaches. You get less sensitive, but it's still pretty repulsive.

By now you're thinking, *Gross! I'm never going to eat at Marion's ever again!* Listen, *every* restaurant has either mice or rats. Never both—always one or the other. At least Marion's had cute little creatures right out of Dr. Seuss. I've worked in places where the rats have substantial girth and a haughty New York attitude—"You lookin' at me?"—and they act like you're intruding on their entrée of garbage while you're attempting to restock your bar. So don't think for a minute that your favorite, seemingly spotless bistro doesn't have vermin. I'm here to tell you, it does. Just be thankful if they don't have nine-pound rats feasting on your garnish before it hits your plate.

In my many years at Marion's I'd seen mice killed in both merciful and gruesome ways. One of the managers had once intercepted one of the furry little critters darting across the sink, to which she responded by baring her teeth and shrieking. Instantly commandeering a meat cleaver, she literally pulverized it with one cruel whack. The look of Joan Crawford going at it with metal hangers was blazing on her face.

One of the waiters thought it more humane to drown them before discarding their lifeless little bodies. He'd take an empty industrial-sized Pepperidge Farms goldfish box, fill it with water, and place the entire glue trap in it with the exhausted little mouse still struggling to pry itself loose.

One of the ex-chefs would step on the animal with his full body weight, leaving blood spurts on the floor and a tiny mangled body to throw out. I caught him doing it once, and God help me, he looked like he was enjoying it.

There were many instances when I'd come in to set up the bar and I'd hear a mouse trying to jump out of my small wastebasket, after having somehow fallen in during the night. I would beg the hesitant dishwasher to discard it, and he would do so by either simply tossing it into the main garbage can still alive or throwing it out into the street.

Anyway, after trailing Maryanne, I was through scrutinizing the pit of Marion's and was anxious to get home. When I asked if I could use their phone, she said, "Whatever." She pointed to it with her face and continued cutting fruit. When I brought the handle up to my ear, about twelve bantam roaches came running out of the handset. Apparently they lived in the nooks and crannies of the phone. I flinched and put the phone down. I told my guide that I was going to go unless she needed anything else. "You're starting this Saturday, right?" she asked.

"This Saturday?" I replied. I'd eaten there on a Saturday and knew the place was a mob scene, packed to the gills. "Uh, sure. I'll be here Saturday."

"Great. Everyone is going to love you. Now, back to work!" she said, motioning for me to leave.

When I tell people I'm a bartender, they automatically think (a) I'm a champagne-guzzling party girl, (b) I'm a tough chick who wouldn't think twice about chucking their ass out onto the cold street, or (c) I'll give them free drinks whenever they come see me. The answer is (b). I've had to be, having to deal with the hundreds, if not thousands, of alcohol-provoked urchins that have graced me with their hostile presences.

There are a myriad of things that can go wrong at a restaurant job, as in any public arena. I consider them occupational hazards.

Anything from uncontrollable drunks who come after you, to questionably dated foods and juices, to diseases that customers bring in are just the beginning when it comes to dilemmas mixers and waitrons must cope with. For example, a waiter, Max, told me that hepatitis and herpes are most easily spread through glasses that customers have used. I've seen many workers stick their fingers in four empty glasses in order to lift them together and place them in the dishwasher—should their hands have even the smallest open wound, they could have contracted a customer's offending virus or disease at that point. It works the other way around too. An infected waitron placing that fork on your table is akin to putting whatever disease he might have on the steak going into your mouth and system. But my concern was naturally for my own safety, just as your health is your priority. For me, the public was enemy number one when it came to germ-spreading, and I was on the frontline.

My biggest fear for years was that one of those deviants would end up committing the unthinkable. And a few have told me two inches from my face that they would rape, cut, and even kill me. I thought they were real possibilities. To freak them out I would always wave them off. "Yeah, I'm shaking now. Fuck off," I'd say, all the while shaking just a little.

There was a ghastly rumor circulating about an ordeal that had impaired a bouncer at an East Side topless club. Apparently he had unceremoniously turned away a customer, reportedly a Mafia type, and the man left infuriated. He returned with a couple of massive cronies looking for a confrontation. When the bouncer brushed him off again, the story goes that they held the bouncer down as the rejected mobster literally *bit* his nose off. I still have nightmares about that one.

Back in the early nineties, vagabonds were still abundant around Marion's. It was the Bowery, after all. Every night I could expect to physically eject up to three crack addicts, winos, or just plain deviants from the local halfway houses. On occasion I'd cut someone off and he'd get violent. It wasn't pretty, and after many pleas for protection I got a baseball bat and continued on as the bouncer. When you're making two or three hundred bucks a night, minimum, you're not going to whine about much.

Not all of the people I hurled out were alcoholics and drug addicts. There were also the purse snatchers, the mentally unstable, "jack-rollers" (muggers), belligerent frat boys on binges, prostitutes, and some numbskulls just looking for a fight.

There were the derelicts who would come in and demand a dollar and if they didn't get it from me, they would badger each and every customer at the bar. I'm not overly unsympathetic, and so, at first, when an exceptionally dissipated man came in and asked for some help, I would sometimes slide him a note or two. BIG MISTAKE. Never give a bum cash if you're the bartender because you will never get rid of him. He'll come back night after night until the finale comes, when you have to physically catapult him out on his ass.

These drifters would always catch me by surprise. I thought everyone deserved a chance, at least a drink when they really needed it. So on some nights, when most of the bar was lined up with hip locals and fabulously dressed drinkers discussing au courant topics, there would sometimes be a Bowery reject or two among them. You couldn't miss them. Much of the time they were charming, and once in a while they were downright cranky. The crusty ones were asked to leave after exhibiting their surly behavior (after I had given them a chance) and the rest hung out like everyone else. I really liked the eclectic mix, preferring it to a crowd that was too uptown or downtown, too fashiony, old-man's bar, or family-style. When the customers mix well a bartender has a better perspective on people and classes—which makes for a more fascinating job.

The seat right in front of where I made the drinks was the hot seat—the most advantageous spot for a person who wanted to corner me and drag me into his world because I was simply there the most. It was difficult to ignore a person in this position since I couldn't exactly move my tools and other necessities around all night; I had to just eat dirt and make him my friend for a couple of hours. That isn't to say it was always a drag, just that it was a mixed bag. There were the few occasions when a fabulous regular, celebrity, or a foxy drinker would park himself there for a quick drink or smoke. But that wasn't the norm, really. Most of the time I was trapped, making eight drinks for the dining room and my bar in front of the most boring rube in the restaurant, attempting to lure me into his take on why his life wasn't going the way he wished—or worse, asking if I wouldn't consider a tryst with a guy like him.

A lot of these drifters who came into Marion's were old men who lived in the Bowery's famous halfway houses. One elderly gentleman, probably in his mid-seventies, wandered in on a packed Friday night and somehow managed to park himself right in front of me.

As I was in the middle of making a slew of cocktails, the elderly man began to flirt with me. I thought it was sweet that a man his age would come on to me, so I humored him. There he was, thick bifocals, the Seventh Avenue Sweep (when the six remaining hairs on the head get combed over and are somehow glued down), a polyester striped shirt (like the ones accountants wear), and beige slacks. I noticed his hands were dirty, his nails caked with God knows what.

"What'll it be?"

"What are you offering?" he said with a devilish grin, looking me up and down. I had to giggle.

"Are you flirting with me?"

He chuckled. "I'll have a Heineken and your phone number."

"My husband would have a problem with that," I said, placing the beer in front of him.

"Come here. I want to tell you a secret," he said, motioning me over. I leaned in close and gave him my ear. "He can't fuck you like I can. Believe me. I fuck like a bull."

I was taken aback. Still smiling, trying not to egg him on, I said, "You know what you are? You're a dirty old man. I never met a dirty old man before—you're my first." He laughed and called me over again.

"I like virgins!" He laughed. I waved him off and pointed to the massive crowd I was still serving.

"I'm really busy right now, Grandpa. I'll get back to you."

After I made another round of drinks for the dining room and my own patrons, he signaled me over. "Come here. I want to tell you something," he whispered as if it were top secret. Moving in close again, he slipped my dangling hair over my ear. "I have a huge cock—and it still works. No, really," he giggled, illustrating the length with his hands. I responded with a grimace, but he continued, "I swear! I will have you begging me to stop, just give me a chance."

"Okay, take it down a notch. The drink's on me, but it's definitely time to go," I said as I cleared his near-empty beer. He shuffled out, all grins and a wink before the door closed behind him.

These old men were not all pervs; some were just pathetic. One fellow who happened upon Marion's two or three hours before closing was particularly memorable. It was a slow night, not a lot of people out in the stormy weather (nothing kills business quite like rain, Oscar night, or major sporting events). He was probably in his mid-sixties and looked real sad. His very thin, silvery hair was pulled over his ears, stringy from the rain and flaccid, like soaked white yarn clinging to his veiny neck. His sneakers were soaked and they squeaked when he walked. So I served him—why not? He was slouching and grubby but certainly not drunk.

"Can I get you a towel, sir?" I asked the sad-looking man.

"No. A beer, please," he said. I served him a Rolling Rock and continued my work. An hour later he was on his fourth beer and continued sitting alone in his thoughts. He never attempted to speak to anyone and the only words that left his mouth were, "Another beer over here."

By the time I was restocking the bar to go home, I realized he had occupied the bar and drank for three hours. There was something off about the scene but I couldn't put my finger on it. I asked myself if there was something he did or didn't do that was nagging me. People who drink a lot of beer act like goofballs within two hours, but he was as still as a church mouse. They started talking to me, to anyone. Not this guy—he barely flinched. I thought that he might be falling asleep and didn't want to go back to his melancholy room at the Sunshine or Whitehouse.

I was almost done restocking the bar for the following bartender, and the old man was the only customer left to ease out. The bad feeling was plaguing me. People who sat and drank like that at least get up to stretch once in a while or maybe ask for the time. And when they drink beer for hours they definitely use the toilet a couple of times.

Spike, the waiter, and I were turning off the stereo and told the man that we were about to close. He asked for one more beer, but I vetoed him, mentioning that it was too late. When he got up I noticed that though he had dried in the warmth of Marion's room, his pants were still dripping. That's when it hit me. Under his stool was an enormous pool of urine. The freak had been peeing on himself, the stool, and the floor for hours!

I yelled, "Hey! You peed all over the place!"

He looked me in the face with his moist eyes and said, "I'm an old man. I can't help it."

"You ever hear of Depends diapers?"

He looked truly humiliated. "I can't afford them."

"We also have toilets, you know! Ever use a toilet? Ugh, just leave," I snapped. It was late and the last thing I wanted to do was mop up someone's foul piss. With his head hung low he walked out into the rain as sad as when he came in. Spike did the mopping, clearly noting my frustration.

To this day I still feel bad about the Depends remark. It was mean-spirited and unnecessary. But when things like this happen, it brings out the ugliest side of me—a side that scares and horrifies me. I can deal with vomit, threats, broken glasses, and even passed-out customers, but a drinker peeing on my bar stool and all over the floor was a first. I saw red and it took all of me not to chuck him out on his soggy butt.

Then there were all the violent, unwarranted, and just plain scary incidents that arose on a somewhat regular basis. The most memorable fiasco I'd faced happened my first year at Marion's. It was a bachelorette party—enough said, I'm sure—that had gotten *way* out of hand.

Ten seemingly ordinary girls had finished their meal and had moved on to some devoted drinking. The bride-to-be was downing Tanqueray and tonic like there was no tomorrow—tomorrow being her wedding day. At some point, she placed her empty glass on the bar and turned around to scream/talk to her friends. I took the tumbler away and resumed waiting on my regulars. Much to my exasperated astonishment, I saw her finger-snapping for my attention and I hesitantly marched over. It was obvious that she was plastered and was going to create a commotion; she just had that look. She asked me what I did with her drink. When I told her that the glass was empty and that I had cleared it, she snarled that she wanted it back. Again, I enlightened her that it was empty and had been cleared, trying the "broken record" technique, which usually got through to lushes on rampages. She was starting to seethe, so I calmly turned away to deal with the other customers before she lost control.

Soon she was experimenting with the "divide and conquer" technique, which was to talk to the rest of the staff and get them on her side in the hopes that they would convince me to give her another drink. The manager shook his head and told her that it was the bartender's prerogative. She moved on to the waiters. When all else failed, she returned and began screeching at me for another T&T. I let her know that she had clearly had enough. One of her friends chimed in and thundered obscenities at me, too. I glanced at the manager to make sure the women had honored their sizable check and told them that they had to leave. She pulled herself together enough to calmly state, "When pigs fly."

I said, "What's it going to be? You can leave or I'll *make* you leave—your choice."

The waiters could see that things were heating up so they rushed over for backup. When the bride-to-be began screaming at the top of her lungs about her goddamn missing Tanqueray and tonic, I began the ritual of easing her out. To my surprise, she took a swing at me but missed. Men never went to punch me, but women often did. I grabbed her hair and twisted her arm back and literally kicked her out, like in the movies. She landed on her ass while Spike, a veteran, had her friend in his arms and did the same with her. We threw their bags full of plastic penises and lingerie out with them. I never expected her to get up, never saw it coming. When I locked the door she continued approaching, like a rabid dog, and kicked the door in, shattering the original fifties glass. Shards were everywhere. I went out to finish her off when lo and behold, a shocked cop was standing two feet away and had seen the whole thing. I'll never again say there isn't a cop there when you need him.

Suddenly our lush became quite amiable and distressed. I was explaining to the officer how we couldn't get the party to leave, and she began a weepy scene right out of *Terms of Endearment.* I balked. After all, the officer had just witnessed her rage while kicking the door in. I demanded a police report. When he asked her for identification, she hurled insults (*bitch* and *cunt* come to mind) and tried to go at me again. He held her back, again seeing her viciousness first-hand, and filed the charges. He even asked me if I would like him to take her in. That really pissed her off. As appealing as that sounded, her wedding was the next day—I could only feel sorry for the poor sot who actually had to marry her.

There are a lot of bizarre people in Manhattan, and bars are a magnet for them. Marion's is a public establishment so we couldn't exactly turn people away, and besides, almost everyone looks harmless at first. So they stroll in and ask for a drink. The really deranged ones show their true colors before the first drink ends, and I can toss them out relatively quickly. Then there are those who are unoffensive until the second or third drink, making them a little more laborious to oust. The booze makes them defensive and sometimes violent.

One late evening, Kurt was having margaritas while waiting for me to close up when a frizzy, redheaded woman sauntered in. She was my age and quite normal-looking. After she ordered a second white wine and a glass of water, I went back to restocking and chatting with the handful of customers who remained. Peripherally I noticed she was cruising my drinkers and especially Kurt. When she wouldn't quit leering at people, I became irritated and looked straight at her—the kind of look only a wife could give. I asked, "It's last call. Can I get you anything else?"

She shook her head, giggled, and proceeded to balance the glass of wine on her head. I grumbled to Kurt, "Why do I get all the goddamn freaks!"

After watching her nearly drop the glass twice, I said, "Are you feeling okay? Please stop doing that because you risk breaking the glass, which does not belong to you."

"Am I okay? *AM I OKAY?* Yes, I'm okay," she screamed in some kind of European accent. "Are *you* okay?"

"Look, I don't want any problems. Just stop doing that to your glass and we'll be fine."

She was on a roll now and was unquestionably getting agitated. "Am I okay? How dare you ask me that! What's wrong with *you*, stupid American woman?"

It was not going well. It was obvious that she was deranged and that the best thing to do was to get her to leave without incident. I took her glass of wine away and calmly said, "I'm sorry, you don't need this drink and now you have to go."

"You stupid American bitch! How dare you," she wailed. Then she grabbed a fistful of goldfish and threw it at me, not very effectively, though I think it was meant for dramatic effect. I instinctively grabbed her glass of water and threw it into her face. She was soaked, her mouth agape, with mascara running down to her chin. Suddenly she went for the bowl of goldfish. I got to it at the same time and we fought for it, the container being pulled like a tug-of-war rope.

"You don't want to do this. Believe me, I will beat the shit out of you. Let go!" I hollered. Meanwhile all eight of my customers, including Kurt, and the waitress were watching this fiasco in horror. She was screaming, "You stupid Americans! You have no passion! No passion, I tell you! You stupid Americans!"

Finally Kurt stood up, towering over her, yanked away the bowl of crackers, and said, "You've got to go."

The soggy lunatic composed herself, called me a slew of other names, and walked out the door, probably looking for another joint to wreak havoc on. My customers all started clapping, having noticed her creepiness from the start.

A friend of Kurt's showed up soon thereafter and said, "Hey, there's a crazy redhead on the corner screaming 'You stupid Americans' at the top of her lungs."

I asked if she looked angry, hoping she, unlike some of my past crazies, wouldn't come back for vengeance. He said that she was smiling like a Cheshire cat.

I have seen so many episodes that they have, with the passing of time, blended into one blurry image of the same lunatic. Besides triggering my anxiety disorder and subsequently depression, the worst part of dealing with these people was that it brought about a social phobia I had to acclimate to. Try to imagine a bartender who is terrified of crowds! It was both a hilarious and unfortunate situation to be in. Before tackling the issue in therapy, I was operating in an almost agoraphobic state. Parties and going out to restaurants were the most difficult situations for me. I needed a lot of coaxing on the part of my friends and family to go to gatherings. And for many months, I needed the calming effects of Xanax to take the edge off and get me out the door. Yeah, it sounds pathetic, and if it hadn't happened to me, I'd agree with you.

Despite all the similarities of the violent freaks, the final incident I had to deal with at Marion's was quite singular—and traumatic for my regulars.

It was odd in that we had just opened—people weren't ordinarily drunk that early in the evening. I had a few customers drinking martinis after their workday. Unlike everyone else, a hefty young man with a ponytail walked in with a conspicuously panoramic smile on his face, clearly not coming in after a hard day of work. Hint: Always worry when a customer comes in solo and looks a wee bit too happy.

"What'll it be?" I asked.

"It's snowing in Hawaii," he said, chuckling.

I wasn't in the mood that day—it was too early. "Do you want a drink or not?"

"Did you hear that the Antarctic melted?" At that point, he was full-on roaring.

My boss was standing by my station, using the phone and shaking his head at me, trying to signal me not to serve him. I was already on it. Wanting to get this oddball out of the bar as fast as possible, I said, "Sorry, you've had too much of whatever you're on for a drink. I'll have to ask you to leave."

"Just give me a fucking beer. Anything," he said, still laughing. "The world is crumbling, so I need a fucking beer!"

"Look, it's nothing personal. I just don't want to get into trouble," I said, attempting to assuage him. My freak-o-meter was highly developed at this point in my career, so I knew it was best to try not to upset him. The object was just to get him out of Marion's. I thought it would be a good move to use the "dramshop" laws as explanation for my unwillingness to serve him. The laws basically say that in over half the nation, commercial servers of alcoholic beverages can be held liable for injuries or damage caused by their underaged or drunken patrons. In some states it applies even to noncommercial servers of alcohol, as in a host of a party or the person playing bartender. "It's illegal for me to serve you when I think you're already drunk or could harm someone or yourself. Nothing personal. So do me a favor, go home and relax."

He remained seated, talking to himself, mumbling quiet obscenities I was meant to overhear. Eventually he got off the stool, grabbed his backpack, smiled, and strolled out. My boss hung up the phone and said, "I just saw him on Fourth Street turning over garbage cans and throwing them into the street."

"Thanks for telling me sooner and helping me throw him out," I said, getting back to business.

Five minutes later my nightmare was realized. The front windows, which essentially made up our exterior, came crashing in with a loud, explosive roar. A girl at the end of the bar cried out in pain and everyone ducked for cover. Lying on the floor—and what had hit my patron in the back—was a liter of coffee-flavored soda. Everyone was shaking and in shock. When we looked out the door, the freak who thought it was snowing in Hawaii was crossing the Bowery. My employers and the manager were too petrified to go after him, and by the time the cops came he was long gone.

People who drink to get drunk need to be watched very carefully. I've seen far too many occasions where I could have been arrested, sued, or harmed by what happened to these sots after a night at Marion's. Although I try not to think about it, I wonder if these people have gotten into automobile accidents, killed or maimed others, beat the crap out of their wives, or even hurt themselves.

It is a statistical fact that 104 million Americans imbibe on a regular basis. Eighty percent of adolescents who succeed in committing suicide are children of alcoholic parents. Forty-one percent of all traffic accidents are alcohol related, and 100,000 deaths annually are attributed to alcohol, making it the third leading cause of preventable deaths in the United States. How can I not be troubled or feel any guilt when the statistics say that I probably had something to do with someone's pain or even death?

Josh was a regular I had for only a short time who, I think, had a brewing crush on me. He would come in weekly and down a bottle of cheap red wine within an hour and hit blotto—every time. Talk about a turn-off. Had he clearly not been such a fierce alcoholic, I most definitely would have toyed with the idea of dating him. But who needed to baby-sit an adult on what should be passionate, carefree dates? Not worth it, not ever.

The trouble I had with Josh was that he could somehow keep it together until the very end, when the lights were turned up and the music came to an abrupt end—signaling everyone to get the hell out. Our conversations were lucid and intellectual, our chemistry light but stimulating. By the time the bottle of wine was over and I was pouring the second Merlot by the glass, he would start slurring, making it impossible to understand most of what he was saying.

I had been a bartender at that point for only a year and was still learning to identify the moment to cut a drinker off—just before he crosses that universal blurry line. I was still oblivious when to stop the pouring despite the clues from our past evenings together: he'd puked twice en route to the john, fell asleep on the bar, his head landing in the goldfish bowl, and once tumbled off the stool he was sitting on. Not the most ideal techniques to use when trying to charm a girl.

Josh had come in for his weekly binge and, as usual, by the time the waiter, Michael, was nudging me to close, Josh was drunker than I'd ever seen him. He was swaying toward the bathrooms, where I assumed he was going to try to pull himself together. I was adding up my money drop for the safe with my back to the coat-check room. I could hear Josh stumbling back toward me and when he made it to the bar, he said, "I'm going to head out. Where's my coat?"

Without turning my head (I was still counting singles), I said, "I hung it up in the coat-check room behind me." I yelled for Michael to hustle so we could leave and then I heard a muffled wail, ending in a resonant thud. "What the hell was that?" I asked Michael. "Where's Josh?" I ran to the empty coat-check room and looked around. "Josh? Where are you? Holy shit!" I yelled. "Michael, get over here!"

I looked down the stairs leading to the stockroom, and there was Josh, lying in an impossible position, his head in a large pool of blood. Bolting down with Michael behind me, I tried to coax Josh into talking. "Josh! Josh, can you hear me?"

"Hey, Ty. I don't feel so good."

"Michael, call 911! Josh, you had a fall. Do you know where you are?" I asked, trying to figure out how much damage was done.

"I'm not sure. Am I at Marion's?" he whispered with a grin. I gratefully smiled at him.

"You've hit your head and we're going to get you to the hospital," I said, wiping the blood from his face, which had already begun to cake. Josh raised a hand, touched his scalp, and chuckled when he saw his blood-spattered palm.

He said, "Shit, I'm bleeding."

"I know. That's why we're going to go to the hospital."

The EMTs showed up within five minutes, put Josh into a neck brace ("a precaution"), and strapped him onto a stretcher. I volunteered to accompany him on the blaring ride through Manhattan and managed to call Josh's roommate, Peter, who was also a mutual friend. The hospital was jammed, but we were admitted immediately (the blood was quite a show). Peter arrived at five in the morning and I was discharged, bloody and exhausted.

I waited months to hear that I was being sued or arrested for negligence or involuntary assault or whatever term is used for being a stupid bartender, nearly causing someone's untimely death. That day never arrived. And understandably, Josh never returned to Marion's. I heard from Peter that Josh was uncomfortable with the thought of entering the restaurant and that I should probably not expect him "anytime soon." He also told me that Josh quit drinking, which was a good thing.

The detail of the experience that never left me was not the gore, or my clothes caked with Josh's blood, or seeing Josh in that illogical pose at the bottom of the stairs, or even the eerie thud that followed his fall. It was what the emergency worker said to me en route to the hospital.

"This guy's a lucky son of a bitch. Sober people never survive falls like that. Drunks bounce off the walls. Drunks never die."

pet peeve no. 16 ⸻⸻⸻⸻⸻⸻⸻⸻⸻⸻▶

> If I cut you off, just try to see through the drunken haze and understand
> that it's for your own good. I'm trying to prevent you from getting date-
> raped, mugged on the way home, getting hit by a car, or into a fight.
> Believe me, it hurts me (in the pocketbook) more than it hurts you. We
> never want to do it, but we're required to by law—so give me a break
> because I'm trying to protect you.

◀⸻⸻⸻⸻⸻⸻⸻⸻⸻⸻

I really disliked cutting people off, but more than that, I absolutely *hated* carding them. The underage crowd inevitably had that certain look when I was approaching, as if they were about to rob a convenience store. Their innocent eyes would be darting left and right. Twirling their hair and slouching if they were girls, sitting with perfect posture if they were boys. There was always the uncomfortable grin.

"Would you mind if I see your ID?" I would ask.

Without blinking they would go digging in their bags or wallets and would always come up empty-handed. Their comeback was usually something like, "I can't believe what an idiot I am! I left it at home! Jeez!" When I refused them, the crestfallen look was painful since I remembered what it was like from my own youthful boozing days.

I've seen it all. Driver's licenses that have obviously been tampered with—the picture eased in through a bent corner, then iron-sealed (I'd pulled that off a few times). The twenty-dollar college badge that had a certain St. Marks Place look to it—with no expiration date (been there, done that). The general proof cards that had in bold letters "IDENTIFICATION" on top, the kinds one would have to carry in Third World countries but never in the United States. I only accepted valid driver's licenses and passports—that's it.

One of the bartenders at our sister restaurant had gotten busted serving a minor, though I considered it an ambush of the worst kind.

It was Halloween night and a guy entered in full drag—makeup, wig, dress, and all. He was accompanied by a friend, also in costume. Immediately after ordering cocktails, the drag queen's companion went to the bathroom. When the mixer placed the drinks in front of the sot in drag, the other one bolted out of the bathroom, revealed his badge, announced that the bartender had served a minor, and the owners were called in. It took months, a couple of court dates, and a hefty fine not to get their liquor license revoked. I'm sorry, but when a cop is running around on what is always a slamming Halloween night with a minor in more makeup than RuPaul just to incriminate an unsuspecting bartender, I call that entrapment.

There's no denying that I appreciate officers when a boozer is out of control and I need more than a warrior waitron to back me up. Episodes like setting up a bartender or trying to close the place down on various petty grounds strengthen the love-hate relationship bartenders and service people have with law enforcers. It's much like our relationship with the dreaded health inspector.

Let's face it. Without health inspectors we'd all be eating food that is rank, sneakily prepared with embellishments to hide spoilage, spiced up to taste "interesting." A restaurant will do almost anything not to have to throw out that case of milk that expired only two days ago. Owners don't think of much more than cost effectiveness when it comes to their kitchens. And when you're thinking about saving pennies, most restaurants don't mind risking a couple of lives to salmonella or botulism. (What are they going to do, come back and complain?) In other words, if all this wasn't required we'd be eating rodent droppings, unpasteurized dairy products, chicken that's contaminated, and God knows what else.

During the health inspector's annual unannounced visits, his primary function was to evaluate food workers' operations, including the way in which they "receive and store foods," how they "process foods, and the temperatures at which they cook, hold, and reheat foods." They utilize a class code, Class A being deemed "critical."

General items are subdivided into Classes B, C, and D, which are not as crucial but are still regarded with raised eyebrows and serious consideration. It takes either four criticals or five generals to flunk an audit. As a consequence of the inspections, "sanitarians" may serve summons for violations of the New York City Health Code or the State Sanitary Code.

Every offense, from not having someone on the premises with the proper course certificate from the Health Academy, to not using gloves when handling food, to not wearing a hair net, to finding proof of vermin or roaches, to mixing cooked and raw foods, and a host of other violations big and small can submerge a restaurant/bar in fines or, worse, get the place shut down for good. New York tries to inspect every restaurant once a year. Restaurants are given up to two chances after failing their initial inspection, but after a third failure the space gets padlocked.

As soon as the badge was presented, I would be asked to get management. I would call the office to tell them we had an inspector in the house. No matter where I was working at the time, the health inspector brought with him a ubiquitous fear of God. As soon as that badge was flashed, a feverish pace of getting the place up to code within seconds, behind the examiner's back, went into play. The first thing I noticed was that all the higher-ups would disappear, breaking up into groups: offices, storage rooms, kitchen, and bathrooms. You never saw porters and dishwashers work so fast.

It was a reflex to make eye contact with the inspector (as with all people entering the bar), which would invariably get him to approach the bar. All men are the same. I would smile and ask him if he'd like a drink. He'd say he was working and he couldn't, but boy he could really use a beer. I'd offer him a soda, which he never accepted, though I could tell he would have loved one. I'm inclined to believe he wasn't allowed to since it probably created a conflict of interest. We'd make small talk about his job. "You must see some pretty wild stuff doing what you do," I'd say.

"You have no idea."

"Any advice?" I'd ask.

Without missing a beat, he'd say, "Don't eat in Chinatown."

Trying to get him to loosen up I'd get more personal. Batting my eyelashes, I'd say, "Are you married?" Thank God, most of them were. Under the pretense of making drinks, I would actually be making corrective adjustments to the bar as we talked. I would remove liquor bottles off the floor, where some were kept for lack of space; get a roll of paper towels onto the rack even though I never used them (I preferred cotton towels, but I was cited for paper on my first inspection); and make sure I had hand soap by the sink (I used the industrial-strength soap kept in the sinks, but regulations commanded hand soap for hands).

"It must be hard for your wife to have you hanging out in bars and restaurants all night."

"She's used to it," he'd say with a grin. "You're good at making drinks."

I smiled and said, "Why, thank you. Too bad you can't have one. I'm told I'm good."

"I'll bet you are," he'd say, to which I'd smile.

"You better believe it."

By then I was sure he was one happy camper. Usually I'd get a call from the offices asking how it was going. "I don't get paid enough to do this!" I'd whisper with a pout. "How much longer?" They'd always say a couple of minutes. I'd roll my eyes and return to the inspector.

"They're just finishing up a meeting. They'll be right up. Why don't you start with the bar area?"

He would remove a pad and squeeze into the tight space. We would brush up against each other, and I'd say, "Excuse me. Am I in the way?" He'd smile and shake his head. After figuring out the corrective drill and maintaining a level of teasing without crossing any lines, the bars I had worked in rarely got fined for anything.

My worst experience with an inspector happened on a sweltering summer night. While I was working the man into a happy state, a drink was returned to me with about twelve dead fruit flies wading at the bottom of the bourbon shot. I shot the waiter a look like *Are you crazy?* and smiled at the inspector. He asked to see its source. I raised the bottle and waved it in front of a light and detected forty dead ones inside, submerged in the brown liquor. He looked at me, shrugged, and began jotting notes on his pad. We got a summons for that.

If there was a house pet it would be sneaked out as the inspector left the front area to go to the kitchen. It was usually my job to let the office know that the examiner was on his way to the back to jump-start the process of making the animal disappear. The pet would be put in the hall of the building or a waiter would have to keep it outside around the corner until the inspection was finished.

Finally a manager would emerge and apologize profusely for the delay. I was out of the woods by the time the inspector was led toward the kitchen. Diners would notice the bustle but, like most of us who don't want to know about sensitive things like the food that goes into our mouths, they kept on chewing.

Back at the nightclub I'd once served a glass of champagne with a mouse dropping stuck to its rim, a roach floating on top of a whiskey sour, a roach frozen in an ice cube, fruit flies in an assortment of cocktails (they're red wine and brown liquor drinkers), an olive that had been nibbled on by a mouse, and countless other repulsive things I hadn't caught. Bars are unclean—there's no getting around it.

It's nearly impossible to manage a vermin problem. You can slow it down, but I've never seen it eradicated. I got to be friends with Marion's exterminator, who came regularly for the sprayings, and he'd always give me a huge wad of glue traps. More than the poison, the inhumane glue traps were the only thing that really worked. They came in banana- and peanut-butter-scented varieties that drove them wild.

Whenever he left, the mice at Marion's would get so delirious from the poison that they would parade out in clusters, wobbling into the dining room and lingering, much to the diners' horror. I'd spent a few nights trying to edge them toward the stairs or out the door—

without much luck. It isn't easy when you know there's a mouse present and the diner doesn't. You try to inconspicuously walk around with a broom, pretending there is a broken glass somewhere near. Or pace with a flashlight, telling the diner or drinker that someone called and said they'd lost their wallet somewhere close.

Every place I worked had these problems, and trying to keep them from customers was like trying to hide a bull in a china shop. But people don't see what they don't want to see—and we took advantage of that.

Fruit flies are always a problem in the summer. During those humid days, take a quick peek at the service area after the bread has been placed and your drink order is being made. Are the waiters spooning something out of your drink? Is the bartender holding a thin, hollow drinking straw and suctioning something out? Fruit flies. At the nightclub, the porter would cover the entire bar in plastic wrap at the end of the night because the flies would crawl into the bottles no matter what stopper we used. I covered my bottles with huge tablecloths. The flies procreated in the pipes, so at Marion's we drowned them with bleach every night, leaving the bar with an unnatural, chlorine stench that gave me migraines. It made a dent in the problem—but I'll bet the bleach going down our pipes was some kind of violation. At the uptown restaurant where I'd worked I'd had to line the entire sink area with sticky insect traps. Every day I'd throw out five or six of them blanketed with roaches and flies. They got into the cocktails, espressos, garnishes, everything. And this restaurant was considered very upscale.

Trying to keep the patrons unharmed wasn't an effortless job. We're talking food and beverages here. I read that at the Health Academy the teachers tell the restaurateur and the hot-dog vendor and the school-cafeteria cook that they are "potential murderers." There's a moral code to follow, which is more important than the knowledge of bacterial identification. Sadly, though, most owners in the business don't put a lot of energy or stock into ethics.

So it was my awful job to placate the people who safeguard your health. And after all the horseshit of having to dally with a man that I was not in the least bit interested in—who was justly trying to protect the public—all I could think about was getting home and taking a long, hot shower to scrub it all off.

You get to know your local crooks when you work at a bar for a long time. They make the rounds, and if they've been successful, they come back for more. One of my managers at Marion's and I implemented a technique when we got suspicious of anyone.

The thief would come in and usually stand by the door. Sometimes he would come up to the hostess stand and ask for a table for two and claim he was waiting for a friend. In that time, he would be scanning the bar for money or panning the floor for handbags. Most of the time he was pretty obvious about it, so we would jump into gear. I would inform my bar customers, loud enough for the suspect to hear, to please take their bags off the floors because "we'd had a rash of purse-snatchings recently." They were always grateful and picked up their belongings.

Sometimes the questionable patron would then take a stroll to the back of the restaurant to "use the bathroom" and browse the floors on the way. I would signal the manager to follow him. When the urchin returned, still there was no friend meeting him. My manager would go up and inquire if it would be much longer, to which he would either give up and leave or wait longer for a more opportune moment.

If he was stupid enough to stay, we would stare him down until he was so uncomfortable he couldn't take it anymore. He would figure out that we were on to him and ultimately make his exit. I made a point to call Bowery Bar, Jones Street Café, and other restaurants in the vicinity and warn them about the suspicious "patron," which they always appreciated and sometimes returned the favor.

Management at Marion's liked to scare the bartenders into thinking they, too, were being watched because they heard somewhere that we all steal. Well, to set the record straight, not *all* bartenders (and waiters) steal. Yeah, I've heard of and have known those who do and the techniques are varied.

My ex-boyfriend, the club owner, once told me that a way he's caught bartenders stealing was that they would pocket the money whenever someone ordered sodas. These drinkers never paid by credit card and we're talking a buck or two at best. That can add up. He had also fired a guy who lifted cash that was left on the bar for the tab, tip and all. Some managers consider giving away drinks as stealing, though most would agree to the "every third drink is free" policy for regulars.

There are a hundred ways to steal at a bar. But if you work a locals bar, you don't need to. Every night is lined up with regulars, and your customers take care of you. If it's a slow night, they take note and leave a twenty or more instead of a fiver. It all evens out in the end; it's all relevant.

One of the owners at Marion's loved to declare that he had hired a "spotter." This is a goon asked to come sit at the bar, have a drink, and watch the bartender *very* closely. He then reports back to the owner. It's usually a friend, so the bartender is not supposed to suspect a thing. Not exactly a morale booster. I smiled and told him, "I have nothing to hide. And when your precious spy finally tells you that I'm clean, maybe you'll shut up about how you don't trust us."

I had a friend, George, who tended bar at a wildly successful nightclub. One night after the club closed, we headed back to his apartment, which he shared with another bartender he worked with. A soon as the three of us entered they marched to the sofa and emptied their bags. They flipped them over and we watched fifty- and hundred-dollar bills float out, landing on the sofa and floor, forming small hills of money.

I looked on in awe and said, "Holy shit." They counted their take, which turned out to be almost three thousand dollars—in one night. I asked, "I'm quitting school and working with you guys!" They laughed. "How the hell do you make so much money?"

In a matter-of-fact tone, they said in unison, "We steal." No guilt or drama—it was just what they did. I didn't agree with it, but their rationale was that if the owners could steal, why shouldn't they? Most managers and owners I've worked with stole either from the house or the bartenders.

George was investing his take on art, which he eventually sold and made a killing. He could have retired, he said, on what he got for those. The other bartender, Jessica, bought a one-bedroom flat in the East Village with hers and paid for some of her tuition at NYU to study psychology. What goes around comes around, I suppose.

So why don't bartenders save all that money and get out? We hate "the life," right? Well, not exactly. It's a complex question with myriad answers. There's the freedom to pursue the creative life. That's what kept me for so long. I wouldn't quit until either my acting or writing took off. Plus I'd rather have every hair on my body plucked off by tweezers, then be dunked into a vat of cheap cologne than get a cubical job ever again.

A lot of bartenders lack the discipline to save any of the riches they earn. It's hard when you're not waiting for a paycheck every two weeks. Essentially, you're getting a huge wad of cash night after night. To unwind after a grueling shift, you go out after work for a drink with your friends and end up spending half of what you made buying everyone cocktails and late-night suppers. A bartender I worked with spent every penny on CDs and going to rock concerts. The cash is there in your hand, ready to spend before you've even had the chance to shower the night off your body.

There were only two lifers I knew personally. One was Sal, an elderly barman at Milano's, and the other was Patrick, who worked at the uptown restaurant. Their stories were similar. Sal was content serving the old 8 A.M. drunks, probably because whatever dreams he had were settled, tucked neatly in his past. Or, as for Patrick, those dreams were never attained so he's continued mixing because he didn't learn another trade.

It's too easy to rely on the cash that fills our greedy palms every night, resulting in a procrastination to do anything else. Most bartenders I know are desperate to do something else—anything. But after last call is served, a couple of drinks in their own bellies and they're out with a few friends till dawn; there just isn't time to do anything else. So they pay their bills and do it over again. Pretty soon it's ten, twenty, or thirty years later and they are officially members of the lifers club. I, myself, cut it pretty close.

Am I, or any sane person, going to give up two or three hundred dollars a shift to make four hundred dollars a week at a mind-numbing desk job? The money is addictive. I wasn't going to give up my summer home, my car, my ability to buy my nephews and nieces their inane Nintendo games or Pokémon toys, or being able to give to charities for the first time in my life. I took great pleasure in sharing the money I made, capital I never had before to give.

You can't go back to Montezuma tequila once you've quaffed Patron Gold. Just like you can't go back to rice and beans or Cocoa Puffs for dinner after you've eaten great restaurant food night after night for over a decade. And it continues snowballing. The lifestyle, which feels an awful lot like hanging out at a party every night, is highly charged and enjoyable. I was meeting the most fascinating people in the world working at Marion's, with its forever sparkling vibe, the magical music that reeked of glamorous days gone past.

Nonetheless, sometimes my colleagues and I would say things like, "This is my last year in a restaurant." I think I said that six years straight. A waiter I used to work with would reply, "Ty, I've been saying that for fifteen years. We'll quit when it's time to quit." But I didn't quit despite other job offers. The Odeon, one of my favorite spots in New York, even offered to create a position for me as a bar manager. They told me I could have any hours I wanted, an assistant, and could hire all of my own mixers. Tempting as it was, I couldn't make the move. Marion's was too sweet a job to leave, emotionally and financially. I did ultimately leave, having experienced the most fun years of my life—but I still get the urge.

Once a junkie, always a junkie.

Neanderthal men could expect to live to the ripe old age of twenty. In the eighteenth century, Western Europeans could assume they would live to thirty, and at the turn of the century, the American life expectancy was forty-seven years of age, with only one in twenty-five clawing their way to age sixty. And women lived shorter lives due to the many dangers of childbirth. These days the figure is more like a whopping sixty-five years thanks to the wonders of medical care, better living conditions, and improved public health. If a baby born today avoided heavy manual labor, eating irresponsibly, exercising too little and becoming obese, he has an excellent chance of living to seventy-five or eighty years of age. And if he is able to maintain a mellow outlook and continue exercising his brain, he should be able to revel in a mostly independent, active life—extended years won't be spent on a rocking chair waiting for death to emancipate him.

Still, people are obsessed with health and with living forever. New York City Mayor Mike Bloomberg had his fun, having quit smoking decades ago, and now has taken the charge to ban smoking in bars and restaurants, saying he wants to protect me and other restaurant and bar workers from the dangers of secondhand smoke. It's already prohibited in California. In Alaska and many other states, smoking is banned in restaurants, but not bars. Delaware passed a sweeping smoking ban in 2002 that included bars, but it was reversed. Some cities in Arizona (Tempe and Guadalupe) have banned lighting up in bars, as has Cambridge (Massachusetts), Helena (Montana), Eugene and Corvallis (Oregon), Austin and El Paso (Texas), most public places in Utah, and most of West Virginia (though this is in appeal). In Oklahoma, an establishment can choose whether it wants to be smoke-free or remain entirely smoking, which seems fair to me. The proprietors know who their customers are and what they want—not the government.

This subject demands a book of its own, but I have better things to do. Just let me say this: I am shocked at the way people are using this issue as a sort of battlefield for their own interests. I want to get a few things straight on the subject.

I really resent any government telling me I can't do something "for my own good." I am an adult and I can make my own choices, thank you. To tell an adult who *chooses* to work in a smoke-filled atmosphere that he or others are not allowed to light up is ludicrous and a slap in the face for anyone who respects the Constitution.

Then there are the thousands of stats we're forced to believe about "environmental passive smoke." And let me just say that the data is extremely confusing with mountains of "evidence" for both sides, which I consider "junk science" clearly used to justify their own needs. For example, I found documentation on the *Buffalo News* Web site that stated when it comes to secondhand smoke, the methodology for measuring its exposure is questionable at best. In November of 2001, Dr. Dean Edell told the *Buffalo News,* "Secondhand smoke stinks—but is it killing people? There was a study of the wives of the smokers—they have crummy health habits. They eat terrible diets of meat and fat, they don't get any exercise, but when they show up with worse health statistics, it's blamed on secondhand smoke, not on all the other factors."

He went on to explain that we still don't know how cigarettes truly affect us and how they cause cancer. "We don't know what causes the increase in heart disease. It's not nicotine—nicotine gum actually helps heart disease patients." He clarified that there is carbon monoxide in any kind of smoke, though it has a highly fleeting effect. It constricts the oxygen's bond to your hemoglobin, but when you take a breath of fresh air, it is exhaled out of your system. He doesn't ascertain the cause of health problems of smokers, but he also doesn't understand why we're on secondhand smoke when we don't know what the firsthand does yet.

He said, "I think we're becoming a really, really neurotic, fearful people, and politicians and the media love it and know how to feed that monster."

"Secondhand smoke kills more Americans each year than cocaine, crack, heroin, homicide, suicide, car accidents, fires, and AIDS," declared one ad in boldfaced type in the March 10, 1998, *Miami Herald*. In the ad, the U.S. Environmental Protection Agency claimed that secondhand smoke kills 53,000 people a year in different categories. But get this—it was a typo! The actual number was three thousand—yet the 53,000 number is still displayed on antismoking ads—and although the American Cancer Society had admitted to its dubious value, many antismoking lobbyists and other such special interest groups continue to use the large number. More junk science to prove the anti–smoking cause.

A U.S. federal court has ruled that the Environmental Protection Agency wrongly declared secondhand tobacco smoke a dangerous carcinogen. The court harshly criticized the integrity of such institutions as the Department of Health, who have lobbied for smoking bans like vigilantes and have exploited public opinion into believing the notion that "smokers are killers." Do you realize how much money is being spent on persecuting smokers for inflicting passive smoke on the poor masses even though nothing tangible has been proven—and that many legitimate and worthy institutions have even disproved the inflated, and in some cases, false stats of some of the antismoking cartels? Billions of your and my money. Hey, how about we clean up the smog in California instead?

I'm just trying to illustrate how you can find stats and "proof" for whichever side you're on—so don't believe everything you read. On both sides, you'll find a lot of junk science, but the issue I care about is freedom of choice.

Smoking in your own yard or car is banned in Rolling Hills, California. Santa Cruz, California, has banned it at the beach. Palo Alto has barred it within twenty feet of building entrances, which extinguishes smoking in outdoor patio and garden restaurants! What's hilarious, though, is that they allow smoking downtown on the sidewalk "as long as smokers keep moving." In New York City, the most liberal-minded city in the country, I wasn't allowed to light up at the U.S. Open—outside! Co-op boards are enforcing new rules discriminating against homeowners who smoke, not allowing buyers to light up in their own apartments. Where the hell am I—Afghanistan?

I was a bartender. No one put a gun to my head. I've given out more free cigarettes to "nonsmokers" who asked for them than I care to mention. News flash: People come to bars to smoke, as well as drink. It's the one place where people can let loose and relax. Being amongst smoke is part of the job, just as grease is for the short-order cook. For bartenders who whine about inane things like the stench of their clothes after work (but they like the rankness of beer?) or in their hair, I just have one thing to say. You're not some doctor or scientist. You didn't spend thousands upon thousands to study to be a bartender. It's blue-collar work, so get your ass to another job. How about getting yourself into a nice cubicle in a smoke-free environment like an office? In fact, they're all smoke-free now, so take your pick. There are *thousands* of other jobs—especially in New York. And if your stinky clothes bother you that much when you get home from work, try doing laundry. It gets that pesky tobacco (and beer) smell right out.

More than anything, taking tobacco out of the environs of a bar is like taking the bubbles out of champagne. People who drink, even many "nonsmokers," enjoy a puff when they are out trying to have a good time. Whether it's the way it tastes, feels, or creates the vibe, they like it. Smoking is part of what makes a bar, well, a bar—a haven for adults to indulge in their vices and, hopefully, cut loose. It's tradition. It's sexy. It shapes the vibe of the space. It goes with cocktails and candlelight. People don't come to bars for their health. If that were the case, they wouldn't be complaining when I cut them off just before they vomit all over my garnish dispenser and bev naps on work nights. Next thing you know, you won't be allowed to drink at bars. They tried that before—and you know how that turned out.

Smoking is still legal, so I believe adults should be allowed to indulge in whatever legal vice in establishments that allow it.

I can't tolerate the current government's we-know-what-is-best-for-you mentality. When the mayor signed the bill raising the taxes on cigarettes up from eight cents to $1.72 (talk about subtle!), he virtually made cigarettes a luxury item. But he got a lot of flack. In the *New York Post*, I read: "I know you love to eat chunky peanut butter with bacon and bananas. How about I come out there and start a campaign to tax that bacon that's going to cause heart disease and tax that super-chunky peanut butter that's going to kill you?" asked agitated activist Audrey Silk of Citizens Lobbying Against Smoke Harassment. "You're treating us as second-class citizens, as if our opinions do not matter."

Don't misunderstand me—I'm not trying to say that smoking is good for you. But I enjoy smoking, and I'm shocked that my right to indulge is in jeopardy in what is supposed to be a free country. Nearly one in four adults in this country lights up—that's a lot of people who appreciate this particular vice. The government constantly trying to protect me from myself is a bizarre epidemic.

Why isn't the government protecting people from secondhand alcohol? Today 104 million Americans drink alcohol on a regular basis and drunk-driving fatalities have always been a major problem. I won't get into all the horrid crimes that are committed where either the assailant and/or the victim were intoxicated. The numbers are too large and belong in another book. It bothers me when I hear smoking is a "disgusting" habit. You want to know what a disgusting habit is? It's the lushes who don't know when to stop drinking until they projectile vomit all over the bar (and sometimes me!), barely managing to get home in one piece. That, my friend, is disgusting.

pet peeve no. 17 - ➤

Don't ask me for a cigarette—*especially* if you're a nonsmoker. You're
not fooling anyone with your "I just quit" or "I only smoke when I drink"

routine. And if you manage to get one, you'd better be tipping extra for it. In Manhattan they're over $7 a pack, which at Marion's costs more than the top-shelf cocktails. If they so generously furnish you that cigarette, consider yourself lucky and do not ask for another and another. Get your nonsmoking sanctimonious attitude over to a bodega and buy yourself a pack.

Sadly, the worst occupational hazards are personal ones for bartenders, particularly alcoholism. Many of the employees at Marion's (and every other place I've worked) had an extreme problem with alcoholism and/or drugs. One chef, Peter, was drinking so much that his hands shook violently when he prepared the food. It was painful to watch him write anything down, the scribbles in jagged spasms, and let's just say I stayed away whenever he was working with his precious knives. Finally he got himself on the wagon, and is now able to have a beer with dinner without any problems.

Paul was another story altogether. His heroin dependence had gotten so bad that he survived burning his apartment building down after having gone to sleep doped up with a cigarette in his hand. Without a place to live, he slept in the restaurant's Belmar Lounge, a private space in the back of the restaurant, curled up on the long table covered with the stained napkins from the laundry bin. Eventually he was living on the streets.

After a few years, most bartenders either cut back on their drinking drastically, or don't drink at all or do any drugs. It's a complex situation. Some of them suffered the effects of constant binging and partying during their shifts, or as in my case, watched too many people destroy themselves at their bars, the juice quickly ripening into an ugly turn-off. This is not to say the latter group didn't once enjoy the wonderful effects of booze, but like anything, it gets tired.

Another friend from Lucky Strike's bar is in AA. "I know this sounds sick," he said. "But I think it's better to help someone hit their bottom." He truly feels that sliding that whiskey to a drunk might force him to find redemption. "I pray for people. I pray for people who are still sick and suffering."

I've known quite a few mixers who couldn't help a nip of scotch for the duration of their shifts. The immediacy of the alcohol, the lure of the high right behind a mixer is sometimes just too much to bear. Those who like the potent encounter of spirits have got to have willpower so as not to become a raving alcoholic. It's too easy to down a quickie, the backwash of someone's drink left over in the mixing glass. I know a bartender who thought it was a big waste when there was a half-ounce of liquor left over and would down much of it. It reminded me of my mother, who would clean off our plates instead of throw the leftovers into the trash.

Mig, the owner and bartender at a local haunt on the Lower East Side of Manhattan, was someone I would often visit on my walks to my own shifts at Marion's. When I happened upon him during his setting-up process, he would be quite lucid, but when I dropped in on my way home he would be wrecked. Mig was one of two things by three in the morning: a charming, sometimes out-of-control skirt-chaser or a miserable aggressor, ready for a brawl. Either he was exchanging saliva with some innocuous strawberry-blonde or taking it outside with a suit that rubbed him the wrong way. I guarantee you, neither would ensue if he could lay off the shots.

Speaking of shots, before management got corporate at Marion's, we would often do shots during the night. Some shifts were more creative than others, as in "rainbow" nights. The challenge was to make shots for the staff during particularly gruesome shifts and we had to cover all the colors of the rainbow. First there was red: Red Devils all around—the sloe gin giving it the vermilion stain. Orange was achieved through the house classic Suburban, thanks to the blood-orange juice hobnobbing with the standard Tropicana orange juice. Yellow was my own creation, the citrus-blasted Brassy Blonde (which on the Marion's drink menu is captioned with "Only Ty and her hair-dresser know"). Green was easy: Midori liqueur mingled with a kiss of pineapple juice for the melon martini. Blue was always tricky because we had to use blue curaçao, which doesn't taste very good—so to dress up the flavor, we furnished the staff with shots of the elementary blue margarita. Violet was achieved through the raspberry martini, which got its color from Chambord liqueur shaken with Stoli Raspberi vodka.

By the time we clinked shot glasses to the melon martini we were all pretty lit and not taking any lip from the customers. A fruit fly in that Manhattan? Tough. You don't want to wait for a table? Go to B-Bar. You don't like my attitude? Good. By the time we made it to the raspberry martini, I was downright ready to do last call and go find myself a silly boy somewhere else.

These days I drink a glass of wine with my food, or the occasional shallow Bombay sapphire martini with Kurt when he's preparing dinner. The flavors are beautiful and mature, though the effects leave me with an uncomfortable feeling. They resemble the onset of panic attacks too much, so I now have an automatic timer that tells me when to quit (I wish more people had one). I have no desire to suck face with strangers, or find some meaningless hunk to drag home—I'm happy with my lot. The urge to drink for stupidity's sake has lost its charm. I've gotten too old for that.

Drinking at home also brought back the dark sensations I had concealed during my last years at Marion's. Menacingly, having that third drink with my husband or friends brought me back to the familiarity of nights drudging through my shift, unhappy and wishing I were anywhere else. Drinking for fun had lost its flavor. Those final shifts were not fun, nor were they glamorous or like some big party I was overseeing. I was sick of entertaining. Those nights were work, plain and simple. And when it starts to feel like work, a mixer should leave—for the sake of the customers as well as for her own sanity.

The last time I drank for the sake of getting drunk was a night at

Marion's I hope to one day strike from my memory. I was six years into my job, drinking two or three Makers Mark Manhattans a shift or a Tanqueray martini on the rocks, when an Irish gal, Gail, decided to drop by. She was quite unassuming, so thinking nothing of it, I served her the first of four Ketel One martinis. By the third she was getting talkative and we became drinking buddies for the night. Between clinking glasses and talking about how "men suck" and "all the good ones are gay," she started slurring, but hey, I was having a good time. It was a Monday night, so it was slow, and it sure beat reading the horoscopes in the *New York Press* or doing the *New York Times* crossword puzzle.

When she got up to go to the rest room, I watched her as she leaned on a chair for balance. She looked like a drunken sorority girl on spring break. If she were in a bikini, she'd have taken it off by now. With not a straight man in sight, she hobbled back to the bar and asked for a "last drink" before heading home. Sadly, she had to be at work at eight-thirty the next morning. I chilled her glass, shook her martini, and as I was pouring it she grabbed the glass before I could finish. Tossing the contents into her mouth, she handed me the glass for the rest. "I notished ya had some leff over lasht time. Dun wanna waste prrrfectly good boooooze."

I shook my head, feeling a little lit too, and said, "Girl, you're pathetic. Here." I poured the rest of the vodka into her glass. We clinked glasses and she made a shot out of it, swallowing it in one gulp. Suddenly she started having a hot flash, sweating profusely, and her face turned clammy and ashen.

"You okay?" I asked. "You don't look so good." She didn't respond, then placed her head on the bar as if to nap. "Hey, Gail. Wake up. You can't sleep on the bar." I pulled on her curly blonde tresses, but she wouldn't budge though she managed to shoo my hand away. I yanked a little harder and her head came up. She turned green, her eyes bugged out, and with a loud burp she vomited like a torpedo all over me. "Shit!" I yelled. Immediately I became nauseous and bolted for the bathroom, my mouth covered, my chest retching, covered in regurgitated pasta. I threw up until whatever I ate was coming out clear and I could puke no more, ultimately dry heaving for a few minutes.

When I got back to the bar, I was dizzy and feverish. After I put ice in my mouth, I noticed that Gail had vanished. She had functioned well enough to get the hell out of there, leaving me to clean up her mess. I had to pay the dishwasher ten bucks to do it for me, but it was money well spent. By the time I closed, I realized she hadn't tipped me at all! My new policy from that day on: if you're going to puke on me, it's going to cost you.

I stopped drinking that day for a very, very long time.

On October 17, 2001, I was walking to work. It was a gorgeous afternoon and I was wearing my favorite red and black vintage skirt and a tight black halter top, thinking to myself, "It feels strange to be in such glorious sunshine. To be alive in Manhattan on such a beautiful day is such an odd blessing." It had been a little over a month since the terrorist attacks of 9/11 and my beloved city had taken on a melancholy vibe. I was doing what I always did, walking to work, though I had begun carrying flowers in my hand. I made it a weekly ritual to deliver a bouquet to my fire department around the corner on Great Jones Street, a station that had lost so many wonderful men to the tragedy. I myself knew a firefighter, a regular named Erik who was a part-time actor, who had perished in the unthinkable disaster that I still couldn't wrap my mind around. Still can't.

I could see the shrine from across the street, candles burning, cards and flowers overflowing, and a handful of princely firemen scattered idle on the sidewalk. Crossing Great Jones Street, I could think only about those men, my local guys, who were now gone and unable to experience the glory of that day. Of Erik.

I suddenly felt a push and fell to the ground, the flowers crushed by my arm. I realized I had been hit on my left side by a massive car.

A parking attendant was driving an SUV backward the wrong way up the street. It would have never occurred to me to have checked that way, as cars would normally drive down from my right. I had collapsed, my leg was bleeding, my head was in a whirl, right in front of the bravest men in New York, around the corner from Marion's.

At least five firemen ran to me and got to work, initially trying to calm me down. I was in shock, and the tears began to flow. In the haze of the moment, I looked up at a woman who ran over and began screaming at the crew, "She wasn't hit! She wasn't hit! She's lying! I saw the whole thing! She just sat on the ground."

"How'd she start bleeding?" one fireman skeptically asked her.

"I'm telling you! She wasn't hit!" she continued ranting. I was sobbing, my leg was bloody, my nice skirt destroyed. And in my delirium I thought maybe I could still make it to work.

"I'm f-f-f-fine. Really, I-I-I'm okay," I said, still wailing. "I have . . . to get . . . to work."

One fireman held me down and told me not to move and that he'd tell my boss at Marion's that I was hit and going to the hospital. "No. I-I-I'm okay. Shit, m-m-my leg hurts! But I'm f-f-fine!"

Next thing I knew, I was strapped onto a stretcher with a neck brace on and was rushed, sirens and all, to St. Vincent's hospital. I asked them to call Kurt, who was still waiting tables, and they promised that they would. I don't recollect much of the ambulance ride, but when I got to the hospital I was given a full run-down. They took a lot of internal tests and I was slowly getting over the ebbing shock of being hit by a car.

When I finally pulled myself together I realized I could get some mighty fine prescription drugs out of the situation. I had nothing a Vicodin or Percocet couldn't fix. I asked for painkillers and the male nurse asked me a few questions before making the recommendation to the doctor.

"Are you allergic to anything we should know about?"

"No."

"Do you have high blood pressure?"

"I will if you don't give me the painkillers," I said and he rolled his eyes. "No."

"Are you pregnant or nursing at the present time?"

"I don't think so. No."

"What do you mean? Yes or no?"

I don't know why I got into it, but I did. "Well, my husband and I have been talking about having a baby lately, but I don't think I'm pregnant. So my answer is unequivocally no."

He raised an eyebrow. "Look, this is heavy stuff and could harm a baby. Why don't we just do a quick test and know for sure, okay?"

I laughed. "I think I'd know if I were pregnant! I'm not nauseous, dizzy or anything. I'm bloated but that's because I'm waiting for my, uh, *friend* to show any day now. I'm pretty sure that I'm not."

He pressed on. "It takes a second." I surrendered and took the cup to pee in.

Within ten minutes the nurse and a doctor took me into the checkup room and said, "No Vicodin for you, young lady! You're pregnant!"

The stone-cold nurse suddenly turned giddy. I was shocked for the second time that day. "I'm pregnant? You're *shitting* me!"

"Nope," he said. "It came back positive."

It occurred to me I had a new life in my body and was compelled to put a hand on the belly I previously thought was premenstrual and distended. Out of the blue, through no effort on my part, a huge smile enveloped my face and I felt like the happiest person alive. I began laughing uncontrollably until my ribs ached. The doctor's stern face cracked a smile. He exhaled and said, "Phew! Most people aren't so happy about the news. I'm glad to see you are."

With my knee still aching, I hopped off the shiny, steel examination table and hobbled out of the room with a new, sweeping outlook. I was going to have the little baby Kurt and I had been talking about for months. No one was going to believe it. I sat down on the beige seat outside the emergency room and caught a glimpse of Kurt running into the room through the diamond-shaped window. I motioned to him and he came running toward me.

"Are you okay? A fireman called me and told me you got hit by a car! Are you all right? What did the doctor say?" He was hurling questions at me, to which I just smiled in response. "What the hell's wrong with you? Are you still in shock?"

"Yeah, you could say that. I have something to tell you," I began.

"Uh oh. What's wrong? Did they find something?" he asked hesitantly.

I giggled. "You could say that they found something. Give me your hand." I took his hand and put it on my belly. "Do you feel anything?"

Because his mother had suffered and died of cancer, he asked, "They didn't find a lump, did they?" He looked genuinely terrified.

"No. Not that kind of lump. Congratulations, Daddy. They found a little baby."

We discovered our child was conceived on the thirteenth of September, making us a part of the much-publicized 9/11 baby-boom generation. It was apropos, getting hit by a car en route to placing flowers for the fallen heroes of my station house, to find out that I was having a 9/11 baby. It was a flawless cycle, albeit dramatic. And a sign that life goes on. It was perfect.

I could finally leave Marion's—on my own terms.

Still Want to Mix?

Drink to me.

KAMIKAZI

2 oz. vodka
½ oz. Triple Sec
½ oz. Rose's lime juice
Splash fresh lime juice

Combine ingredients into a mixing glass and shake
well. Serve in 4 shot glasses or serve as a cocktail in
a chilled martini glass. Garnish with 2 lime wedges.

So, being a masochistic fool, you still want to bartend? Well, as Benjamin Franklin once said, "There can't be good living where there is not good drinking." The living is often good but it usually involves good bartenders, which are not made overnight. Like any profession, it takes experience to get it right, to deserve the many guests who will come in one evening and look crestfallen when they find out you took that night off.

It's not exactly brain surgery but a lot goes into this walk of life, and it goes way beyond the ability to mix a few ingredients together.

On any given night people could observe me reach for glasses and bottles without ever looking, manage seven intricate and laborious drink orders, smoke a cigarette, seat a diner while the hostess is flirting in the back, answer phones (callers are put on hold indefinitely), and reapply my lipstick. God forbid if I have to take a leak and I'm five deep! Multitasking (and being able to hold it) is the most important quality to possess.

Like I said, it's experience more than anything, but if you think you need academic instruction in the matter there's always bartending school—something I do not recommend. But people always seem curious. First of all, it's very expensive and you end up learning how to make drinks like Howling Orgasm or Black Dingo—drinks that no one will ever order and I wouldn't make even if they did. When I'd ask a patron what went into a mixture with a name like that and he didn't know, I'd always say, "If you don't know what's in it, it shouldn't go in your body." Sensible enough, right?

Schools offer functional curriculums on fruit peeling for the perfect twist, how to make the notch in the lemon so it sits on the rim of the glass, orange slices that will light up your life, garnishes for every mood. Let me save you some money.

For the twist, slice the skin of the lemon or lime from end to end lengthwise in half-inch strips with your paring knife, then slice them again into thinner strips ready for twisting. Make sure to rub the skin on the rim of the glass so that the drinker tastes the oil, then twist it strongly so that the oil laces the alcohol and the shape holds. More obliging mixers will even light the skin with a match so that the oil drips into the drink, though I never had the time for such theatrics.

To make the perfect lemon, lime, or orange wedge, cut the fruit in half lengthwise from tip to tip. With your paring knife, make a slash across the vein of the fruit but *not* to the skin. Then take the half of fruit (now with a slit in the middle) and cut into wedges. The small slit will allow the fruit to slide onto the rim of any glass.

Your dispenser should also carry maraschino cherries, pearl onions, and the almighty olive. That's it.

Ever seen one of those ads for these schools? Usually there are scantily clad women with large breasts falling out of their halters and the words "MEET PEOPLE" under it. "FUN FUN FUN," says one of the school sites, and every picture looks like a big orgy. This particular school offers a ninety-two-piece flash card set with recipes, letters of recommendation, job placement assistance, and the almighty bartender's diploma. Flash cards? Huh? And I have yet to observe a bartender sporting a diploma.

If you insist on going to bartending school, I recommend Dale DeGroff, who is, for lack of a better word, *God* to bartenders from coast to coast. He's called King Cocktail for good reason. First of all, he's been at it for thirty years—now that's devotion. He has a website and teaches several courses ranging from a tour of the great bars of Manhattan to the fine art of mixing with none of the pretenses you'll find at other schools.

As a bartender I'm not of a classy background or philosophy, but Dale is. He accepts all of the glorious trappings and traditions while I believe in making the shift go as fast as possible so long as the drinks are perfect. The one thing we have in common is that we take immense pride in our mixing abilities. He's famous for a multitude of libation techniques, has served every living celebrity known to humankind, and is the man to go to when a reporter needs a liquor or bar quote for a story. He was also the first, at the Rainbow Room, to resuscitate the cocktail menu from its early days as a supper club staple item. Most of all, he's famous because he's Dale DeGroff, legendary mixologist supreme.

During the humble beginnings of my bartending career, an epicurist friend, Francis, never failed to compare any and all bartenders who served him to the legendary DeGroff. By the time he brought Dale to Marion's, I was positively intimidated. I imagined a sort of god would walk through the doors—experienced, large hands, wisdom dripping from his lips, and a condescending attitude to boot. When Dale finally arrived, I thought I should kiss his hand or something. I took pronounced care when I made his cocktails and bent over backward to make the experience exceptional. There was always a clean ashtray handy, complimentary appetizers, the never-ending cocktail that was always refilled just before he finished.

He was unbelievably gracious and laudatory of my drinks, which made me feel like the greatest bartender on earth. His laid-back disposition made it easy to talk to him and, before I knew it, he became a mortal human being like the rest of us. I am pleased to say we even became friends. In fact, during a visit to my house in East Hampton one summer, he stayed over (after a bacchanalian evening) and slept on my couch! He may as well have been Mick Jagger for all I cared— that's how cool I thought that was.

So if you insist on studying, don't hit the *Village Voice* listings— find Dale DeGroff and you will be learning from a legend. You can even purchase his beautifully crafted and noteworthy book, *The Craft of the Cocktail*, which will surely become a staple for anyone who reveres the art of mixology. It includes all of the classic and more contemporary cocktails that all bartenders need to know. My very own creation at Marion's, the Brassy Blonde, is even listed. The book will be worth every penny.

If you decide not to study, there are just a few imperative lessons to learn, such as the twenty essential cocktails I teach people when they beg me for lessons. Letter of recommendation? Marion's has yet to adopt a placement service to fill a bartender opening and I've yet to meet a bartender who's having FUN FUN FUN. I'm not trying to burst any mixology bubbles here, but let's get *real*—it's a laborious job. We'll get to the twenty drinks later to get you started on that first real bar gig, so you can pass on the bar school and learn-at-home videos.

It's better to get out there and experience life (see theater and film, travel and read) so that you'll have more to talk about with your fabulous regulars. Go to parties and learn how to flirt to the extreme. Buy sexy outfits! People can get a Sidecar anywhere, but when they want to linger on a bar stool for hours and imbibe every night, they want someone engaging shaking their drinks to pass the time with.

An interesting bartender is more valuable than someone who can make a Cat's Purr or a Twin Peak. They're also going to make a helluva lot more money.

One thing people do after a few years of bartending is launch a hyper regard for the noble world of booze. I, myself, couldn't have imagined how intricately designed the flavors would be, the years it would take to get a liquor to taste like it did. The determining oak barrels it takes to age a scotch to a peaty finish. The time it takes for a wine to ripen, full and complex. One vodka will have a smooth edge while the next has a medicinal essence. Rums could be sweet, flavored, or so intricate they are considered a sipping medium to be served in a snifter. Single-malts could be smoked in peat moss for a weathered flavor, giving off a trace of Scotland marsh, while others are smooth as silk yet go down like fire.

Cocktails should also be seasonal; I learned to love bourbon so much that the Southern-style Manhattan, with its warm, soothing effects, turned into my favorite winter drink, while the crisp Tanqueray martini reigned supreme during the hot, sweltering months. I tried different classes of bourbons for my Manhattan, finally settling on the sweet-edged Makers Mark as the best for it—heavy on the sweet vermouth and two cherries to soak up the love. What a way to end a drink! The same goes for my gin martini—olives absorb the liquor so intensely they're practically the best part.

Not all bars are what they seem. If you're serious about mixing, take a good look at the places you're considering working at. Just because the place is packed on a Friday and Saturday night doesn't mean the job is at all worth showing up for the rest of the week. Sometimes those are the best shifts and they're probably taken by the

veteran barkeeps, so beware. "Trailing" is when you follow the exist-
ing bartender around for free for a few hours, learning the bar's ins
and outs from someone who knows them well. Bartending takes a lot
out of a person physically, emotionally, and psychologically—it's
worth investigating before trailing for the job.

If you're considering a job at a nightclub, first find out if the bartenders pool their tips. Pooling is when all the mixers empty their tip
jars into one big pile of money, which they divide equally after the
busboys are paid out their percentage (usually 7 to 10 percent, which
they split among themselves). If they don't pool, then you are taking
home exactly what you have in that jar minus whatever your little
helpers, barbacks, get.

I had an unfortunate experience that taught me that lesson but
good. When the huge, multilevel nightclub Webster Hall opened, I
was one of those people who waited on long lines just to get an interview. My ex-boyfriend got me in and I got the job starting on opening night. The guest list was miles long; the club was advertising at a
frenetic pace and was the first big New York endeavor since Peter
Gatien (Limelight, the Tunnel, Club USA) got most of his clubs
closed down amidst allegations of various drug violations and tax
evasion. I was expecting to make anywhere from six hundred dollars
to a thousand opening night. I prepped for hours, working with busboys stocking up, cutting fruit, lugging beer cases, and generally
cleaning at what was to be my station: the revered VIP lounge.

In the old days of clubbing the VIP lounge had its cache and
working it could easily net a grand—and I was clinging to those illusions that night. I was prepared to work until 6 or 7 A.M. but it would
all be worth it, right? Of the fifteen bartenders, I was the only one on
my floor. Expecting celebrities and A-listers I was downright giddy
and the envy of all the bartenders hired—they were going to work in
twos on the dance floors, where the common folk were.

When we opened I could hear the commotion downstairs. It
sounded packed and the wood floors vibrated along with the bass of
the music below. My floor had a tarot-card reader, a cocktail waitress

chain-smoking with the busboy, and a security guard with a guest list that had the thickness of the Yellow Pages. I was psyched. Three hours later not a single person had come to my floor. Were they being too strict at the door? Were the celebs and coveted A-listers not showing up? Four hours later a trickle of silly Jersey girls showed up, dancing with each other in between smoking weed with the tarot-card reader. I asked one of the girls if it was busy downstairs.

"Are ya kidding? It's crazy down there! I couldn't breath, jeez!"

"How did you find the VIP lounge?" I inquired, bored to tears.

"Someone told us we could smoke pot in here. Want some?"

"No. But thanks," I said, discouraged.

Suddenly one of the girls shrieked, "Oh my gawd! Is that who I think it is? Holy shit!"

Finally, I thought, I was going to see some action. A wildly notorious tattooed rock star sauntered over to the bar and looked around the vast but empty room, a pretty girl hanging on his jacket and every mumbled word. I knew this was going to be a hideous night when the one celebrity who came to my bar the whole miserable night turned to me, opened his mouth to order, and proceeded to vomit all over the condiments. I could do nothing but look up to the chandeliered ceiling and curse whatever force put me in that God-forsaken place that night. There I was, wallowing in a rock star's regurgitation—it doesn't get lower than that. Worst of all, he didn't leave a tip! Not that he drank, mind you, but Christ, he just puked all over the garnishes and ashtrays.

Believe it or not, it got worse. At six o'clock in the morning, after I had served about fifteen people the *whole* night, I was told by the manager that the house did not pool their tips. I asked him to repeat himself because I thought he said that the house *didn't* pool.

"That's right. We don't pool. We rotate the bartenders," he said, emptying my cash register.

"But I worked eleven hours and made thirty-three dollars all night. We have to pool or it wouldn't be fair," I protested.

"That's why we *rotate*."

I must have turned purple because he practically sprinted out with his money and didn't even attempt to console me. I took the thirty-three dollars I made and left, never to return. The moral of this tale is make sure the club pools or you'll get stuck working for almost nothing while everyone else makes all the money.

And if you're the new guy, you'll get the less desirable shifts to begin with whether the place is a club, bar, or restaurant. If you end up interviewing for a restaurant gig, make sure that the shifts available are decent. If you agree to a schedule that consists only of Sunday, Monday, and a brunch shift—and most places will start you off on the lowest possible rung—then you will not make enough money to survive in Manhattan. We're talking thirty to eighty dollars a shift.

Be wary when they say better shifts always come along. That's code for, "We can't keep a bartender so they're always quitting." Or they fire them at the drop of a hat. There's something wrong when they're losing bartenders that fast and believe me, it'll be a waste of your time.

Go to the establishment on a Friday or Saturday night. If it's slammed, you'll make a lot of money on those nights—a given for any place. Obviously, if you can hear a pin drop or if it's dead as dirt, pass. Try a Wednesday or Thursday, because if the place is brimming with customers it means it has a loyal local following. Regulars will be your bread and butter, so take note on those nights when transient, bridge-and-tunnel types don't flock to restaurants. Also, if the place advertises more than one specials nights, they're positively desperate for customers.

If the joint is packed Thursday through Saturday night, check to see how many bartenders are on. If there is more than one working, you'll be splitting all your money with him. In other words, the tip jar will have four hundred dollars and you'll be walking home with two hundred minus whatever is tipped out to the barbacks, busboys, and sometimes even the hostess. If you are looking to make serious cash, you want to be the only one on.

At my uptown bar gig, the owners insisted on two bartenders for every shift except brunch. They thought the service was better, but all I ended up accomplishing was catching up on my reading. On my Monday shift I would have to split the one hundred dollars made with the bitch of a bartender I had to mix with, and skulk home with a paltry fifty bucks minus whatever I paid out to our helpers. She was invariably tormenting me to leave early so that she could pocket whatever was left after the majority of diners dashed out for their Lincoln Center shows.

Look around. Who's drinking at the bar you're considering working at? Suits sprinkling the joint equal drunken brawls and light tippage. Does the place have an extensive wine list? People are going there to *eat*, not drink. Your customers will be diners waiting for their table to free up so they can go sit down. You're just their stepping-stone to the real drinking they intend to do that night. Eurotrash bars are awful! You'll be drowning in cheap cologne, climbing over BMW motorcycles to catch a cab, and get relentlessly handled by men you wouldn't touch with a ten-foot pole. Plus they haven't a clue how to tip. Are the lushes sitting at the bar as gay as the roaring twenties? You'll be making truckloads of money and have a blast doing it. They're some of the finest tippers in town—and they will provide *you* with great advice for a change.

Do you see a lot of your favorite bartenders hanging out somewhere in particular? You want that job more than anything in the world. Nobody tips like other bartenders—and you can commiserate all night long and get great bartending wisdom.

The worst is when a restaurant or bar gives you hope. They tell you that you're wonderful, just the kind of bartender they need. You're asked to come in to trail one of the other barkeeps. That's code for come in and work for free so we can tell if we want you or not. That seems fair to an extent—just make sure it's only once or twice and then only for a few hours at most. If you find you've been trailing twice a week for a month or more and for long, arduous hours, chances are they're using you for free help. Sad but true, there are corrupt bar owners who don't mind for a minute wasting your valuable time and dashing your bartending dreams.

Use your instinct. Is the mixer you've been trailing nice or competitive? How does she feel about management? What is she saying about the place? Do the managers treat you like transient help? If it feels wrong, it probably is, so get out of there pronto.

Ever notice that some bars have ladies or other specials night? It's a lot like happy hour, where you get discount drinks from so-and-so time through whenever, or the situation is buy-one-get-one-free. First, it's usually on a slow night or early in the evening, so the main goal is to get living, breathing human beings in the place. Before Marion's incorporated a specials night, I would be standing around reading magazines all night, dreaming about what I could be doing if I didn't have to work on this crappy shift I could never get rid of. You look at the clock every five minutes and the night seems to be moving in slow motion.

Most bars and restaurants have implemented events like this, and most of the time it serves the owners more than the bartender. If the place is empty on a Sunday or Monday, then you've got food rotting in the walk-ins, kitchen and wait staff to pay for doing nothing, and other overhead concerns that just aren't worth it.

The bar is the most profitable end of the restaurant business because the markup is so unbelievably high. You're paying eight dollars for a glass of house red wine that cost six dollars wholesale for the bottle. So if they get six glasses of wine out of it, then the house just made a forty-two-dollar profit after subtracting the cost of the bottle. And that's just wine. Imagine what they make off hard liquor. Plus, at times our liquor distributor will get unbelievable deals that reap the restaurant even more money. He ends up going to Chile for a free vacation because he pawned all that cheap Chilean wine on us, beating out the other distributors. And let me say, he's enjoyed *a lot* of free vacations because of Marion's low-end price point selling his merchandise. I used to mix on Monday nights and they were dreadful to work. I'd usually make around a hundred bucks, which just didn't cut it when the other nights reaped so much more. Management suggested a specials night and so Metro Monday was born. Casey, the other head mixer, had created the Metropolitan because we couldn't give the new Absolut Kurant away. He basically substituted Kurant for Citron and garnished it with a lime instead of a twist. If you like Robitussin cough suppressant, then you'd *love* the Metro.

Metro Monday turned into the most frightening shift of my week. The idea was that it was buy-one-get-one-free *all* night. It lured the cheapest, scariest mob I'd ever seen—and these people were locals. It used to be that bridge-and-tunnel types could drive me to the edge of insanity, but these people made me actually yearn for the accents and Jersey girls. When you give away free booze, you wouldn't believe the types of reckless, alcohol-deprived sots who come crawling out of their hovels. What was funny was that most of them didn't even like the taste of the Metro, complaining all night that it tasted like "swamp water," "cat piss," and my personal favorite, "rotten lime juice laced with cough syrup." But they kept on drinking and drinking. It got so busy that I was making "swamp water" by the pitcherful, hoping to catch my cigarette ash from falling in as there was no time for breaks except when making the dreadful cocktail.

For all the business it brought in, I probably made an extra thirty dollars because these people were cheap. And it wasn't as if they ordered food at the bar—shit, they were there for the free booze. Why ruin the fun and absorb the alcohol with actual sustenance when you can get so tanked that you're hugging the toilet after your tenth Metro? Cutting off people left and right, adding my grat to their checks because the crowd thought a $1 tip was fine for six drinks, and working so hard I had "waiter's foot" every Monday left me begging management to end the insanity. Tough, they said, and it went on for two more years.

So when you hear about some buy-one-get-one-free deal, there's a catch. You could be drinking vile-tasting concoctions the joint couldn't give away for free, which is what we did.

On the rare night that not a soul ventured in, usually during the summers when people are frolicking in the Hamptons, I would call some friends in and have them sit by the windows up front in our lounge. It always attracted people. I would fuel my friends' appearance with free cocktails and they were happy to oblige. That was better than Metro Monday. Smiling at cute boys who walked by helped, as they would come in and have a few on the house—and stayed for the free entertainment: me. Anything but Metro Monday. Begging the only two people at my bar not to leave as they donned their coats, refilling their drinks, forcing them to stay, worked. I did anything to make the place seem busy to attract other patrons walking by, just to get a new following going so that the hateful Metro madness night finally bit the dust. Eventually my shift's crowd evolved into a wonderful blend of acquaintances, cute boys, and East Village locals who became addicted to the place. Mission accomplished.

pet peeve no. 18 --->

> Bartenders don't like being told how to make a drink—especially those of us who have been doing it for a long time. It drives me to the brink when people tell me that I'm not making a drink the right way. It's like telling a chef that he doesn't know how to boil water.

<--

There are basic bar essentials (either at the job or at a home bar) all budding mixers should own, and they start with the tools of the trade. Because martinis are all the rage at the moment, let's start with the shaker. I don't like a shaker that is made entirely of stainless steel. I prefer a glass shaker so I know how much I'm pouring (I hate backfill). My husband is always making his twice-weekly sapphire gin martini and I'm constantly draining the two ounces left at the bottom. The top that goes on preshaking can be either the stainless-steel cap with the little nub that comes off with the spout for pouring, or the one I prefer, a stainless-steel twenty-eight ouncer with the vinyl coating for a good grip on shaking.

The handy bottle cap opener—a device constantly brought home by bartenders because they're always sticking them in their back pockets for fast use—is invaluable. You'll be opening a lot of beer bottles, Pellegrinos, and the like. I vote for a natural beechwood handle and heavy-gauge nickel-plated stainless-steel opener. Same goes for the corkscrew for the many wines you'll be uncorking. I'm not a fan of the wing corkscrew—you know, the one you screw in, then pull down the wings until the cork pops out. Too much work goes into it. I'm partial to the pull type, also called the "waiter's" corkscrew, that works like a car jack. Make sure it's got a sharp, straight-edge fold-out knife for foil cutting and a tight fit on the mouth of the bottle for easy gravity. Most nights at the job, depending on the establishment, you'll be opening up to thirty or forty bottles, so make it your friend. The key to this tool, I've found, is to be quite butch about the process. I can't tell you how many nimble waitresses have come running to me from a disgruntled table of wine extremists because they couldn't seem to pull the plug out. I'd command them to emote masculinity and pretend they're a man. To stop being so girly about it. Screw it in, give it all your body weight, pull, and pop! You can't pull out dozens of corks by being demure and feminine.

There are many more basics, such as the classic cocktail strainer for all the martinis you'll be pouring. It should be four-prong stainless steel with a six-inch-long handle. The long bar spoon for those who prefer stirred cocktails also comes in handy for a multitude of other tasks (i.e., spooning olives, picking dead fruit flies out of a returned drink, pulling the cigarette butts from your condiments, and even unclogging the drain). It should also be stainless steel, have a rubber stop at the end, and be the standard eleven inches long.

I don't really understand the jigger, which is supposed to measure the alcohol going into the mixing glass. Never used one in my life. Never even seen one used at a bar. It looks a lot like a soft-boiled-egg cup, only made of stainless steel. One side holds exactly one ounce and the other an ounce and a quarter. If you insist on using one, or if the bar requires that you do, it should be triple weld, and some come with long handles for easy carrying. Marion's had always had a freestyle, heavy-handed approach, much to the owners' distress, in which we used the four-count method: counting to four with a half-second pause in between made for a perfect pour. Eventually you will be able to pour by sight, but until then, learn the four count.

You'll need a lot of bottle stoppers, especially for champagne, which goes flat rather quickly. It should be nickel-plated with a superseal plug. Be careful removing these from champagne bottles as I've seen them fly off with force and poke bartenders in the eye— myself included. The bottle pour spout is indispensable for all the liquors you will be working with. I like the steel top with the rugged black plastic plug. It adjusts to a wider range of bottle sizes. I absolutely despise the ones that stop pouring after an ounce. I mean, is this stupid plastic *thing* going to tell *me* when my concoction is going to taste right? Plus, when I have used them, nearly 95 percent of the drinks have come back because there wasn't enough alcohol. Whoever thought of it was a cheap bastard.

The muddler is a pretty common tool nowadays. It's a long, wooden sticklike object used in mashing condiments (fruits, sugars, or ice) for classics such as the Old-Fashioned and the mint julep. It's construction should be of solid wood and be exactly eight inches long.

Making a comeback is the three-tier margarita glass-rimmer. The trays fan out for easy-access glass rimming, with a tier for kosher salt and a tier for sugar (for Sidecars, daiquiris, coffee drinks). The top opens to a round, flat sponge that gets soaked with Roses lime juice or just plain water so that you can wet the brim of the glass before dipping. It's an old-time classic and considered a staple for any bar.

The bar spill mat is compulsory, if you're a slob like me, to protect any counter from getting wet, sticky, and damaged. Some bars use folded napkins but the mats clean easily and make you look more competent to boot. They fit any standard bar rail, and if you've got a really groovy sixties bar in the corner of your studio apartment, you'll want one if you don't want to defile your counter.

Spirits are the heart of the bar, the point of its existence. One or two of each of the following is necessary for your bar to be considered fully stocked. I would splurge and get top shelf (name brands) as opposed to well liquor (cheaper brands) because your drinks will taste better, people will appreciate them and tell all their friends that you throw a kicking party. Just trust me on this. I'll give you my choice top-shelf names if you choose to go this route.

Vodka: Ketel One and Stolichnaya

Flavored vodka: (a big trend and used in different variations of the Cosmopolitan) Absolut Citron, Stoli Oranj, Stoli Raspberry, Stoli Vanilla.

Gin: Bombay Sapphire and Tanqueray

Rum: Bacardi light and dark

Flavored rum: Captain Morgan's

Blended scotch: Johnnie Walker Black and Dewars

Single-malt scotch: Maccallans (smooth) and Lagavulin (peaty)

Bourbon: Makers Mark and Knob Creek

Tequila (*To'killya*): Cuervo Gold and Sauza Conmemorativo

Sweet vermouth: (go Italian here) Cinzano

Dry vermouth: (take the French route here) Noilly Prat

Brandy/Cognac: Courvoisier VSOP and Remy Martin VSOP

Aperitif (there are many to choose from but these are my must-haves): Campari, Lillet, Dubonnet, a dry sherry, port (Fonseca), Bonnie Dune dessert wine, Bailey's, Kahlua, Franjelico, Sambuca, and Fernet Branca.

Flavorings and mixers are equally as important if you're preparing cocktails or mixed drinks. The fundamentals are: Angostura bitters, Rose's lime juice, grenadine, worcestershire sauce, cocktail olives, pearl onions, maraschino cherries, salt, and sugar. The array of juices are simple: cranberry, grapefruit, orange, pineapple, and tomato; you will also need cream for White Russians and the like. Additional garnishes should be kept to a tight but small selection: limes (wedges), lemons (wedges and twists), and oranges (slices).

There you have it! Whether you are debuting a cozy neighborhood pub to impress your girlfriend, practicing to be a bartender, or if you're just setting up a cool bar in your living room, barring any kooky themes, these are all the gadgets and ingredients you will need to be a grand success.

There's more to the job than mixing drinks and socializing. You'll be sporting a lot of different hats, depending on the bar. If you feel uncomfortable with any of these extra responsibilities they throw at you, it's best to look elsewhere.

Some nights you're the joint's security man, or "beefeater," so to speak. You have to have a thick skin to cut someone off, to which he will without exception reply, "I'm fine, no really, I'm FINE!" After the diplomatic cut-off, an argument will inevitably ensue and you're hurling the sod out the door into the night, praying he makes it home alive. Sometimes I paid for a cab out of my own tips after fishing for an address in his wallet. A manager is not always available, and playing bouncer was always my least favorite part of the job.

Most nights you're playing the house policeman. When you hear the words, "Can I have a Midori Sour?" you will *have* to card. The underage crowd always ask for the sweetest possible drinks. (Look out for the Negotiators here—there's no changing prices to accommodate a light wallet. Plus, they won't tip you.) Same goes for when someone orders an Amaretto Sour, SoCo shot, Red Devil, sloe gin fizz, Screaming Orgasm, peach schnapps shot, Sex on the Beach, Buttery Nipple, Toasted Almond, WooHoo shot, or the notorious Lemon Drop. (I also card when someone asks how much a beer costs, just to fluster him. Yeah, it's mean. But not only is he giving it away that he's probably underage, but he's also telling me that he won't have enough to tip me later.)

And yes, you do have to be a counselor.

There was a certain bartender at my favorite Irish dive, Milano's, called Sal, who I'm guessing was in his early sixties. He'd been around. He worked the morning shift and catered to other older gentlemen starting their days at eight-thirty with stout and shots of scotch. He was cynical and fun to watch, his catchphrase being "Hope it chokes you" as he put the drink in front of his regular. He told me you had to be a psychiatrist to be a great bartender; and as far as clichés go, he's right on the money.

Where else do people go when they lose a loved one, get a divorce, are depressed, file for bankruptcy, or any other difficult human experience you can think of? You guessed it. They're parked right in front of me telling me all about how they were left standing at the altar, whether I give a shit or not. Some nights the patron would be on his third cocktail, spewing his guts, and I'd be making drinks for everyone in the dining room plus all the others sitting at the bar. Did he know I was too busy to listen to his saga of having to put his dog down? Did I care? Probably not, but that's why he was there, for *anyone* to listen to him. Let's face it, I was trapped. I'd be throwing him glances between shaking a martini and nodding sympathetically, pretty much hoping I was going to make a decent tip out of this.

If it wasn't a busy evening, not very often at Marion's, I would give customers my full attention. *And* give a shit. I have lended a caring ear when regulars needed to relate their horrific breakups, with updates every time they came back—which was daily or weekly— and have stood up for their rights in the relationship. I have held in my arms customers who had lost friends and swayed them until they stopped sobbing. I have watched people meet and come back a year later for their wedding reception, thanking me for making their dreams come true by playing matchmaker. I will prick up an ear when they tell me in graphic detail their sexual problems and ask what I would do if I were them. I've played liar's poker with customers who had no friends and frequented the bar for any connection with a human being; and in between losing twenty dollars to me, they would tell me about their childhoods or how lonely they were.

As Sal said, performing as a psychiatrist is a sure way to reap vast amounts of money, though while I was doing it I did aim to give the customers mindful attention. But be warned, it gets tiring after a while.

You could say that through all the bullshit, bartenders are also entertainers. They're on that platform to make sure you have a good time. The flirting is part of that, but it's not where it ends. Not all bar relationships are tinged with sexual innuendos. A great bartender must love to talk to people. But what do we talk about?

As I've said before, the best bartenders know a little about *everything*. We must read the papers, because discussions about current events are common at the bar. We must know something about religion, politics, and public happenings. We must see movies, plays, and read books. It doesn't hurt to know about astrology (what's your sign?), art, fashion, history, and travel. A basic knowledge of cultural milestones is essential. For many of the guests at your bar, you *are* the entertainment. And if you're not in the mood—fake it.

The owners would tell us, in the rare staff meeting, "You are the show, so make it grand!" They wanted us to don wigs, push-up bras, false eyelashes, boas, and vintage, sexy clothing. We were told to be foxy, crusty, and absurd all at the same time. They begged us to put together little shows and perform them on certain nights.

On some evenings the place could pass for the Moulin Rouge: people getting up and dancing on tables, martinis spilling, cigarette smoke gliding above our heads (back when you could still smoke at the tables), waitrons getting drunk—hell, we were all drunk—and lip-synching to songs by The Supremes and other divas, the disco ball spinning, and the world in which the diners were eating their steak au poivre was somewhere in France in another time. It was this philosophy, of joie de vivre and bohemian optimism, that gave Marion's its allure and luster. And longevity.

A couple of hopeful mixers had asked me to teach them how to bartend and I obliged by having them come by Marion's at opening time when it was still relatively slow. Within three one-hour lessons on Monday nights, they were well on their way to shaking classic cocktails at any establishment in New York City. I explained to my students that there were twenty essential drinks to know to set their new career in motion. The rest of the knowledge comes *on* the job because every establishment is different, with disparate customers, wine lists, beer choices, etc. So here are the twenty cocktails you *must* know before you walk through those doors for an interview:

CLASSIC DRY MARTINI
3½ oz. gin or vodka
1 drop dry vermouth

Stir or shake and strain into a chilled cocktail glass. Garnish with one or three cocktail olives. For a WET martini add ½ oz. dry vermouth. For a PERFECT martini add ½ oz. sweet vermouth and ½ oz. dry vermouth and garnish with a twist. For a DIRTY martini add a dollop of olive juice. For a GIBSON substitute olives with pearl onions.

MADRAS
1½ oz. vodka
3½ oz. orange juice
1½ oz. cranberry juice cocktail

Pour over ice in a highball glass and garnish with a lime wedge. For a SEABREEZE substitute orange juice with grapefruit juice. For a BAYBREEZE substitute orange juice with pineapple juice.

MANHATTAN

2 oz. blended whiskey
1 oz. Italian sweet vermouth
2 dashes Angostura bitters

Stir and strain into a chilled cocktail glass.
Garnish with a cherry. For a PERFECT MANHATTAN
add 1 oz. dry vermouth and 1 oz. sweet vermouth
and garnish with a twist. Down South (and my preference),
BOURBON MANHATTANS are the choice.

MARGARITA

2½ oz. tequila
1 oz. Cointreau
½ oz. fresh lime juice

Combine ingredients in a mixing glass with ice.
Shake well and strain into a chilled, salted cocktail glass.
Salting the rim: Rim the edge of the cocktail glass by
rubbing a lime wedge on the outside rim of the glass,
then dip it into a saucer of coarse salt.

APPLE MARTINI

1½ oz. premium vodka
½ oz. sour apple schnapps
½ oz. Triple Sec
Splash fresh lime juice
Splash Rose's lime juice

Combine ingredients in a mixing glass with
ice and shake. Strain into a chilled cocktail glass.
Garnish with a twist.

MELON MARTINI

1 ½ oz. citrus-flavored vodka
½ oz. Midori
Splash fresh lime juice
Splash Rose's lime juice
½ oz. pineapple juice

Combine ingredients in a mixing glass
with ice and shake. Strain into a chilled
cocktail glass. Garnish with an orange slice.

BLOODY MARY

1 ½ oz. vodka
2 dashes worcestershire
4 dashes Tabasco
Pinch of salt and pepper
¼ oz. fresh lemon juice
4 oz. tomato juice

Combine ingredients in a tall glass and stir to mix.
Garnish with a wedge of lemon and lime.
Dash of celery salt is optional, and New Yorkers
add horseradish.

GIMLET

2 ½ oz. vodka or gin
½ oz. Rose's lime juice
Splash fresh lime juice

Shake ingredients with ice and strain into a
chilled cocktail glass or serve over ice.
Garnish with a lime wedge.

GREYHOUND

1½ oz. vodka and grapefruit juice

Pour together into an iced highball glass and garnish with a lime wedge. For a SALTY DOG rim the edge of the glass by rubbing a lime wedge on the outside rim of the glass, then dip it into a saucer of coarse salt. For a CAPE COD substitute grapefruit juice with cranberry juice. For a SCREWDRIVER substitute grapefruit juice with orange juice.

IRISH COFFEE

1½ oz. Irish whiskey
Coffee
Lightly whipped cream

Combine whiskey and coffee in an Irish coffee or Collins glass. Ladle one inch of cream on top. Garnish with three coffee beans.

COSMOPOLITAN

2½ oz. citrus-flavored vodka
½ oz. Triple Sec
¼ oz. fresh lime juice
½ oz. cranberry juice

Shake all ingredients with ice. Strain into a chilled cocktail glass. Garnish with a twist. For a METROPOLITAN, substitute the citrus vodka with Absolut Kurant and garnish with a lime wedge.

LONG ISLAND ICED TEA
½ oz. vodka
½ oz. gin
½ oz. rum
½ oz. tequila
½ oz. Triple Sec
¾ oz. fresh lemon juice
½ oz. sour mix
Splash Coca-Cola

Combine all the ingredients except Coca-Cola and stir.
Top with Coca Cola and serve in a Collins glass.
Garnish with a wedge of lemon or lime.

SEX ON THE BEACH
1½ oz. vodka
½ oz. peach schnapps
2 oz. cranberry juice
2 oz. pineapple juice

Shake and strain into an iced highball glass.
Garnish with a lime wedge.

COLLINS
**(*Tom* is with vodka or use whatever the
customer wants as the base liquor. Some like
gin, and I've even made a tequila Collins.)**
1½ oz. base liquor
1 oz. sour mix
¾ oz. fresh lime juice
Soda

Shake gin or vodka, sour mix and lime juice with ice and strain
into an iced Collins glass and fill with soda. Garnish with a
cherry and an orange slice.

SOURS

(Whiskey, Amaretto, Vodka, Bourbon, or Gin)
2 oz. base liquor
¾ oz. fresh lime juice
2 oz. sour mix

Combine all ingredients in a mixer with ice. Shake and strain
into an iced rocks glass. Garnish with an
orange slice and cherry.

FRENCH MARTINI

2 oz. premium vodka
½ oz. Chambord
1½ oz. pineapple juice

Shake all ingredients with ice and strain into a chilled martini
glass. Garnish with a twist.

BELLINI

1 oz. peach schnapps
4 oz. champagne

Pour the peach schnapps into the bottom of a champagne glass
and top with champagne. For a KIR ROYALE substitute peach
schnapps with crème de cassis. For a CHAMPAGNE
COCKTAIL combine champagne with an Angostura
Bitters—soaked sugar cube.

SPRITZER

White wine with ice and a splash of club soda. Garnish with a
lemon peel. For a KIR omit club soda and add ½ oz. crème de
cassis to the white wine.

SIDECAR

2 oz. brandy
½ oz. Cointreau
Splash fresh lime juice
Splash sour mix

Combine ingredients in a mixing glass with ice.
Shake well and strain into a chilled, sugar-rimmed cocktail
glass. Garnish with a twist.

WHITE RUSSIAN

1 oz. vodka
1 oz. Kahlua
1 oz. heavy cream

Combine in a mixing glass and shake.
Serve in an iced rocks glass. For a
BLACK RUSSIAN, omit the heavy cream.

With this minimal familiarity with the most popular cocktails, you should be well on your way to an award-winning mixology career. And for insider bar terms, here is a brief glossary that may come in handy:

86: To cut a drinker off, as in: "They're 86'd." Or refers to something the bar has run out of, as in: "86 Kahlua and Stoli." Can also mean to banish a customer forever, as in: "You're 86'd, now get the fuck out!"

Baby-sitter: Refers to the manager or the person in charge of the current shift.

Back of the house: Usually a term used for the kitchen or can also refer to the office.

Break down: To clean and close up the bar for the night, as in: "I'm breaking down the bar for the night."

British: Means getting stiffed (a waiter checks the charge slip for the tip and says to the bartender, who is looking on, "The tip is British!").

Buy-back: Refers to a free drink, usually the third drink for regulars, which is a standard policy for most bars. Also see "COMP."

Call liquors: Name-brand liquors (e.g., Absolut, Dewars).

Campers: Customers who linger for hours not ordering anything.

Card: To check that a customer is of drinking age.

Church: A person's sexual orientation, as in: "He belongs to my church."

Comp: A free drink or other item. Also refers to the act of giving the free item.

Cut off: To stop serving a customer who is too intoxicated or clearly out of control.

Dirty: To add olive juice to a martini that is already being served with an olive as a garnish.

Drop: To deliver the food to the customer, as in: "Ty, did you drop the appetizers yet?"

Dupe: Refers to the ticket or pad of paper ("dupe pad") that a drink or food order is written on.

Extreme bartending: When bartenders do tricks to impress silly girls and potential lovers. Usually entails flipping bottles, throwing utensils between two mixers, and setting rinds aflame to create a show for the audience, their customers. See Tom Cruise do it in *Cocktail.*

Fire: To notify the kitchen to start cooking the order, as in: "Chef, you can fire table ten."

Floating 20: The twenty-dollar bill that one bartender tips another when visiting his bar, which will be given back as a tip when the receiving mixer returns the favor.

Floor: Refers to the dining room, as in: "I'm on the floor to-night."

Four count: Refers to the oral or mental counting by a mixer to measure the amount of liquor in a drink, usually for three or four ounces of liquor.

Grazing: Customers who sit for hours and eat the bar snacks or empty the garnish dispenser.

Hair of the dog: A cocktail to have in the morning should you have a hangover. For it to alleviate the agony you're going through, it should be a shot of whatever wrecked you the night before.

In the weeds: Used when describing the frenetic pace at which you are working. Usually describes a state when it's so busy you can hardly catch your breath. Also called Getting SLAMMED.

Last call: Final offering of alcoholic beverages before the establishment closes down. Often a bartender's favorite two words.

Lifers: People who work in the service industry for decades or their whole life. Also the worst nightmare of anyone pursuing creative dreams (e.g., acting, writing, etc.).

Mixer: Bartender.

Mixology: The field of bartending.

Neat: To serve a drink without ice.

Orphan: See REGULAR.

Perfect: To make a drink with both dry and sweet vermouth.

Pooling: When two or more bartenders combine their tips for the night in order to divide them equally between them.

Postal: To lose your temper with a customer.

Regular: Commonly used to describe a customer who frequents the bar more than once a month. Regulars are also referred to as ORPHANS. Think Norm on the sitcom *Cheers*.

Rocks: Ice; also to serve a drink with ice, as in "on the rocks."

Spotter: The spy who is hired by management to watch a bartender to see if he is stealing or giving away too many comps.

Stiff: When a customer leaves less than 10 percent or no gratuity at all, as in "I got stiffed." See BRITISH.

Stock: To replenish items that have run out.

Suits: Wall Street–type customers; patrons who come in wearing business attire, but don't let that fool you. They almost never tip well.

Tab: An open-ended bill that will be paid at the end of the visit or at some other point with the approval of the bartender or manager.

Tippage: Tipping situation (aka grats or gratuity).

Top shelf: See CALL LIQUORS, as in: "I'll have a top-shelf margarita."

Up: To serve a drink without ice in a martini or cocktail glass, as in "a Sidecar straight up."

Waiter's foot: When you're on your feet so long that they ache painfully. Can also feel like the arch of the foot will collapse.

Waitron: Refers to a waiter or food server.

Walk-out: Describes a patron(s) who runs out without paying his check or tab.

Well liquor: Cheap or no-name brands as opposed to Call or Top-shelf liquors. Many a broke customer has said, "Just make the martini *well* vodka."

Wet: To add more dry vermouth to a martini.

Whiskey dick: The inability to get an erection after consuming too much alcohol.

THE MASTER NEW YORK BAR REGISTER

(Ty's Favorites)

Double Happiness – Old speakeasy with fab interior and cool scene: 173 Mott Street

Boiler Room – Gay bar/lounge with great beer on tap: 86 East 4th Street

Botanica – Dark neighborhood bar with cushy couches: 47 Houston Street

Milano's – My favorite dive with the best jukebox: 51 Houston Street

Tom & Jerry's (aka 288) – Local bar with great mixers: 288 Elizabeth Street

Fanelli – Neighborhood pub before loft prices skyrocketed: 94 Prince Street

Blue Ribbon – Great raw bar and bartenders: 97 Sullivan Street

Raoul's – Hip local French bistro: 180 Prince Street

Bubble Lounge – Sexy lounge and wine bar: 228 Broadway

Odeon – Tribeca Art Deco institution: 145 West Broadway

Chumley's – Old speakeasy but stay away from on weekends: 86 Bedford

D.B.A. – Legendary dive with great tequilas and beers: 41 First Avenue

Von – Rustic neighborhood lounge: 3 Bleecker Street

Temple Bar – Dark and sexy, with martinis *almost* as good as mine: 330 Lafayette Street

Beauty Bar – Great kitsch and martinis, plus you can get your hair done: 231 East 14th Street

Opium Den – Great deejays and booths with a Persian vibe: 29 East 3rd Street

Spring Lounge (aka Shark Bar) – Neighborhood dive bar: 48 Spring Street

Wonder Bar – Funky, informal gay haunt: 505 East 6th Street

Bob – Living-room-style local bar with great tunes: 235 Eldridge Street

continued on next page

Sapphire Lounge – Smallest dance club and cheapest drinks: 249 Eldridge Street

Kush – Moroccan bar featuring belly dancers and great wine: 165 Ludlow Street

Tonic – Lounge with live music: 107 Norfolk Street

Max Fish – Classic Lower East Side dive: 178 Ludlow Street

You may end up working at a kooky place like Marion's and be required to sing, wear silly outfits, and maybe even perform with drag queens. Like my bosses always said, "The restaurant is your stage," whether you like it or not. If you want to make any real money, get into it—you might even enjoy it.

Marion's frequently put on themes for the joy and titillation of its fantasy-embracing clientele. When Pan Am went under it became a Marion's theme in which they purchased paraphernalia like uniforms, decoratives, Pan Am pins, and the like. Dinners were served on Pan Am trays and waiters asked, "Coffee, tea, or me?" Which leads me to the theme the Mile High Club. We were required to dress as if we were slutty stewardesses with neckerchiefs, polyester striped shirts, and micromini skirts. Customers asked incessantly if I'd like to join them in the john.

pet peeve no. 19

> For Chrissake, if your favorite bartender is leaving, and she's given you what seems like a million free drinks, go in on her last night and wish her good luck and farewell—especially if she begs you not to. It's a relationship you nurtured and partook of for many years. And despite everything she says, she really does want to see you.

There was the Playboy Mansion, a notorious failure, though it sounded good in theory. The men were to dress in silk pajamas and the girls in a bunny suit, tail, cuffs, bow tie, etc. Male customers were relentless in their crude conduct and women sneered with deep glares of hatred. I was interrogated by customers who asked morality-based questions, in addition to how I felt about women's lib. One of the managers, an ex-bunny in real life, was asked to play cocktail waitress. She was tormented by the patrons and lasted one day as a Marion's bunny. Nothing gave me more pleasure than, after three or four shifts of this misogynistic hell, to ball up the bunny ears, tail, cuffs, and bodysuit and slam-dunk it into the trash bin.

The least successful theme was Cowboys & Cowgirls. We wore the hats—even ordered extra to give away to customers—loads of flannel (not sexy enough for a bartendress), denim (yawn), and decorated the place. The thing that most customers complained about was the dreadful music. There were two tapes playing in a kind of loop: hours of Hank Williams, Loretta Lynn, Dwight Yoakam, and the like. Our clientele was accustomed to the melodies of the lounge, vocalists of the swing period; Billie Holliday lamenting through a tune, Diana Krall sparkling, and Frank Sinatra tempting them with love; so you can imagine this came off as torture for our poor cowpoke patrons. They bellyached to no avail, and I never made so little money through a theme before. No amount of batting my eyelashes could make up for it.

The climax was the annual Kahiki Lounge, which you already know about. *Everything* changed. We even hired cabana boys and drag queens to pass around small shots of the cocktails to diners. Martinis were at a minimum and frozen drinks took over. Pupu platters abounded, bringing an all-new meaning to *fire hazard*. Hurricanes, piña coladas, daiquiris, margaritas, and other predictable frozen cocktails served liberally made my life a sticky hell. I cursed other bartenders who worked in Mexican restaurants who only need pull a lever and *voilà!* the perfect margarita.

New Year's Eve was always a crowd pleaser. The exalted night came with a theme and people came dressed for the occasion. Just to name a few: Glam Rock, Seventies Prom Night, Black & White, Blue Moon, and my personal favorite, 007 James Bond. I was going to be the Goldfinger girl, so I dressed head to toe in gold lamé and spray-painted my hair. I bought gold skin powder, which I applied to the visible parts of my body, and I was confident that the effect was going to be quite glossy. Much to everyone's mortification, by eleven-thirty the powder had turned to a blotchy, shabby brown from all the sweating I was doing—seven deep and drunkenness overflowing. I glaringly resembled someone impersonating a black woman. To this day my spray-painted Doc Martens are hanging on a nail high up in the Marion's kitchen.

"Be bright and jovial among your guests tonight," Macbeth said. It's a restaurant's mantra. Even if you feel like shit, *smile*. Even if you've got cramps and are PMS-ing like Medusa on LSD, *smile*. Even if you say you can't do this any longer, flirt like you've been on a deserted island for ten years. Even if you're seven months pregnant and can no longer see into the beer cooler, work those maternity tips by engaging everyone's whims.

Still sound like fun?

pet peeve no. 20 ....➤

> People who don't know how to have a good time. If you're in a crappy mood, stay home.

◄...

Yeah, you can make a lot of new friends, meet potential lovers, and rake in the bucks, all while having the time of your life. Just remember to enjoy the rest of what the world has to offer. Don't waste your newfound riches on getting drunk every night like so many bartenders I know—it's too easy to destroy yourself in this line of work. Instead, travel around the world, buy a cottage, see some theater, or write a book. You'll finally have the time and money to do such previously unimaginable things if you time it all right.

If there's anything I learned as a mixer, it's that life is hard and you will see it up close and double-magnified standing behind that bar. Just remember, the patrons you serve are not just drunks, sots, and lushes. They're human beings, despite how you're going to feel

about them on some nights. They're going to be annoying, belligerent, and sometimes even dangerous. It's your responsibility to keep
people from getting out of control and, despite themselves, getting
them home in one piece. In most states, you're liable for their safety.
Their madness, sadness, and joys will be shared with you, whether
you give a shit or not. I like to believe that the slurring guy sitting in
front of you isn't what he appears to be—that it's the booze talking
when he tells you he's in love with you, or barks that you're a bitch,
and especially when he warns you to watch your back because he
promises he'll be back to get his revenge for cutting him off.

A good bartender takes everything with a grain of salt.

Last Call

A bottle of wine contains more philosophy than all the books in the world.

LOUIS PASTEUR

THE BELMAR

(After-dinner cocktail named after the resort town in
New Jersey where Marion Nagy summered)

2½ oz. Stoli Raspberry
1½ oz. Kahlua
½ oz. cream

Shake all ingredients in ice and strain into a chilled
martini glass. Garnish with a maraschino cherry.

It had been almost a year since my departure from Marion's when I went back to discuss the book with my surrogate fathers. It was three in the afternoon and it prompted the memory of the autumn day I rode down on my bike to interview for the bartending gig that changed my life. I felt that something was weird that day. Quickly, unbelievably, I realized when I walked through the doors that it was *exactly* the same day that I started my job twelve years before. It hit me like a drink thrown in my face. October 15. How odd. I felt a heavy pang of nostalgia.

I was coming back to the place where my Marion's family, the ones who had shown me unconditional love for a decade, had duly nudged me to move out and make a life for myself beyond their sheltering walls. The animosities were slight but apparent, like seeing an estranged father after eight years of a rebellious void. The love simmered low, alive and well, after all that time.

The chairs were still up on the tables, the familiar smell of the previous night's beer clung to the walls as the new dishwasher mopped the floors. It was beautiful to once again see the bottles sparkling in the sunshine streaming through the front windows—I had the urge to wipe down the bar but had to restrain myself. In the distance, from the Sky Lounge, I could hear Frank singing a duet with Dean, and martinis being shaken by a strapping, heavy-set man while Marion Nagy table-hopped, air-kissing glamorous Hollywood legends. Can someone be myth and tangible at the same time? Marion Nagy was. And her little gem on the Bowery endures, giving New Yorkers what they need more than ever because of the tumultuous times they live in: fantasy by way of a leap into a more innocent time.

My thoughts were interrupted by my baby's cry, breaking into the hustle and echoes that defined the fabled nights of Marion's Continental Restaurant and Lounge. I looked over as my son's smile burst through the tears, as it invariably does after he's gotten my attention. I realized I had moved on from this place.

It wasn't easy knowing that Marion's had moved on as well. All the countless nights being told by my regulars that I *was* Marion's had been an illusion, a romanticized hope that I was important in some way. I believed my own hype. From what I was told, the regulars were still coming in droves, drunk and happy to be a part of the Marion's fantasy. They had hired a new bartendress who was being told the same flattering bullshit, and she's probably believing every word of it, as I did. In truth, there was a part of me that hoped the place couldn't survive without me. That my customers would stage a revolt and leave the bar forever.

Alas, that has not been the case.

After leaving Marion's, I had decided it was time to let go of a lot of the baggage that kept me from giving my whole heart to anything. I realized my family—like my coworkers, friends, regulars, and customers—were fallible. My life had been a confusing mix of Eastern and Western ideals that I had to synchronize so that they could coexist peacefully. And they do for the first time in my life.

Serving alcohol had been an invisible weight on my shoulders, religiously and because I thought my parents would collapse from knowing my secret: that I was a bartender. I have come to terms with Islam, and 9/11 helped me do that. My version of God couldn't possibly hate me for serving booze when there are so-called Muslims bombing innocent people going to work. Besides, I like to think I was there for hundreds, if not thousands, of people in need of a diversion from their ordinary, sometimes hopeless-seeming lives. I gave up organized religion and continue to pray to a gentler God, one who doesn't judge so cruelly. Life is too short for guilt, resentments, and regrets. When it comes to my serving alcohol, my God has other things to worry about.

Looking at my son, his grin wide with comfort and trust, I understood that I am still serving, and am more important than ever. I sat at table 10 and waited for the owners as Kurt handed me a bottle to give Kyle. He dove into it like so many drinkers had their martinis. The venue may have changed, but the work is the same. He looked up with his drowsy eyes, milk dribbling down his chin, and sighed in solace. I beamed in self-satisfaction at my son, my favorite lush—my best regular ever.

Acknowledgments

To Kurt, my better half, good-luck charm, and best friend. The support and kindness you've generously given me continues to reveal the person I'd always been afraid to be. Thank you for loving me, especially when writing this book took over my life. You've shown me that anything and everything is possible.

My fearless agent, Douglas Stewart, for drinking Sapphire gimlets and not bailing when the windows came crashing in—literally. Your faith in me is astounding and your friendship priceless. For Sally Kim, a great friend and the bravest of editors, for taking the leap for a brassy New York bartender with a manuscript. I don't know how, but you turned this mess into something I'm so proud of.

To the Piatt family for putting up with me when the going got tough—especially Reyhan, whose summer was spent making sure I got in some serious daily writing hours, and joined me on the necessary cigarette breaks. Most of all, for caring for a certain Muffin Man when Mommy was too busy. My wonderful mother, Emine, for doing what few Islamic women I've known have done: encouraged her daughter to be a writer even when she couldn't read a lick of it. One of these days I'll translate it into Turkish for you. Guillermo Nanni for teaching me proper curse words in "Spanglish," which was an important part of my bartending career. Mariamne Singer for holding my hand through hell until I found myself. I'm afraid to contemplate where I'd be today without you. And Deniz and Ariel for teaching me to have fun—*no matter what*. For Paul and Ange, wherever you are. That you're together, drinking Ketel One martinis and having more fun than ever.

For my Marion's family, who for ten plus years plied me with love, support, dirty jokes, and shots. In particular, the wacky and wonderful waiters and bartenders for letting me into their exciting lives. You lent me your strong shoulders too many nights to count. But, hell, we sure had a lot of laughs, too. And Michael and Richard, my phantom dads, who never gave up on me, even when they should have. I'll always remember the unconditional love you lavished on me.

For Bob Pollard, Elliott Smith, Ron Sexsmith, Tom Waits, and Ryan Adams for making the music that sustained me through the toughest summer of my life. You guys rock—thank you.

For bartenders everywhere, past and present—my brothers and sisters who have upheld the second oldest profession with dignity, dedication, and a sense of humor. Remember the next time you're cutting a drunk off that what you do is give the lonely companionship, the self-destructive guidance, and your regulars friendship.

And, of course, the regulars—you know who you are. Thanks for trusting me enough to let me into your lives. It was truly a privilege to serve you, and I miss you terribly.